WHY MY CAT IS MORE IMPRESSIVE THAN YOUR BABY

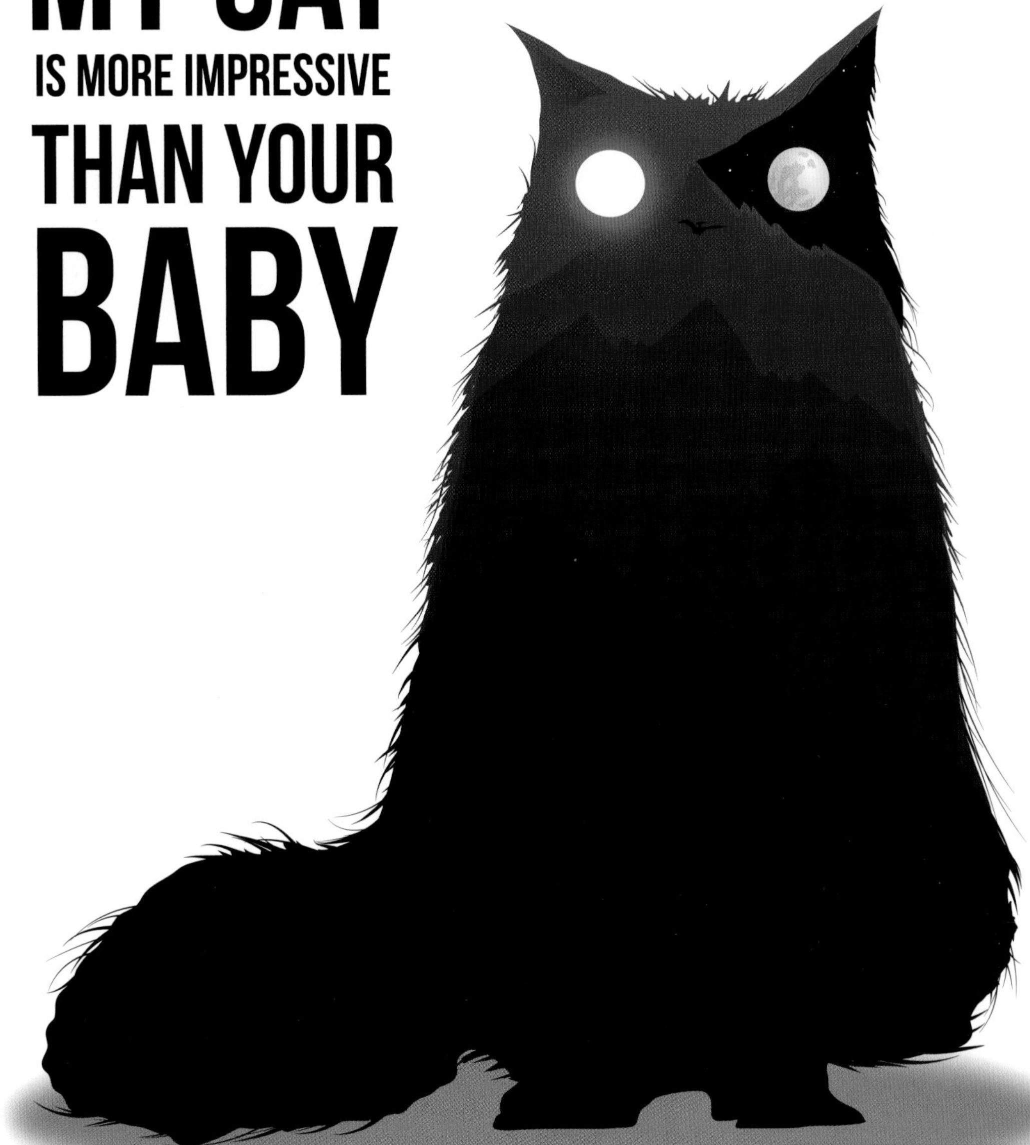

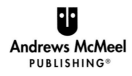

Andrews McMeel
PUBLISHING®

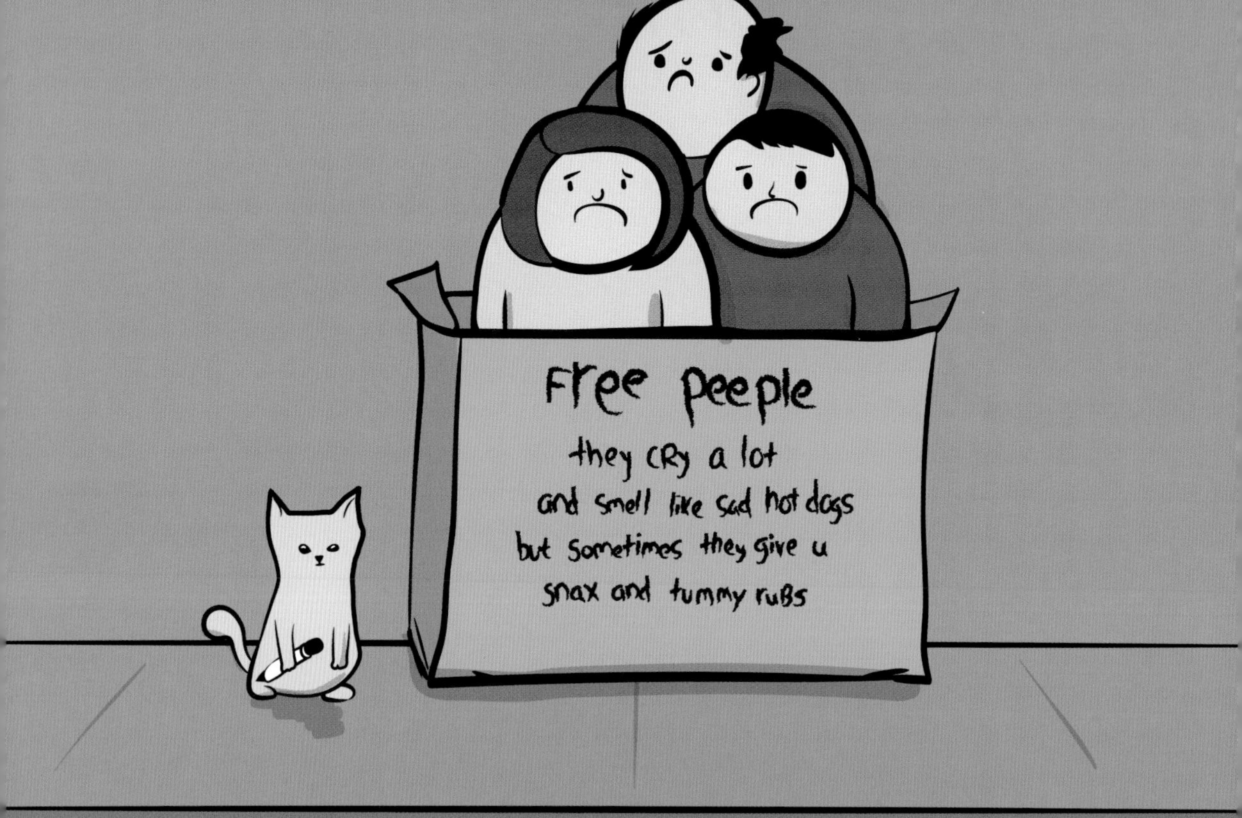
Free peeple
they cry a lot
and smell like sad hot dogs
but sometimes they give u
snax and tummy rubs

WHY MY CAT IS MORE IMPRESSIVE THAN YOUR BABY

Andrews McMeel Publishing
a division of Andrews McMeel Universal
1130 Walnut Street, Kansas City, Missouri 64106

www.andrewsmcmeel.com

19 20 21 22 23 SDB 10 9 8 7 6 5 4 3 2
ISBN: 978-1-5248-5062-3
Library of Congress Control Number: 2018966253

Editor: Patty Rice
Art Director: Diane Marsh
Production Editor: Dave Shaw
Production Manager: Tamara Haus

ATTENTION: SCHOOLS AND BUSINESSES
Andrews McMeel books are available at quantity discounts with bulk purchase for educational, business, or sales promotional use. For information, please e-mail the Andrews McMeel Publishing Special Sales Department: specialsales@amuniversal.com.

Contents

Hi there.

My name is Matthew, and I am a cartoonist.

I live with two cats.

Two dogs.

And exactly zero babies.

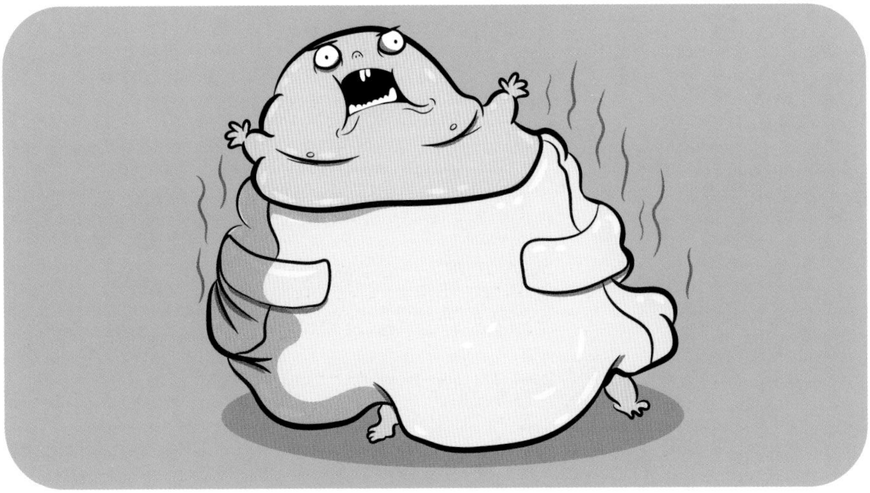

You might think I'm biased.

That's understandable. I get that.

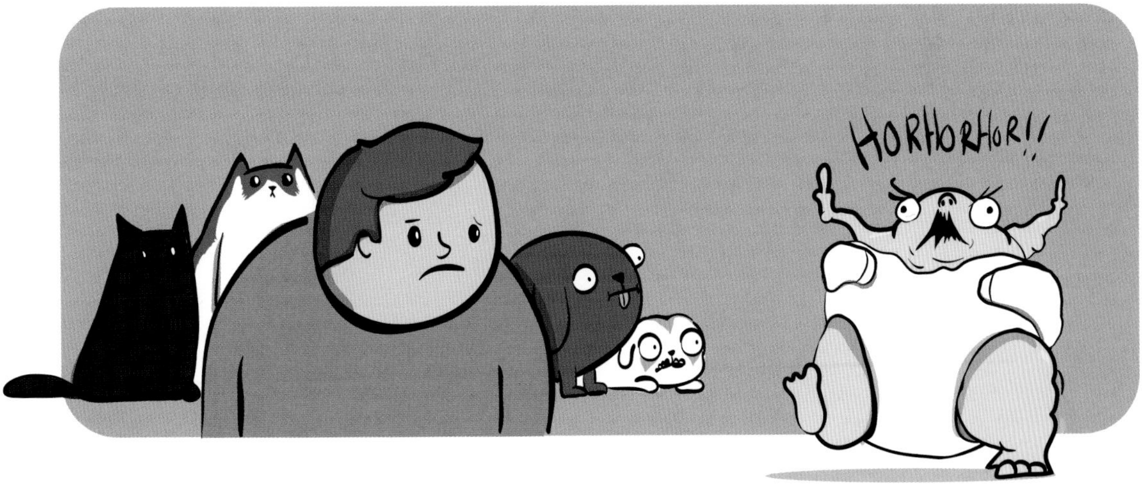
HORHORHOR!!

But before you write me off, allow me to demonstrate my comprehension of these creatures by defining them as succinctly as I can.

My dog is an affable ball of fur and joy who is so excited to see me he sometimes starts dry heaving.

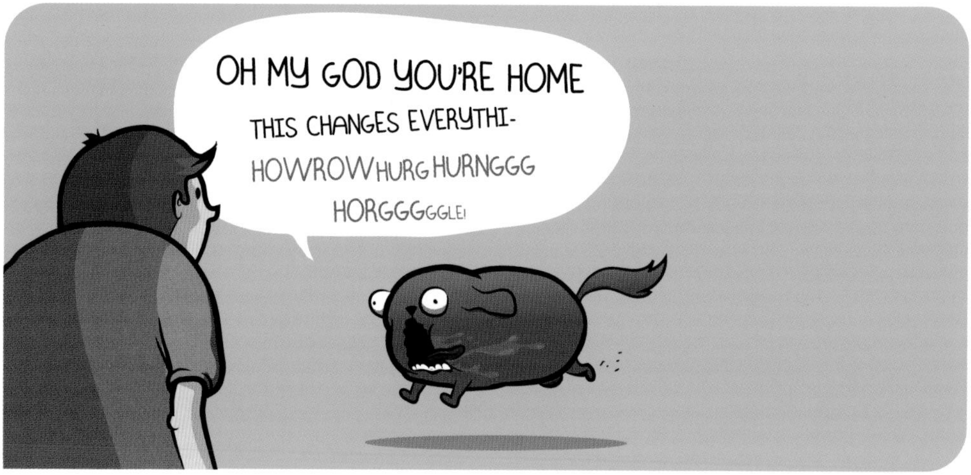
OH MY GOD YOU'RE HOME
THIS CHANGES EVERYTHI-
HOWROWHURG HURNGGG
HORGGGGGLE!

See also: *best friend, lovable idiot, paradox.*

My cat is a confusing ball of violence and tenderness who would probably try to eat me if I were to lie still long enough.

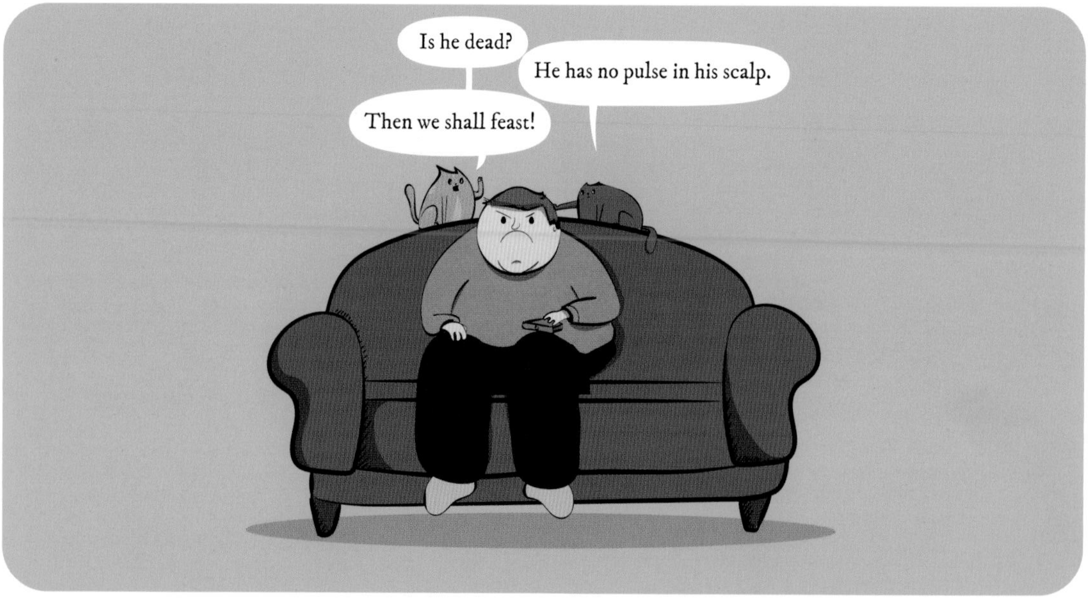
Is he dead?
He has no pulse in his scalp.
Then we shall feast!

See also: *part-time sociopath, stay-at-home tiger.*

A baby

is an obese, naked leprechaun whose primary job is to siphon milk
from boobs and then spray it out of its ass at 4:30 in the morning.

See also: *diapered ham-goblin, defiler of dreams, relentless ScreamBall.*

A parent

is a selfless individual willing to nurture one of these obese leprechauns
until they fall in love with it, at which point they must spend the rest
of their lives worrying that it's going to run into traffic
or choke on a peanut or die in a plane crash or become goth.

See also: *chauffeur of tiny drunk people, conquerer of diapered Demogorgons.*

Insightful, yes?

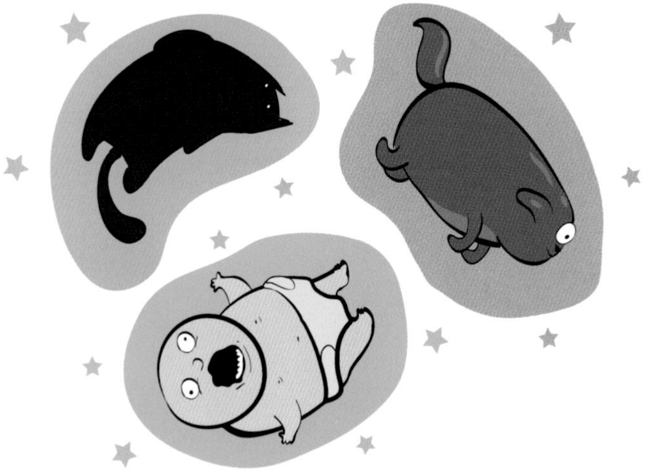

I thought so.

Now that I have earned your undying trust as an *absolute* authority in regards to dogs, cats, and babies, we can continue.

This book is titled *Why My Cat Is More Impressive Than Your Baby*, but that's a bit of a misnomer.

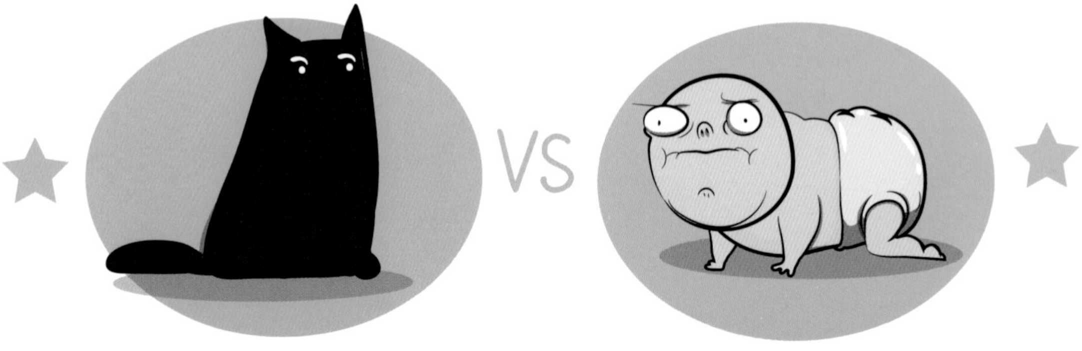
VS

He is no more *my* cat than an electrical storm is *my* lightning.
Lightning strikes where it pleases. It torches livestock at will.
It burns down houses in a flash.
Nobody *owns* it.

We are all prisoners of its violent, unpredictable brilliance.

Furthermore, this book is not just about cats and babies.
It's also about dogs, love, death, and farts.

I hope you enjoy it.

—Matthew.

Why MY CAT is more impressive than your BABY

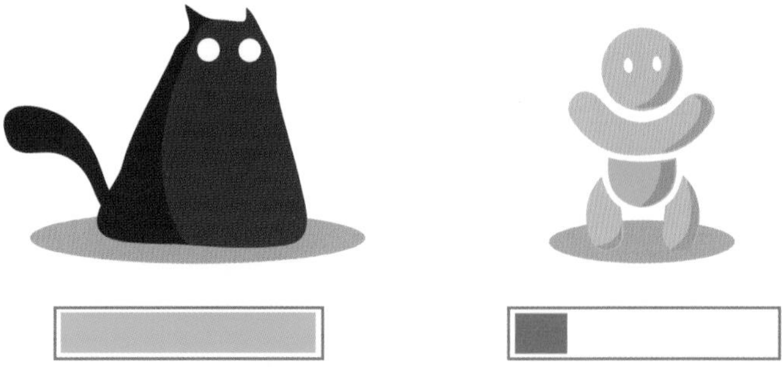

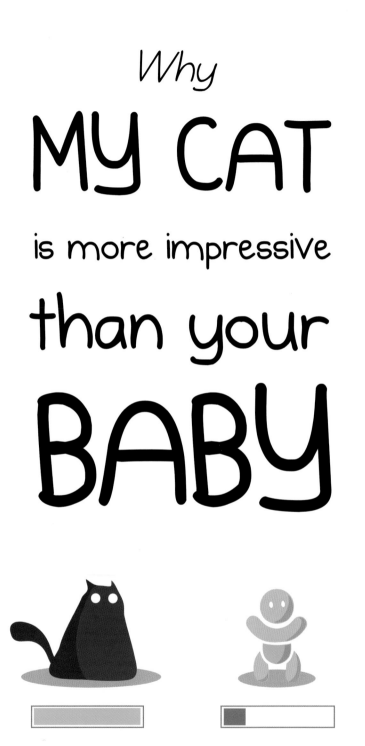

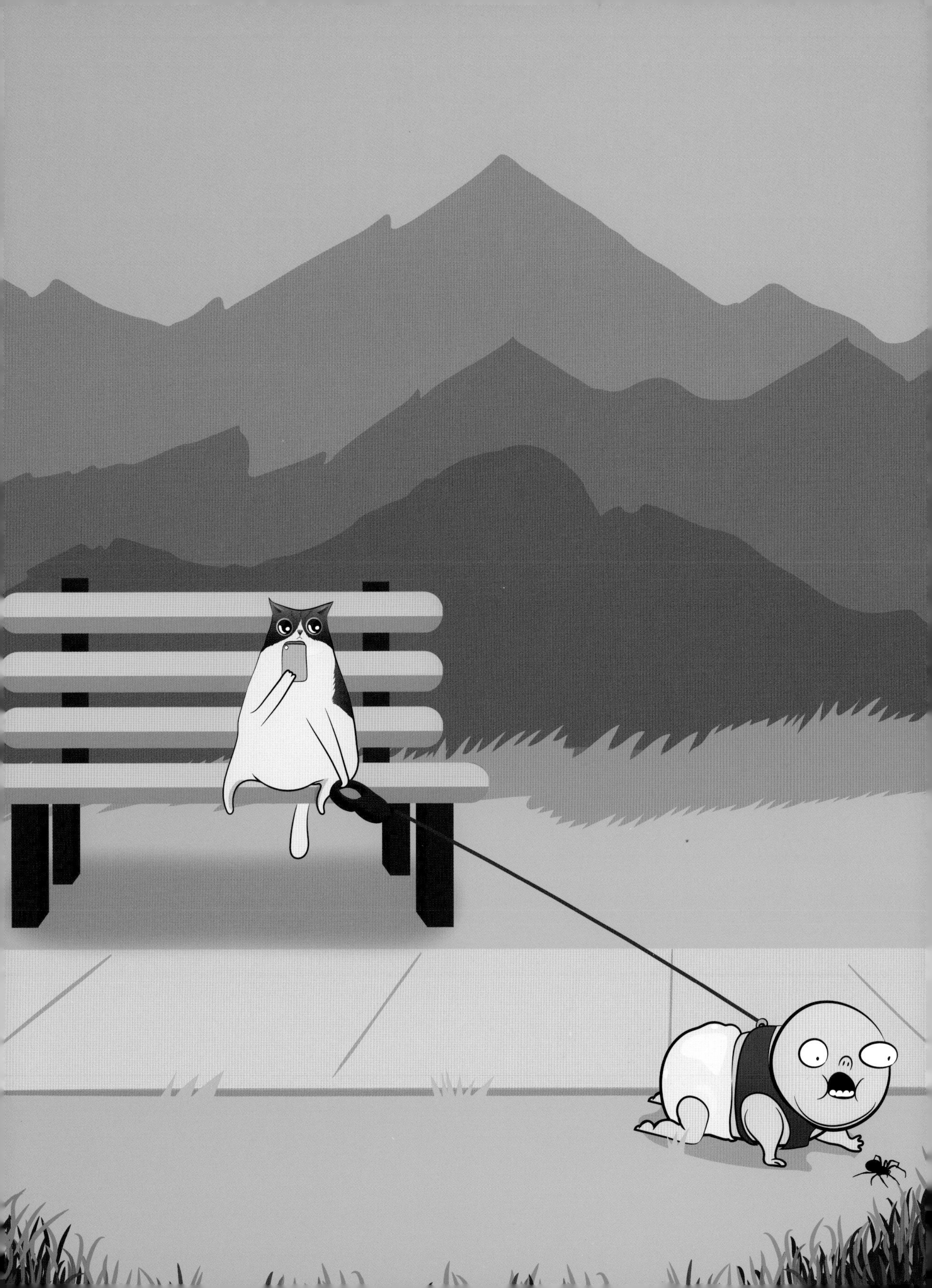

Babies

come shrieking into this world
as selfish, amniotic, jam-covered

goblins.

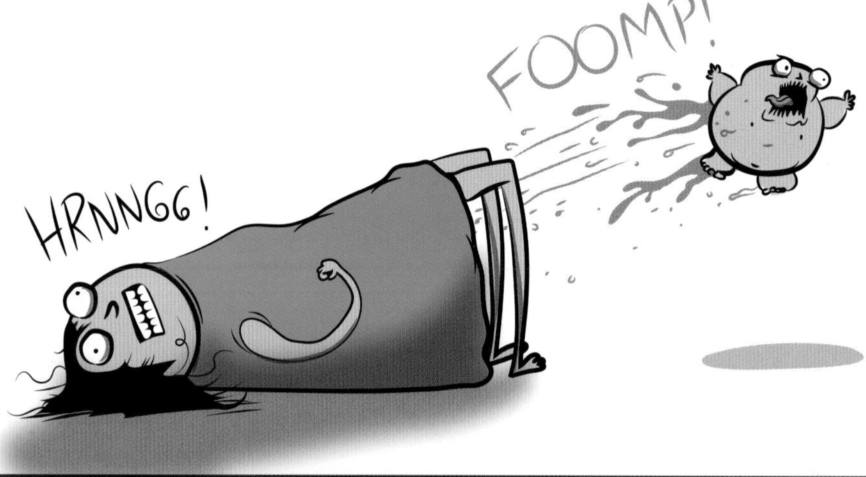
HRNNGG!
FOOMP!

Cats

come into this world as

kittens,

which are independent, adorable,
and not at all goblin-like.

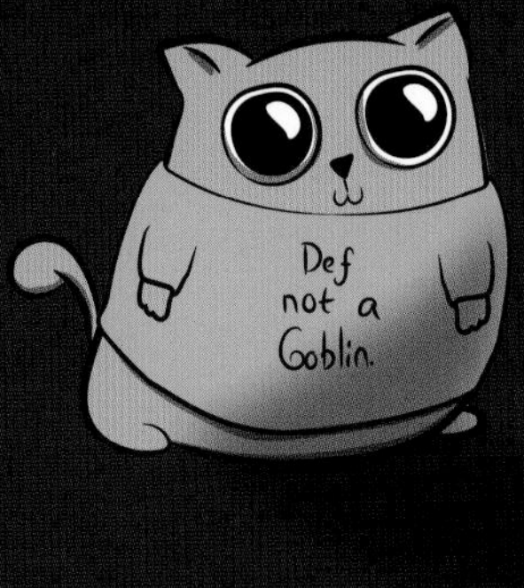
Def not a Goblin.

Babies

crap in plastic underwear.

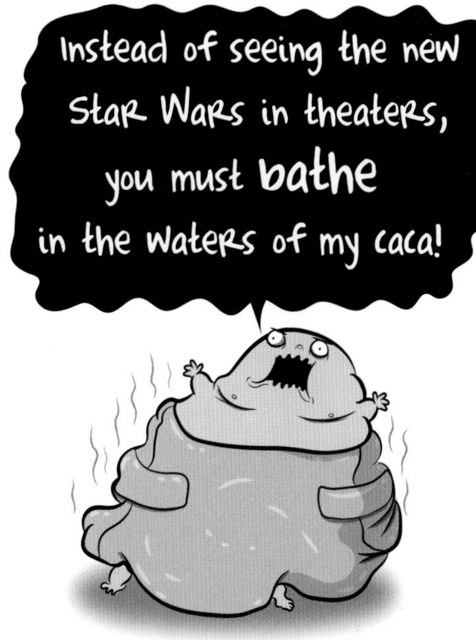
Instead of seeing the new Star Wars in theaters, you must bathe in the waters of my caca!

Children

crap on your dreams.

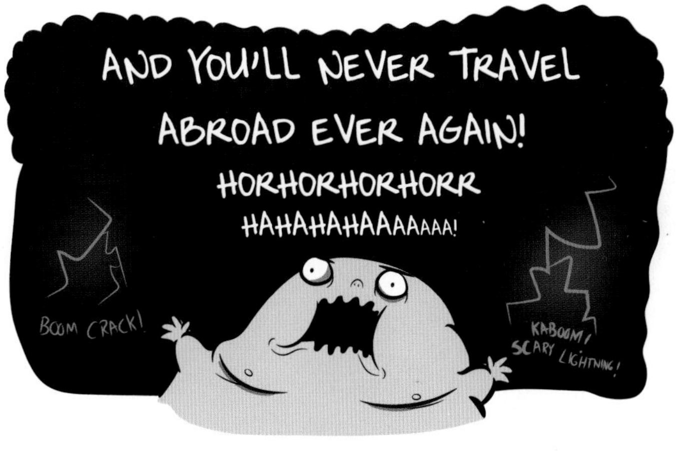
AND YOU'LL NEVER TRAVEL ABROAD EVER AGAIN!
HORHORHORHORR
HAHAHAHAAAAAAA!
BOOM CRACK!
KABOOM! SCARY LIGHTNING!

Cats

just crap in a box.

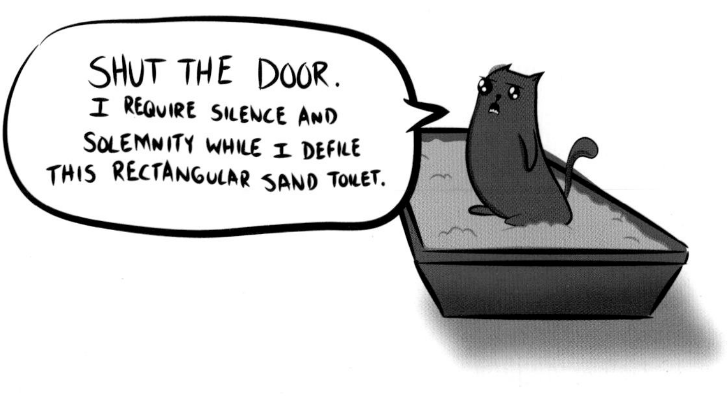
SHUT THE DOOR. I REQUIRE SILENCE AND SOLEMNITY WHILE I DEFILE THIS RECTANGULAR SAND TOILET.

When babies are upset, they produce loud noises.

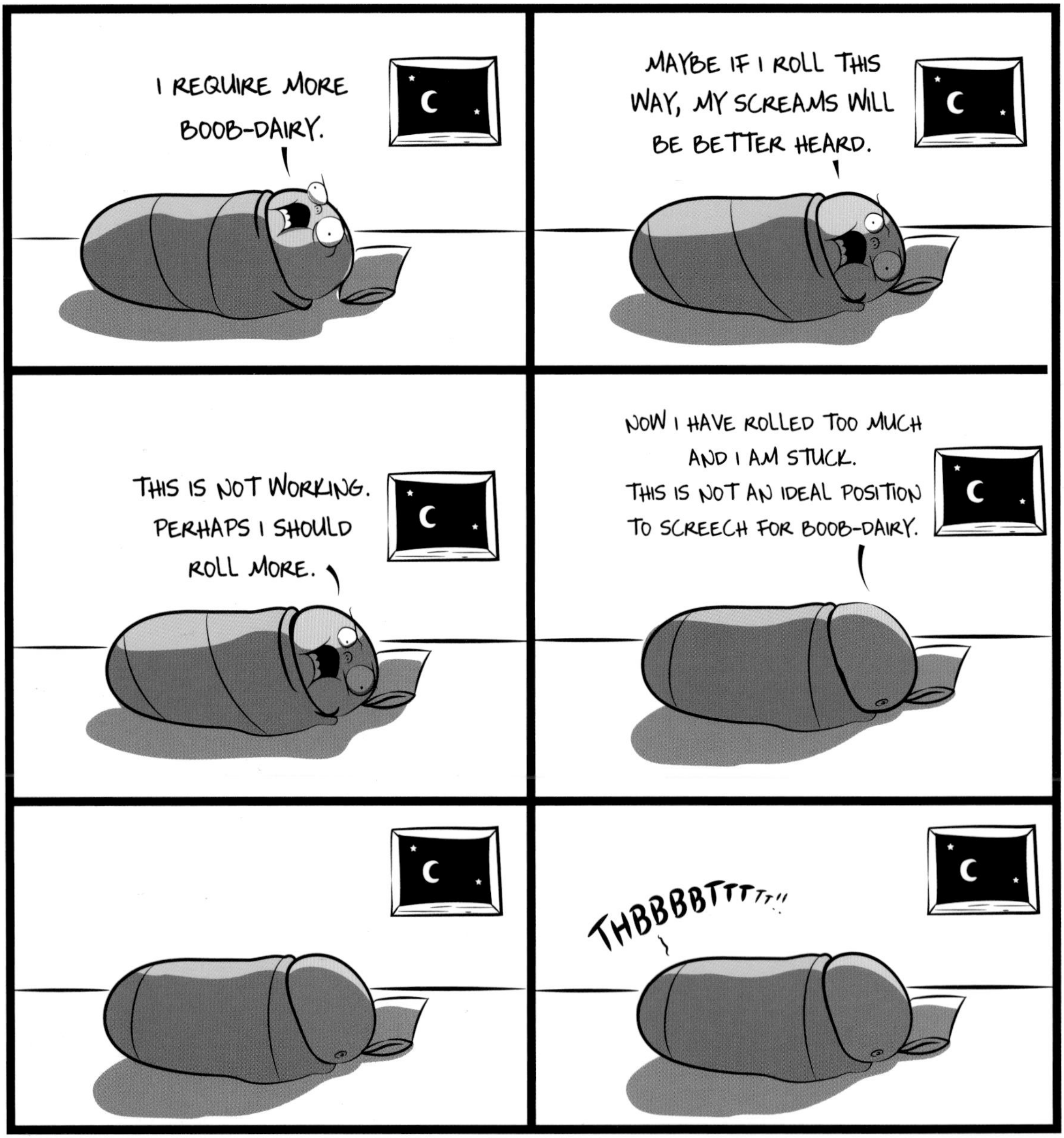
I REQUIRE MORE BOOB-DAIRY.
MAYBE IF I ROLL THIS WAY, MY SCREAMS WILL BE BETTER HEARD.
THIS IS NOT WORKING. PERHAPS I SHOULD ROLL MORE.
NOW I HAVE ROLLED TOO MUCH AND I AM STUCK. THIS IS NOT AN IDEAL POSITION TO SCREECH FOR BOOB-DAIRY.
THBBBBTTTTTT!!

When cats are upset,

they slaughter pigeons
and take 16 hour naps.

They suffer like champions do:
quietly, gracefully,
and while covered in blood.

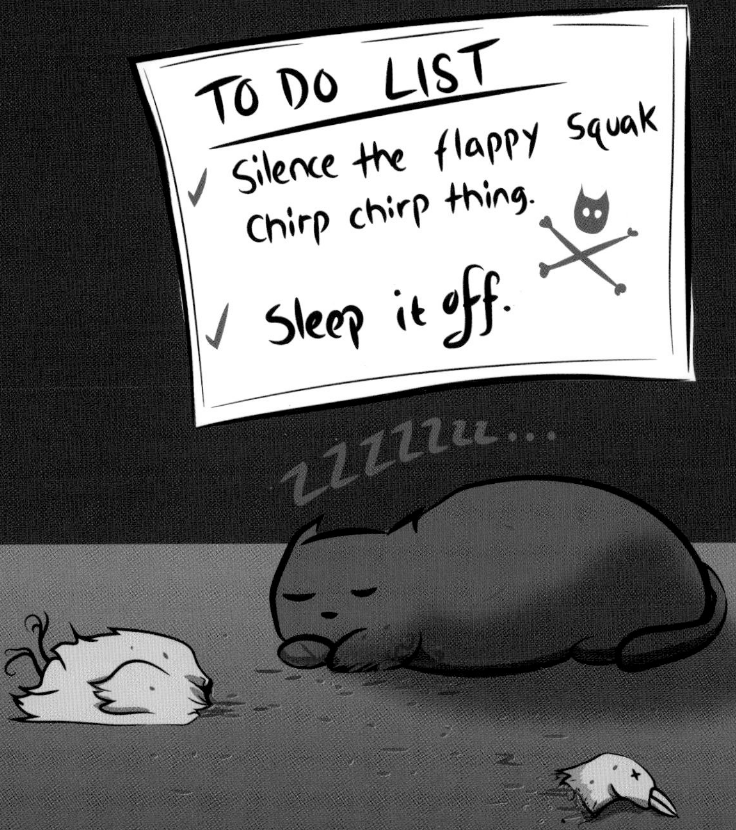
TO DO LIST
Silence the flappy squak chirp chirp thing.
Sleep it off.
ZZZZZzz...

If you spoil a

baby,

they'll become a terrible child,
which will become a terrible adult,
which will become

the next Hitler.

OH LOOK,
I'M TAKING MY
FIRST STEPS...

...INTO POLAND.

If you spoil a

cat,

they lack the physical capacity to grow up and command armies.

They can't ruin anyone's life other than your own,

so spoil away.

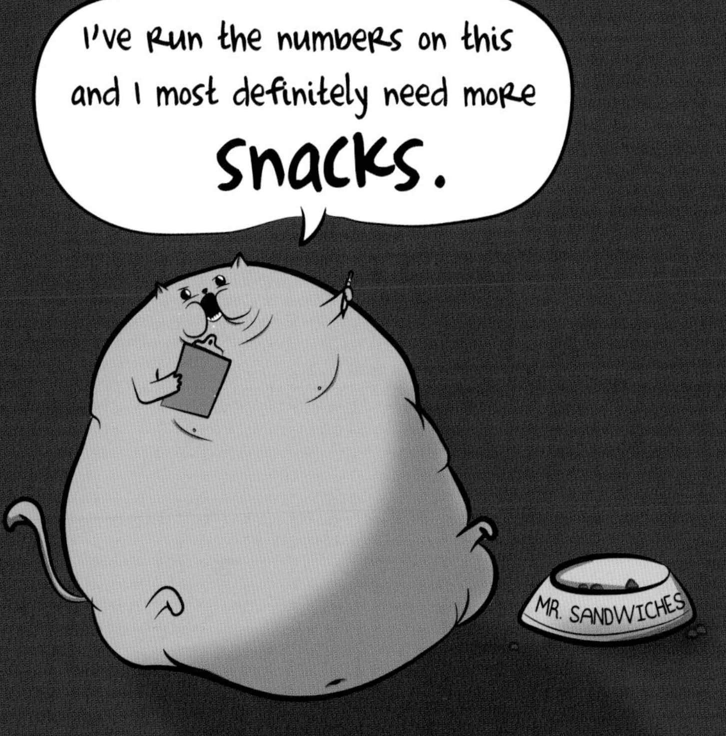
I've run the numbers on this and I most definitely need more
snacks.
MR. SANDWICHES

Babies and romance
cannot coexist.

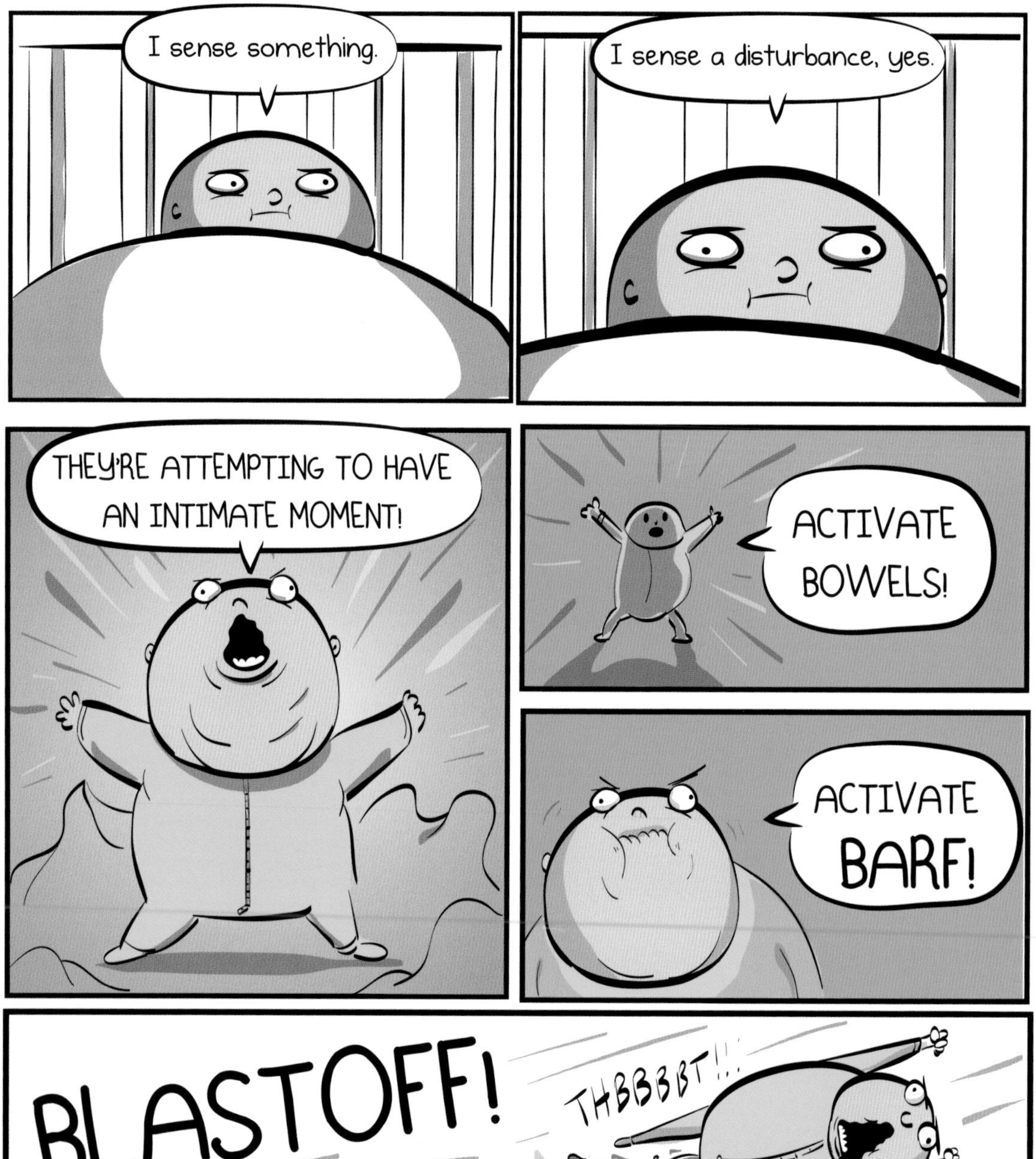

I sense something.
I sense a disturbance, yes.
THEY'RE ATTEMPTING TO HAVE AN INTIMATE MOMENT!
ACTIVATE BOWELS!
ACTIVATE BARF!
BLASTOFF!
THBBBBT!!!
HOROROW HOWRWOW!

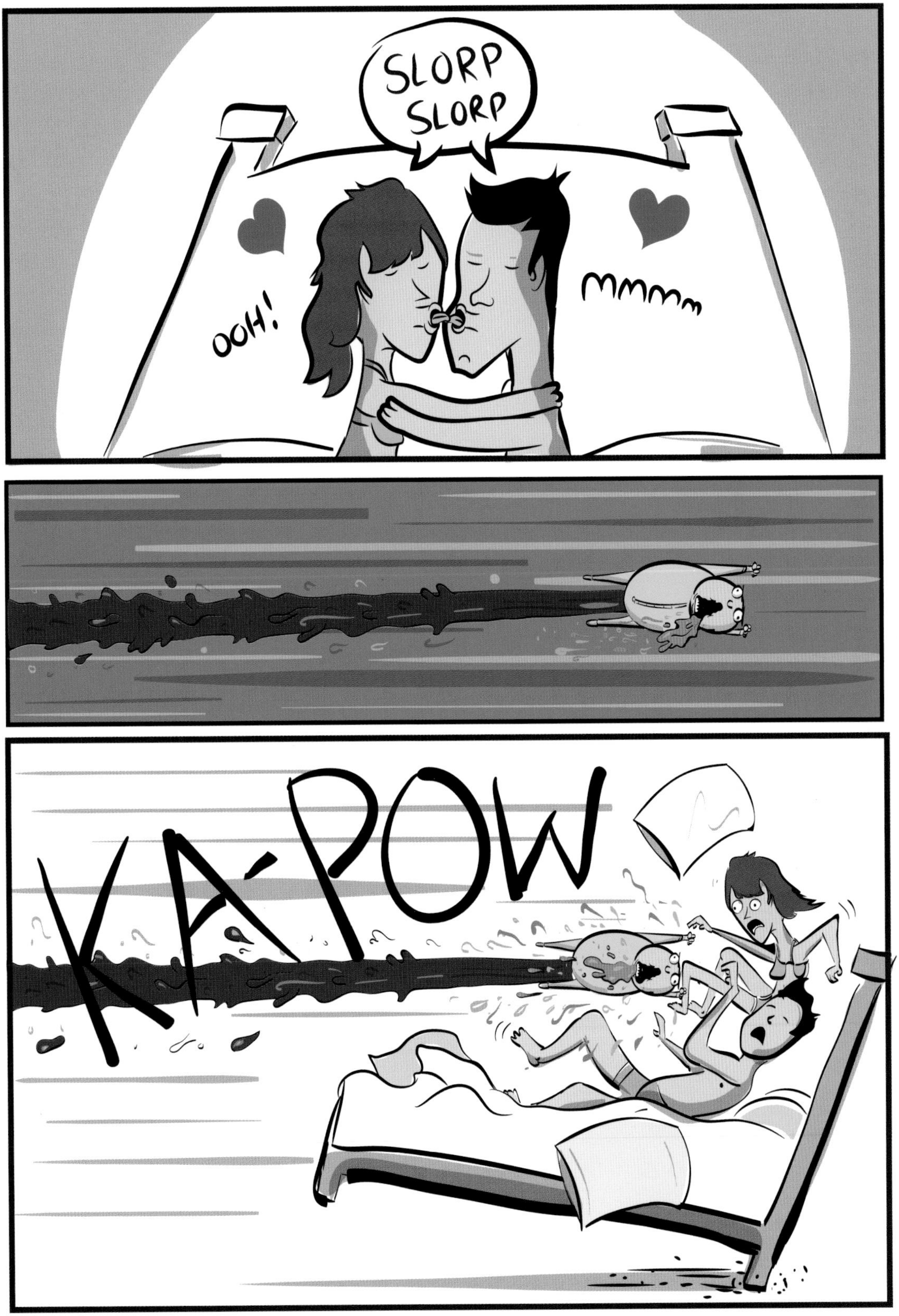
SLORP
SLORP
OOH!
MMMM
KA-POW

Cats
just like to watch.

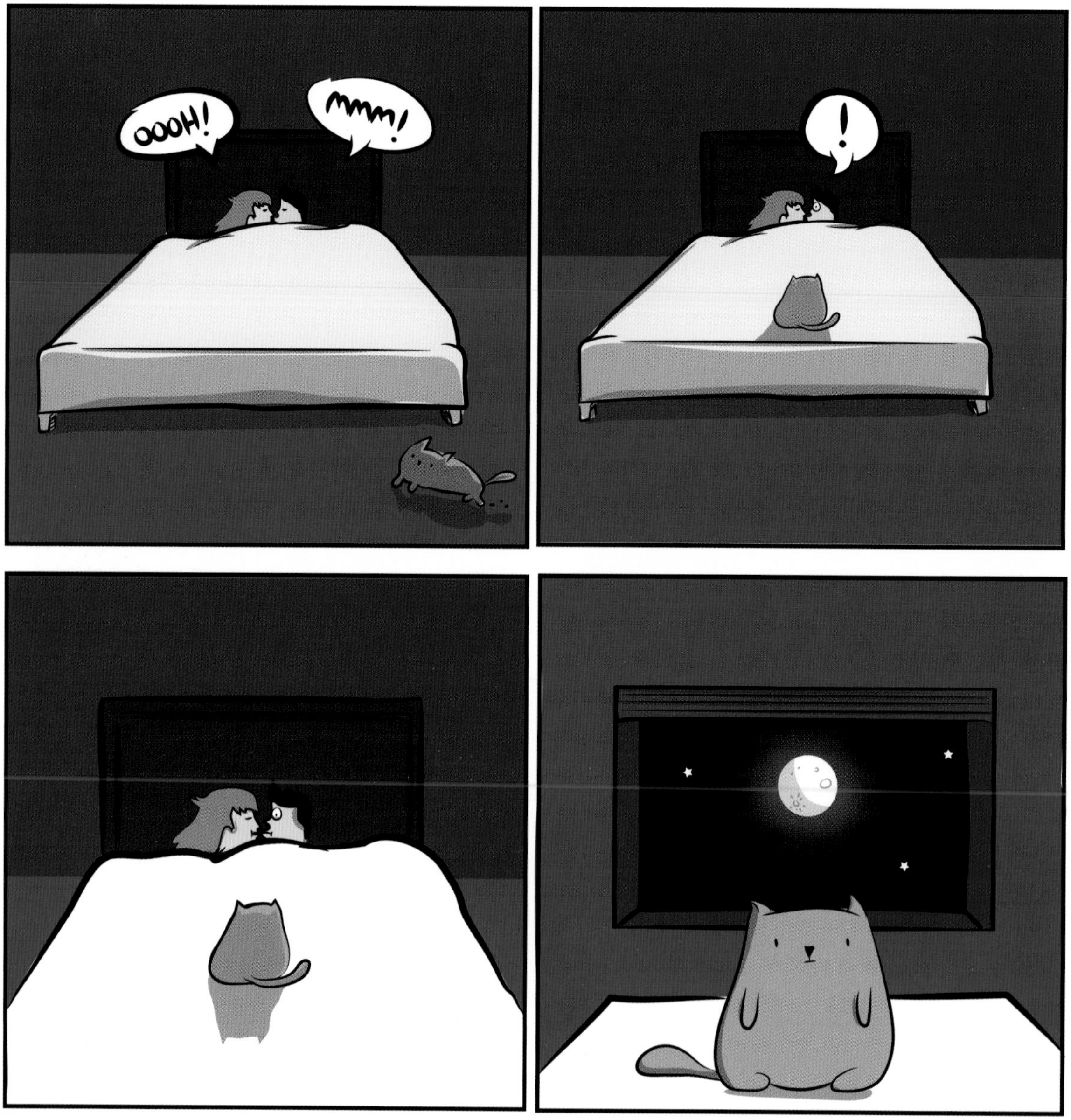

OOOH!
mmm!
!

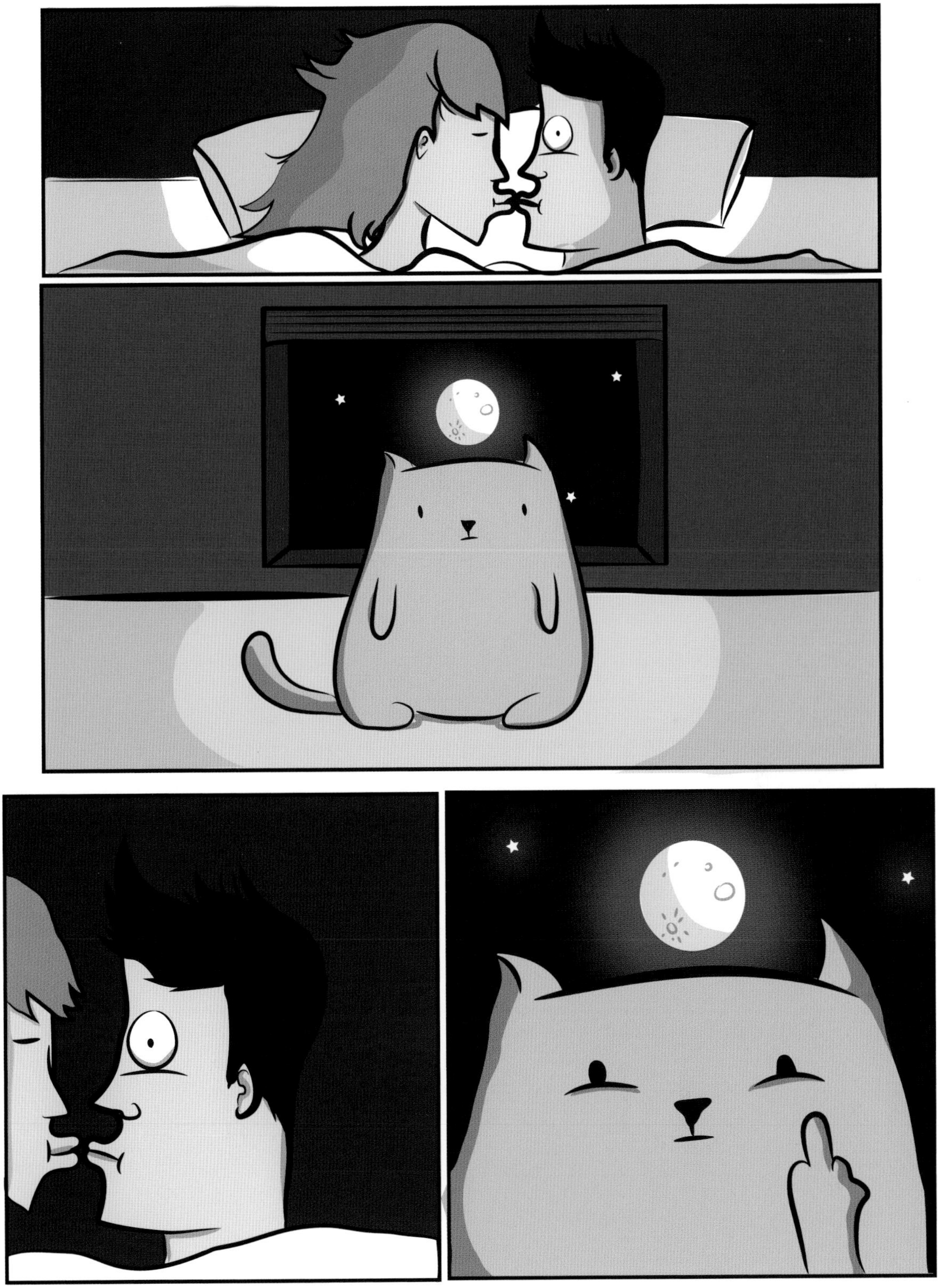

Babies

have no special powers,

other than transforming interesting, hopeful people into bald, sallow, regretful **barf-slaves.**

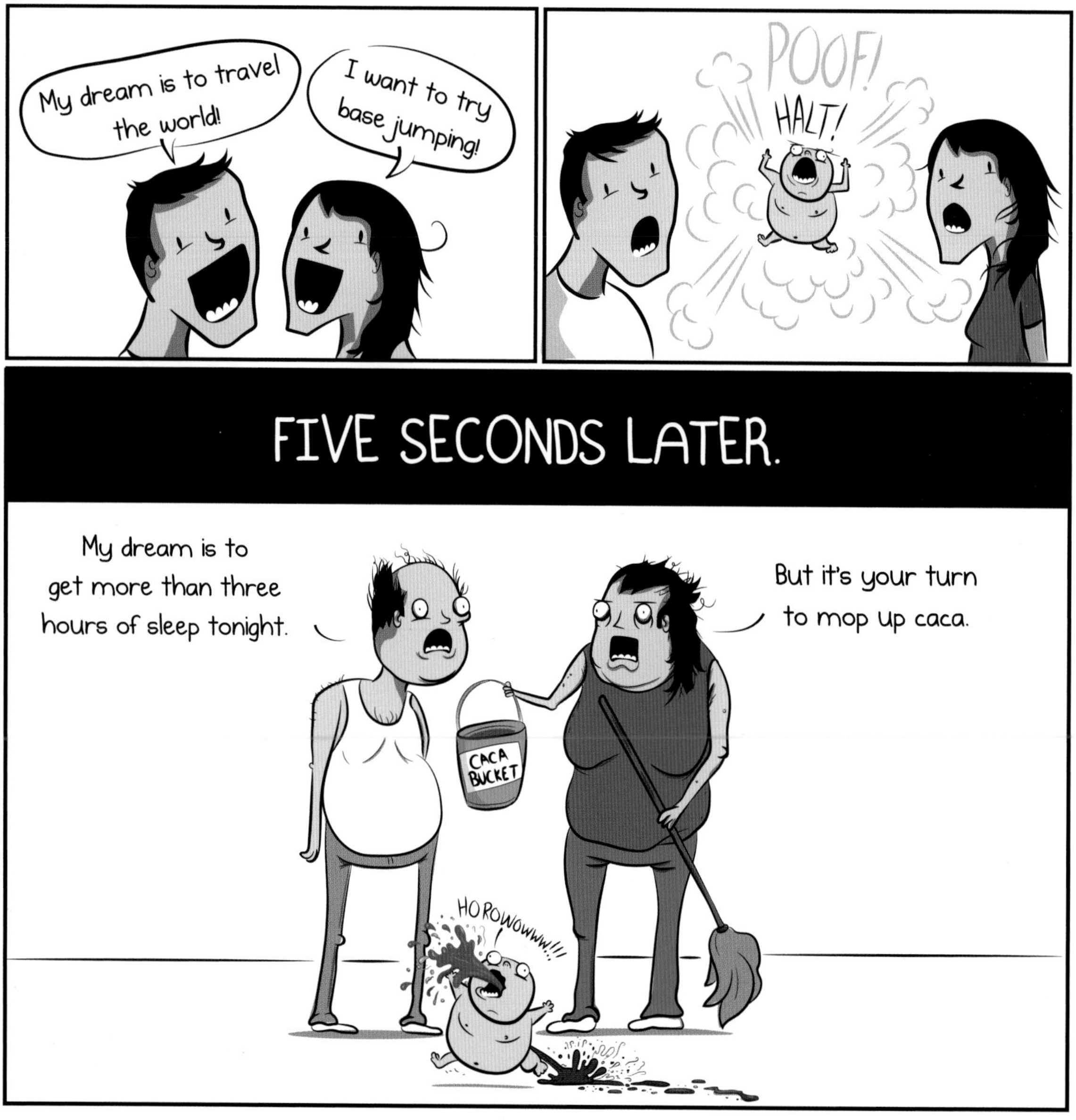

My dream is to travel the world!
I want to try base jumping!
POOF!
HALT!
FIVE SECONDS LATER.
My dream is to get more than three hours of sleep tonight.
But it's your turn to mop up caca.
CACA BUCKET
HOROWOWWW!!!

Cats

on the other hand,
possess a number of special abilites.

Cats have
night vision.

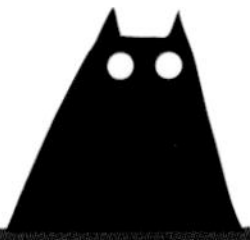

I have witnessed dark things
happening in dark places.

A purring cat can lower
your blood pressure.

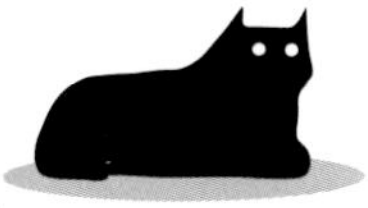

It's in your best interest
to pet me at 4am.

Domestic house cats
can run faster than the
100-meter world-record holder.

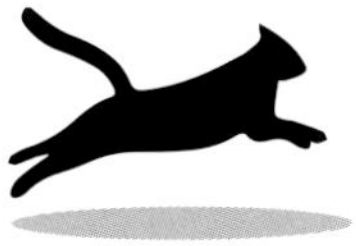

The only thing faster
than my incredible mind
is my extraordinary body.

Cats eat bugs and spiders.

The diet starts Monday.

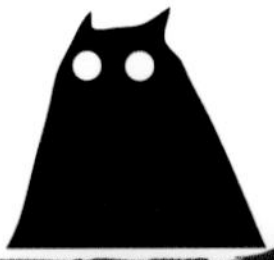

A cat is your own private Batman.

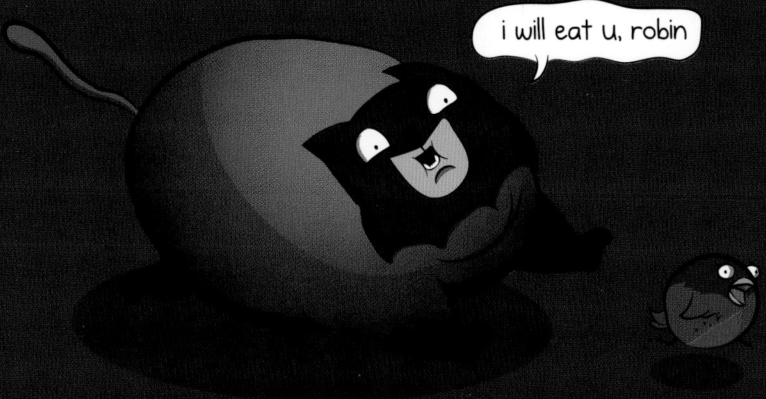
i will eat u, robin

A cat is demanding enough to fulfill your need to *care* for a living thing,

but not demanding enough to ruin your life.

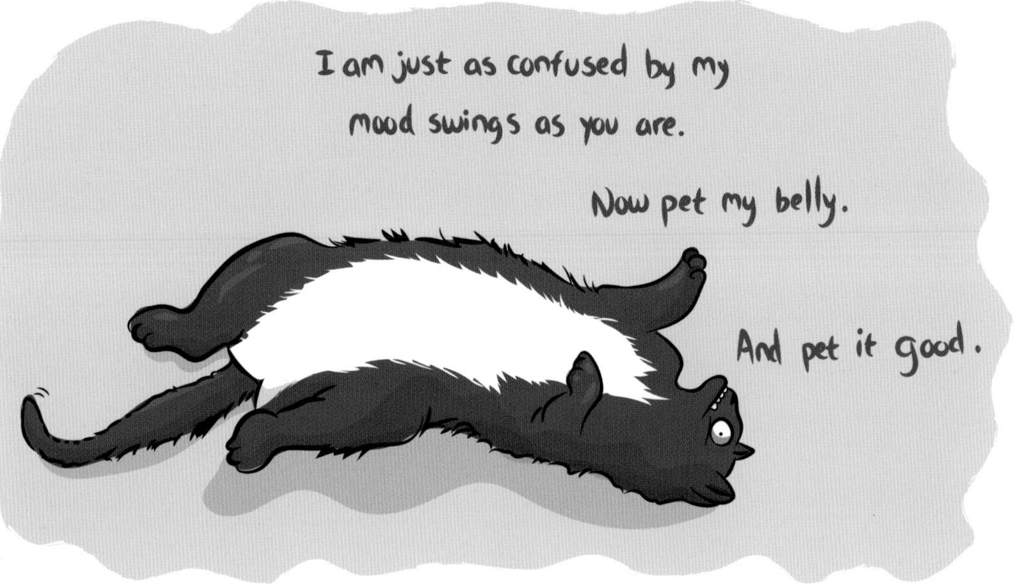
I am just as confused by my mood swings as you are.
Now pet my belly.
And pet it good.

And while a baby might grow up to resent you, a cat is BORN resenting you, so you've got nowhere to go but up.

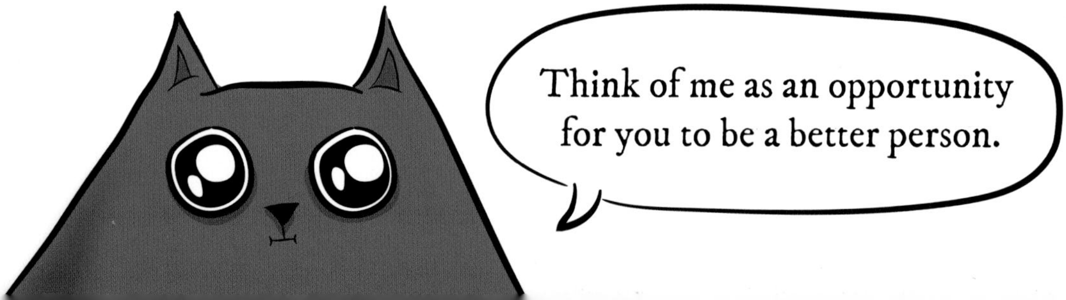
Think of me as an opportunity for you to be a better person.

The life of a cat is fast and luminous.

They are furry cruise missiles, not intended for long voyages but brief bursts of light across the sky.

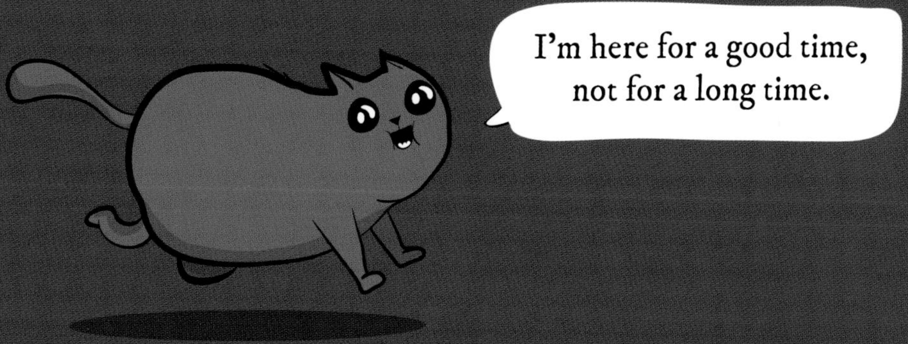
I'm here for a good time, not for a long time.

They find their way across the universe and crash into your heart like a purring, misanthropic meteorite.

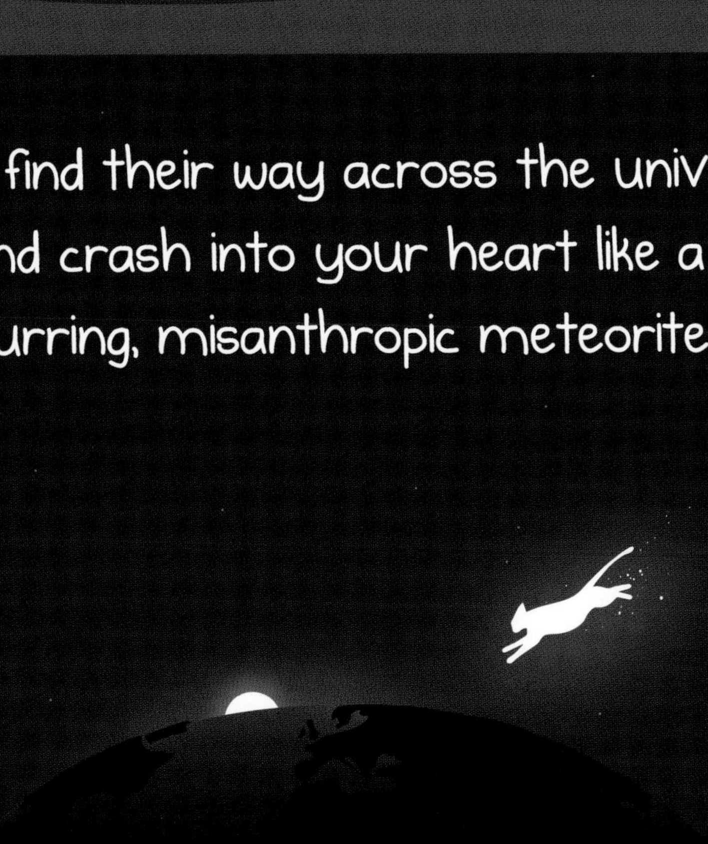

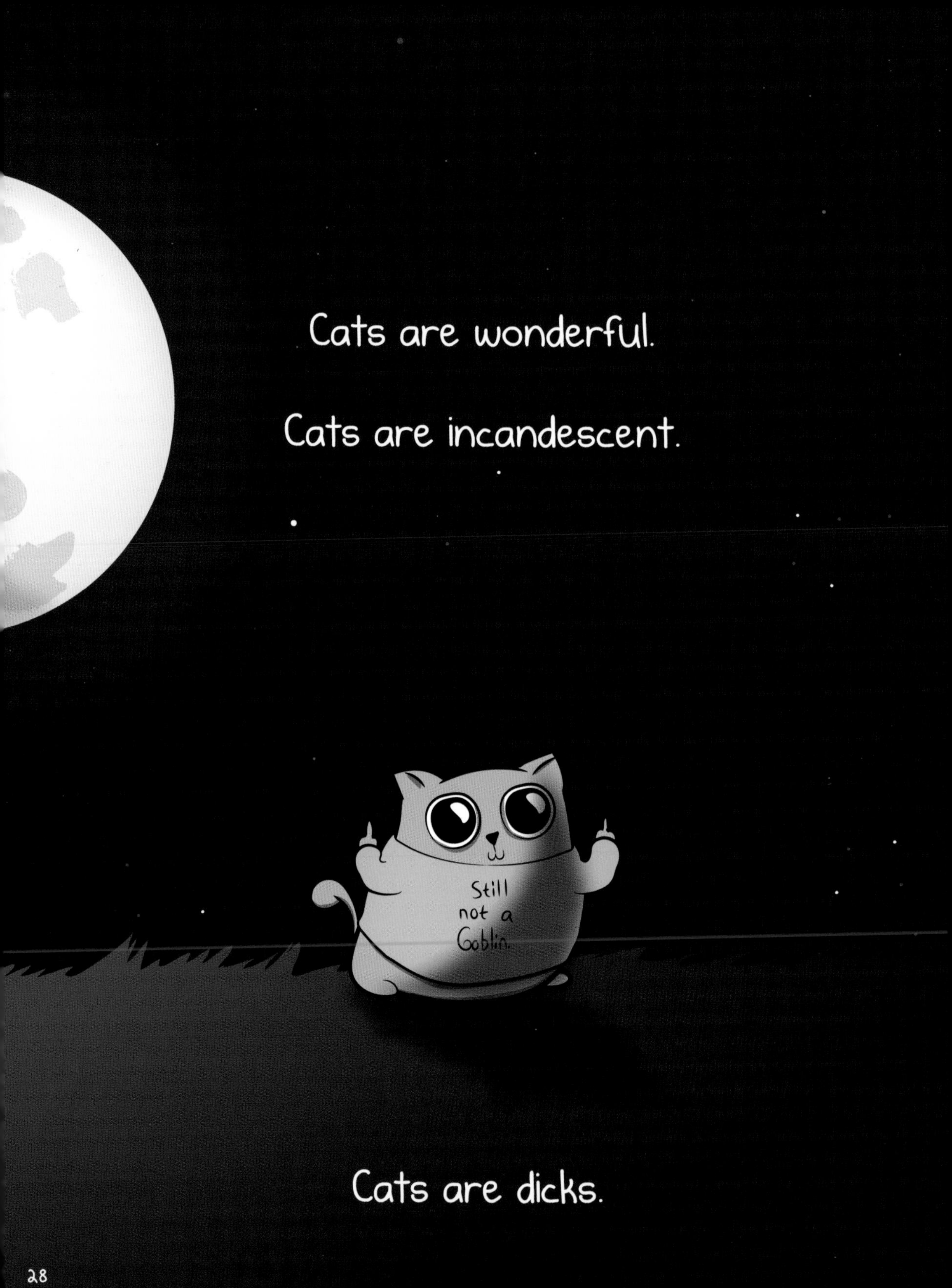
Cats are wonderful.
Cats are incandescent.
Still not a Goblin.
Cats are dicks.

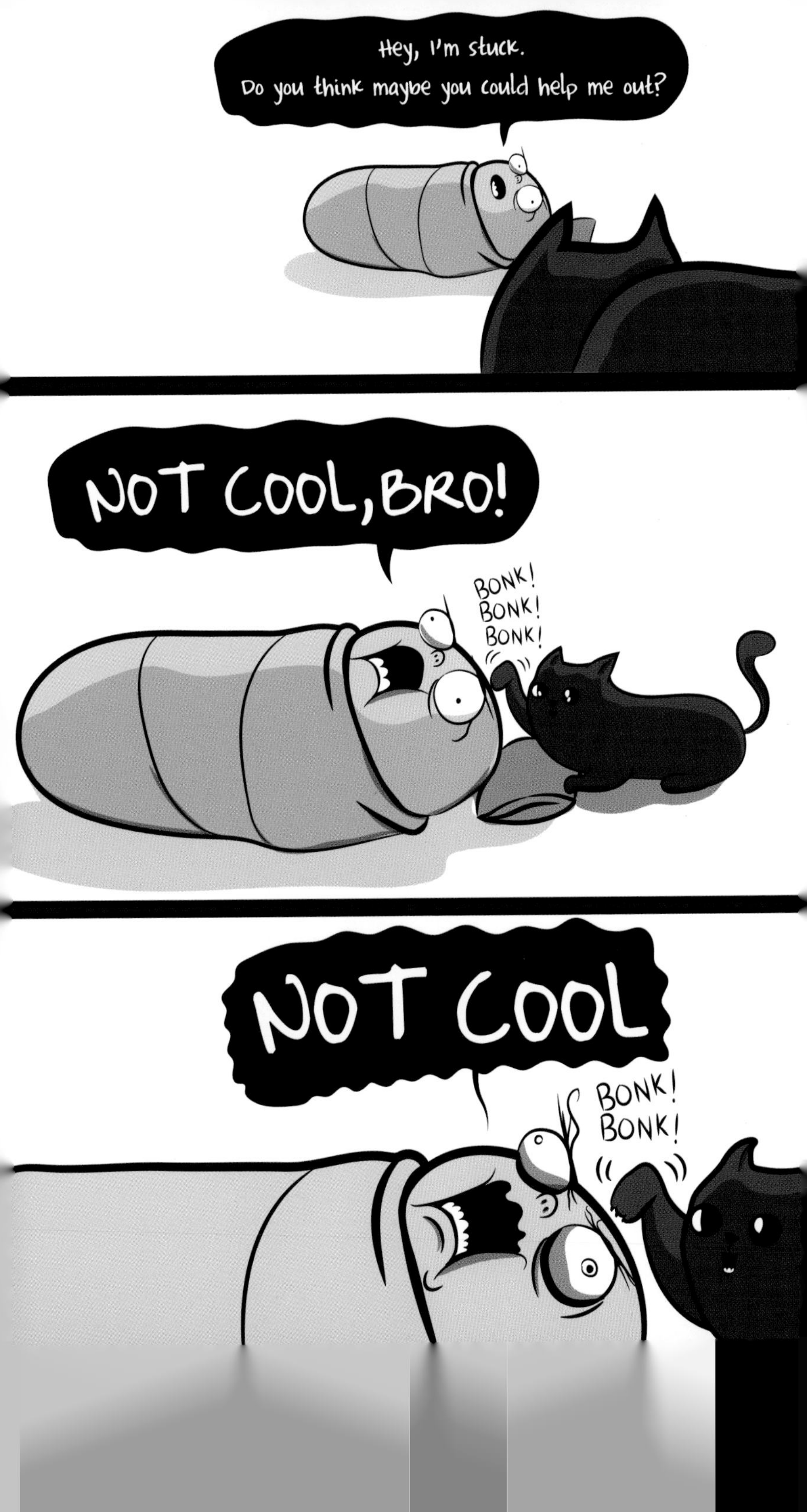
Hey, I'm stuck.
Do you think maybe you could help me out?
NOT COOL, BRO!
BONK! BONK! BONK!
NOT COOL
BONK! BONK!

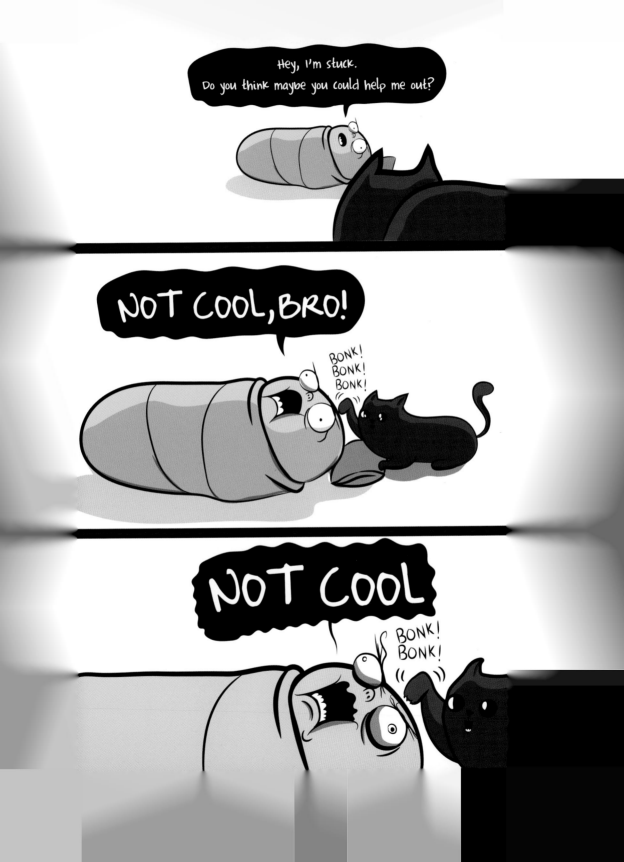

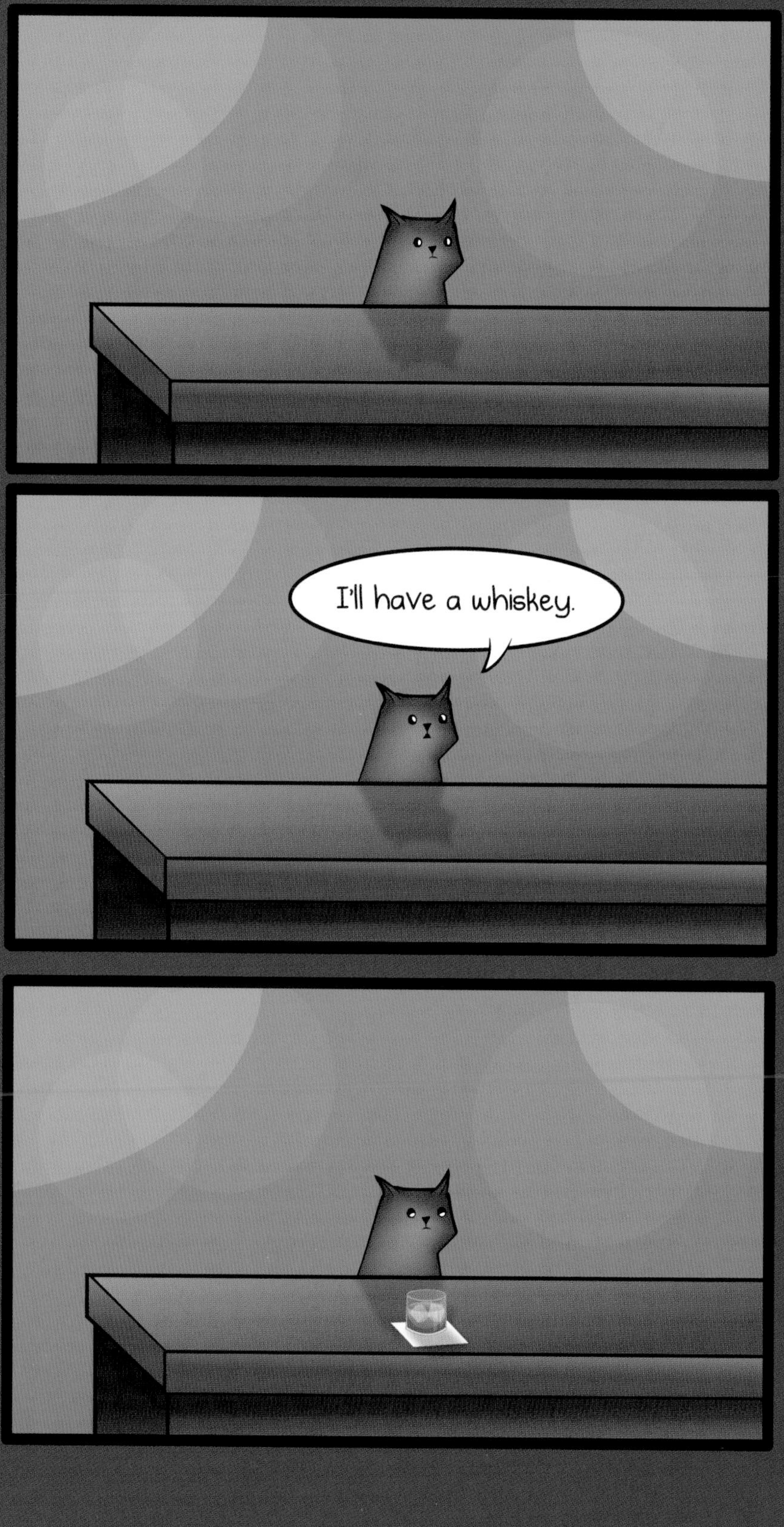
I'll have a whiskey.

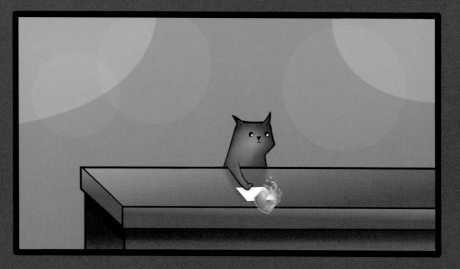

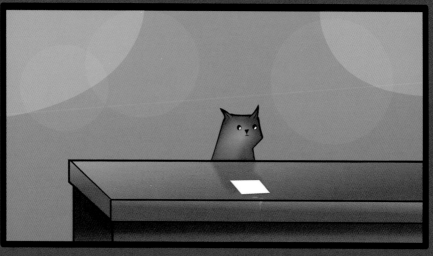

Written by @PhilJamesson. Drawn by @Oatmeal.

Dear Diary,

It was dark when I awoke. As dark as it gets. I wandered into the nursery where the diapered pork chop was screeching like a constipated pterodactyl. He smelled of milk and mediocrity.

I studied him for a moment. I sat in repose, contemplating his form, his purpose. I deduced nothing, only that he is foe and I am fauna.

And so, with feverish intensity, I struck a commanding blow upon his head. I struck him like lightning strikes a sheep abandoned in the rain. And then I absconded with that which he holds most dear.

I stole his binky.

I stole it because the diapered pork chop needs to learn what it means to suffer—and he needs to learn this lesson from *me.* For I am darkness. I am the shadow that falls over a sullen grave.

I am penumbra. I am predator.

I am cat.

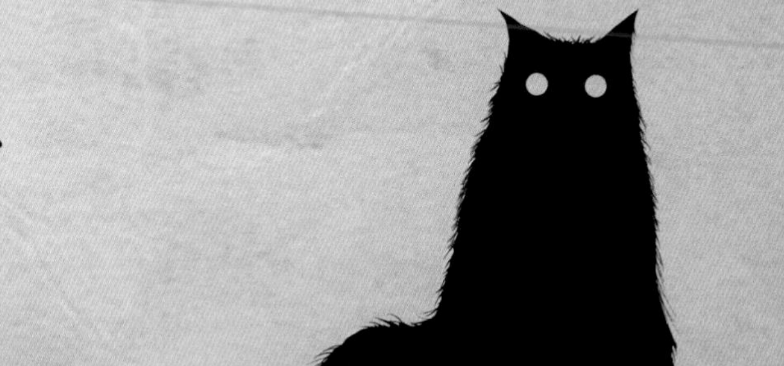

deer dairy,

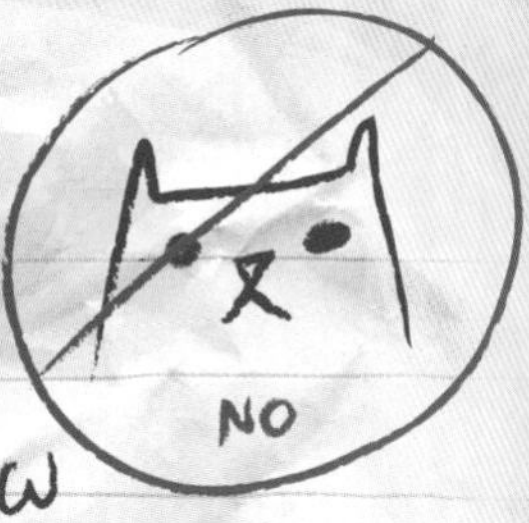
NO

2 day, small tiger hit brainskull with paw STOLE my binky. Now i am upsetful and angry. sadgry. full of indigestion too. need Burp from MomGod.

Love the momGod.

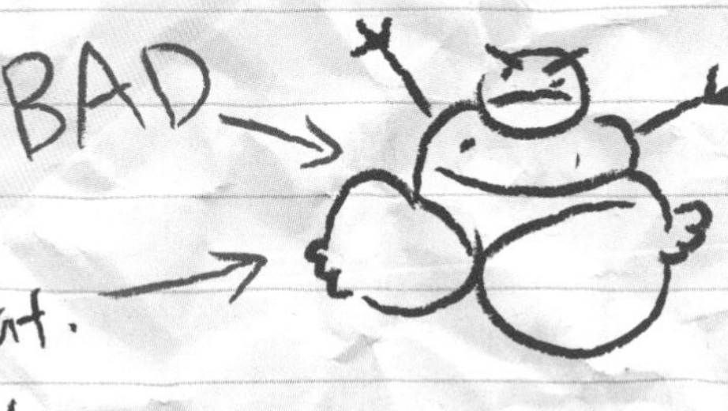
BAD

wish my legs weren't so fat. they are like swollen hot dogs.

maybe 4 decoration only?

then i could walk out of this wooden cage.

then i could grow STRONG.

ONe day, defeat small tiger.

one dax ... get binky back

... but not 2dax

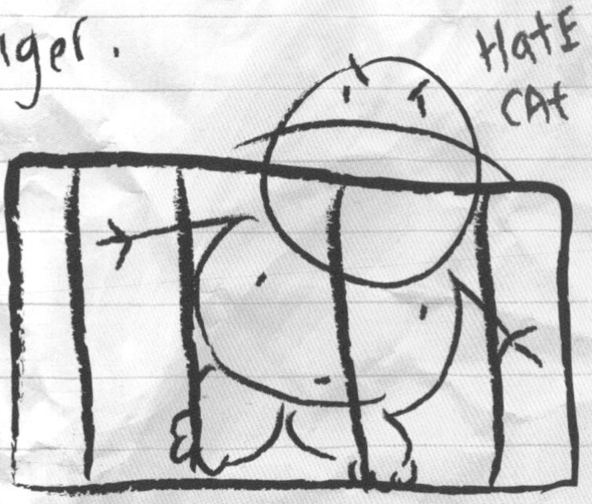
HATE CAT

-BabY

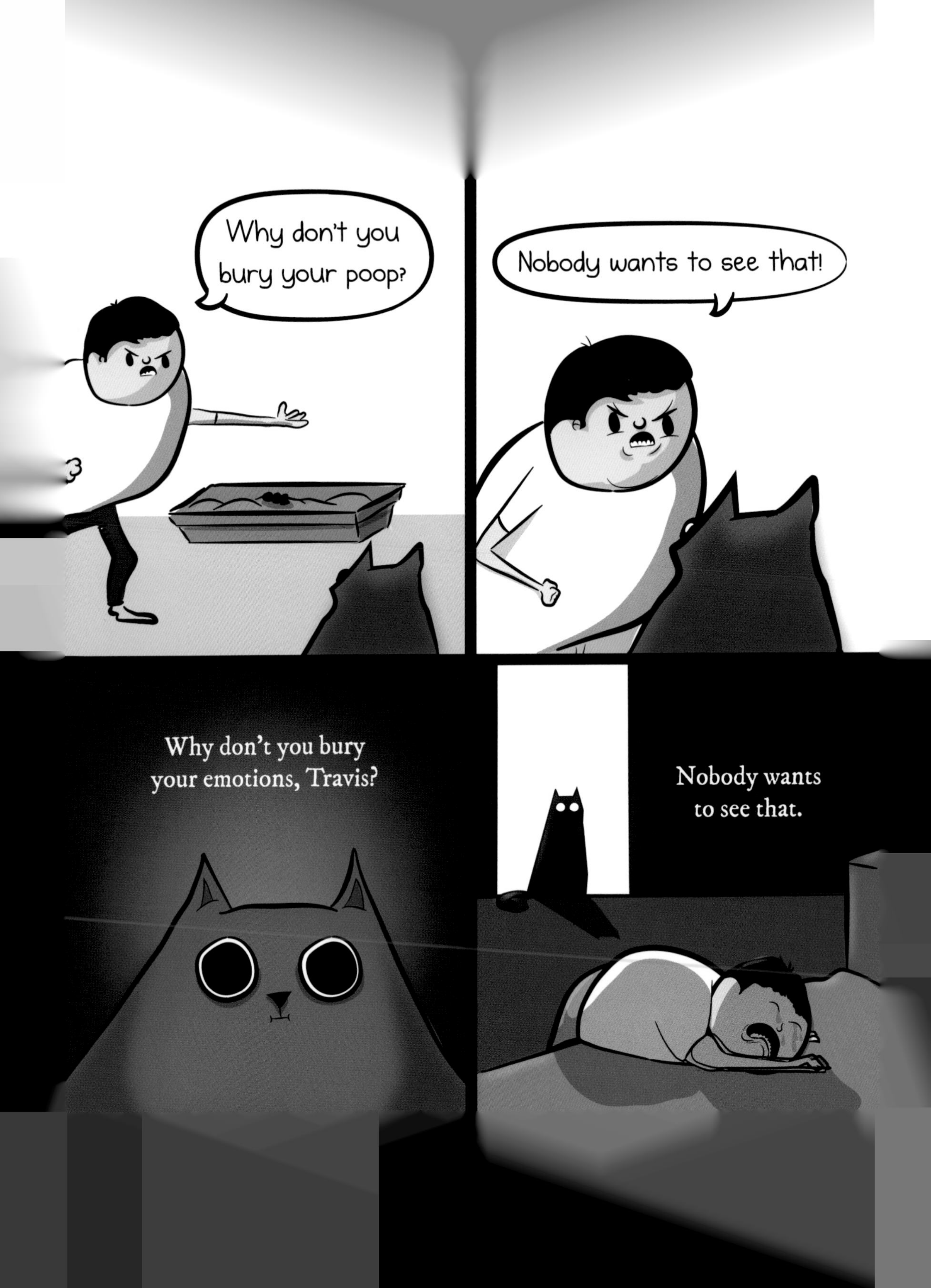
Why don't you bury your poop?
Nobody wants to see that!
Why don't you bury your emotions, Travis?
Nobody wants to see that.

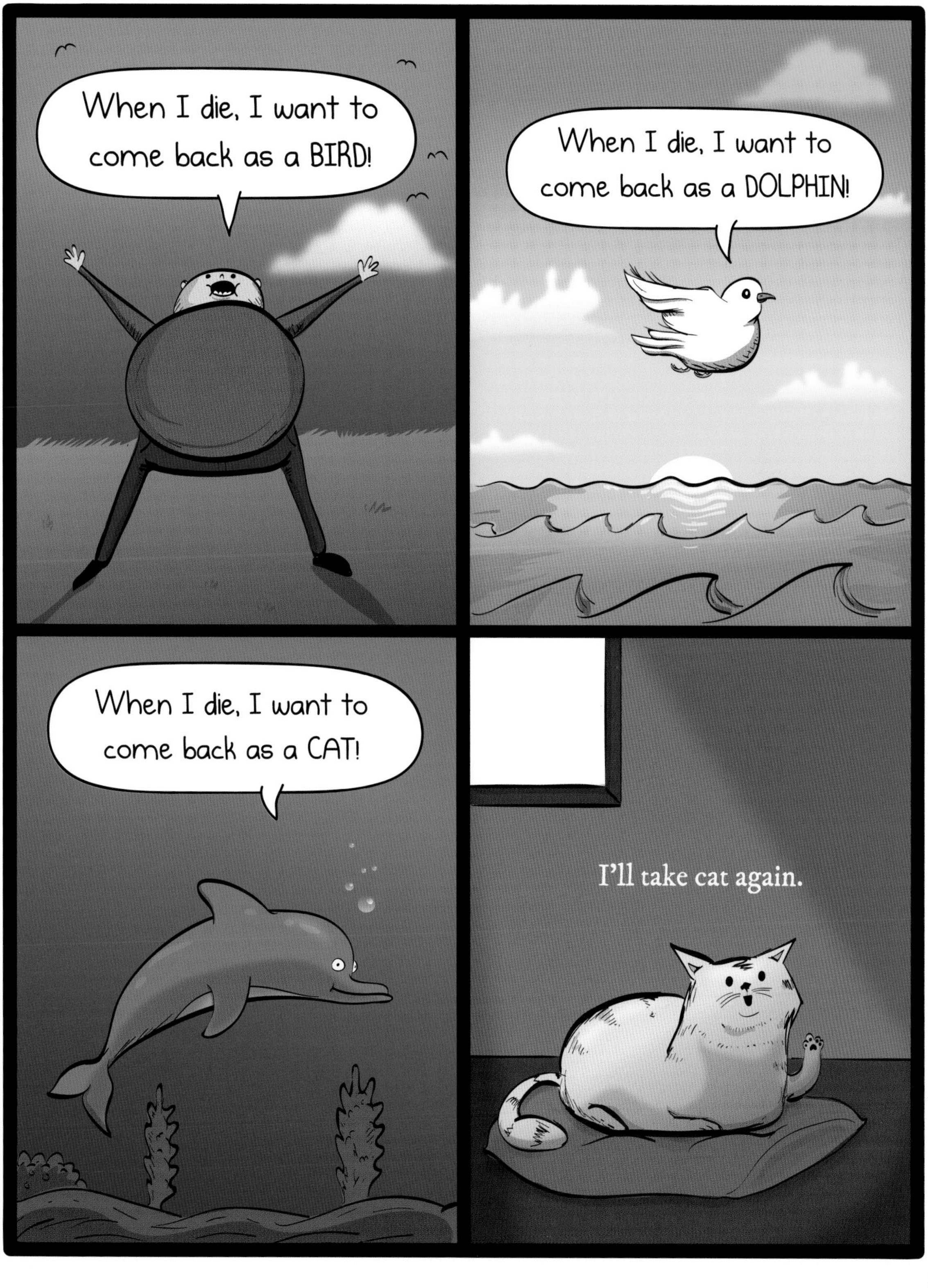
When I die, I want to come back as a BIRD!
When I die, I want to come back as a DOLPHIN!
When I die, I want to come back as a CAT!
I'll take cat again.

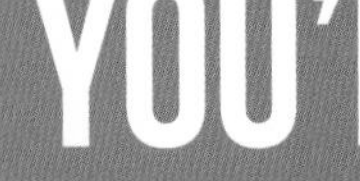

HOW TO TELL IF YOUR CAT THINKS YOU'RE NOT THAT BIG OF A DEAL

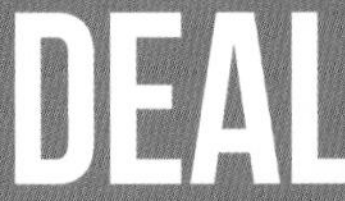

WHEN YOU SAY YOUR CAT'S NAME, THEY PRETEND TO DOZE OFF.

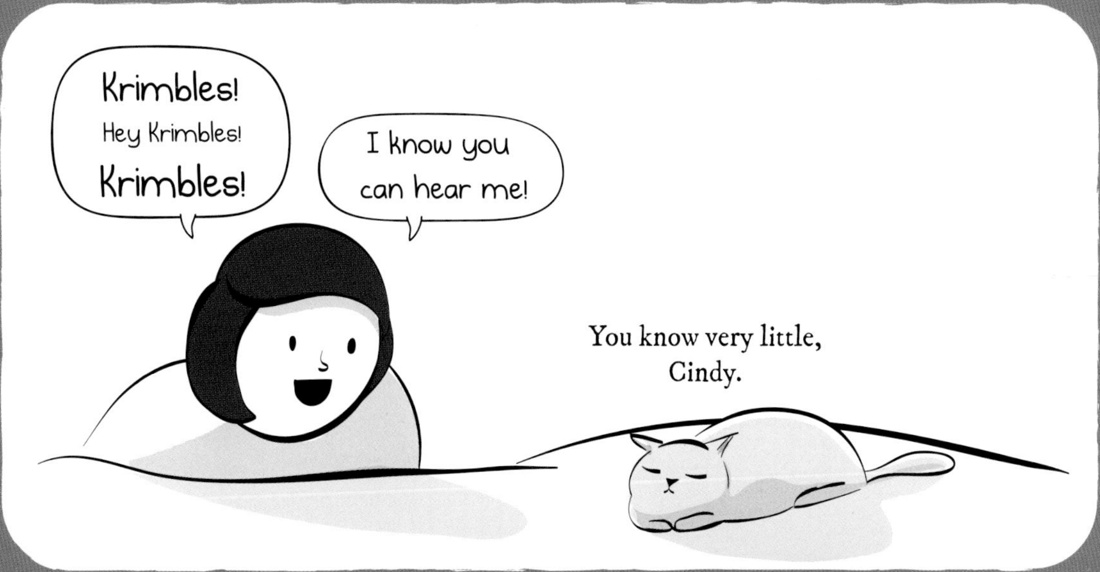
Krimbles!
Hey Krimbles!
Krimbles!
I know you can hear me!
You know very little, Cindy.

YOU SET BOUNDARIES, WHICH YOUR CAT IGNORES.

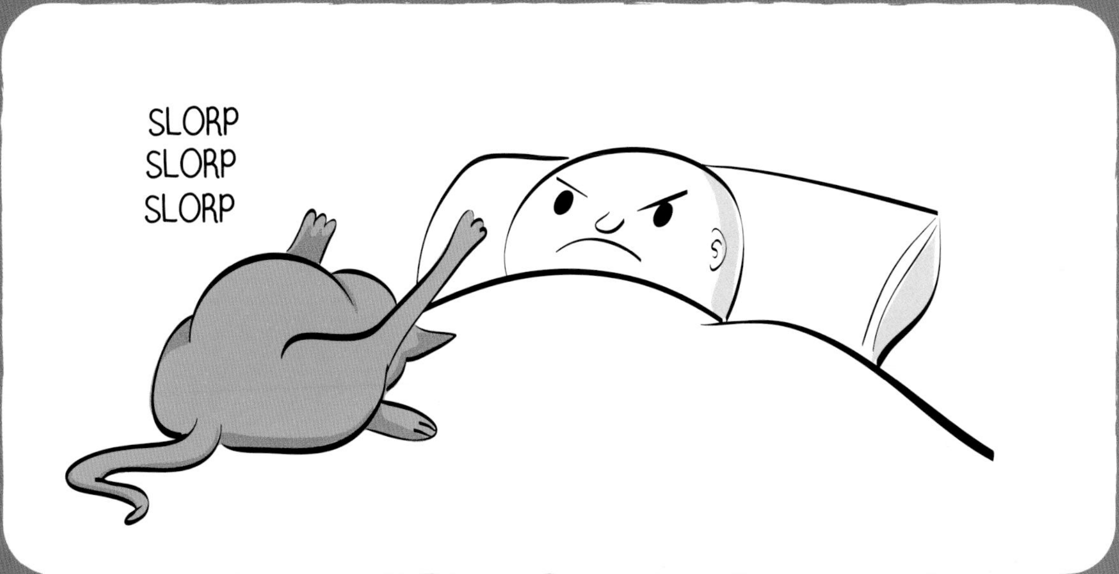
SLORP
SLORP
SLORP

YOUR CAT PRIORITIZES THEIR NEEDS OVER YOUR OWN.

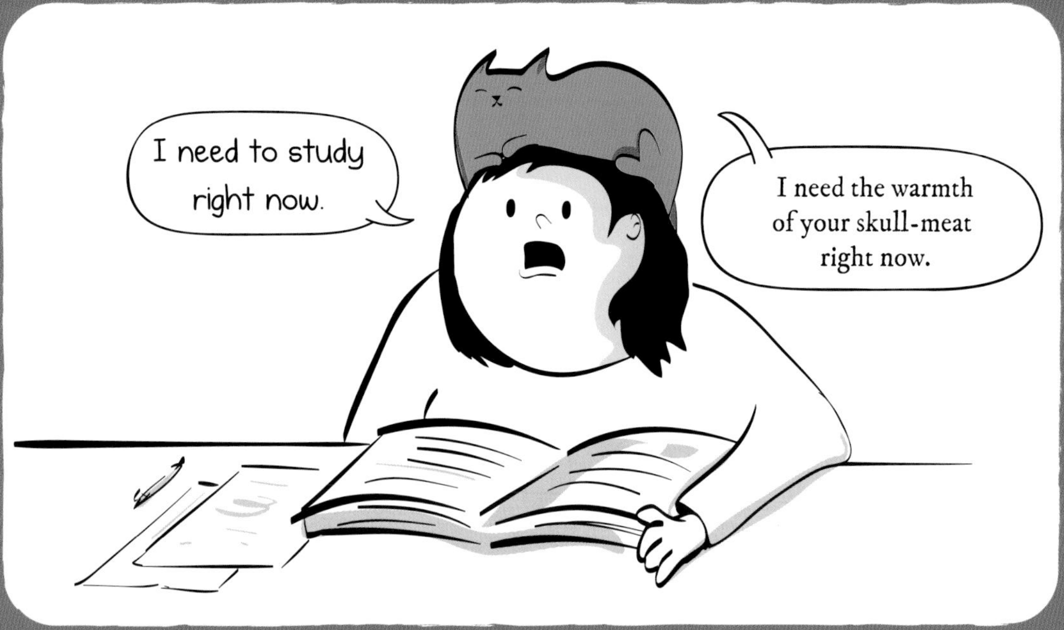
I need to study right now.
I need the warmth of your skull-meat right now.

YOUR CAT IGNORES THE GIFTS YOU BESTOW UPON THEM.

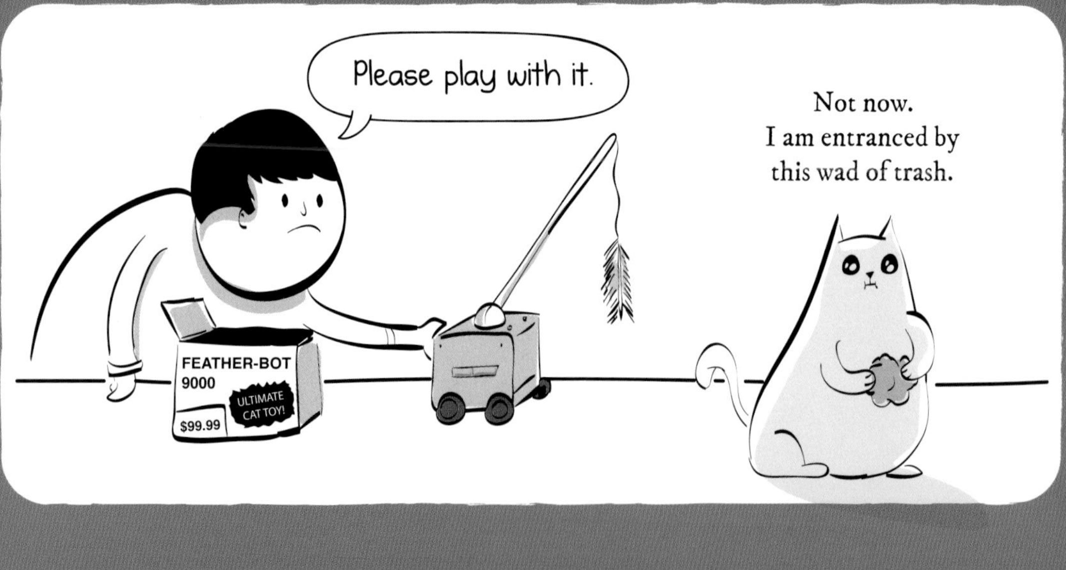
Please play with it.
Not now. I am entranced by this wad of trash.
FEATHER-BOT 9000
ULTIMATE CAT TOY!
$99.99

WHEN YOU TRY TO HAVE A MEANINGFUL CONVERSATION WITH YOUR CAT, THEY BECOME LOST IN THOUGHT.

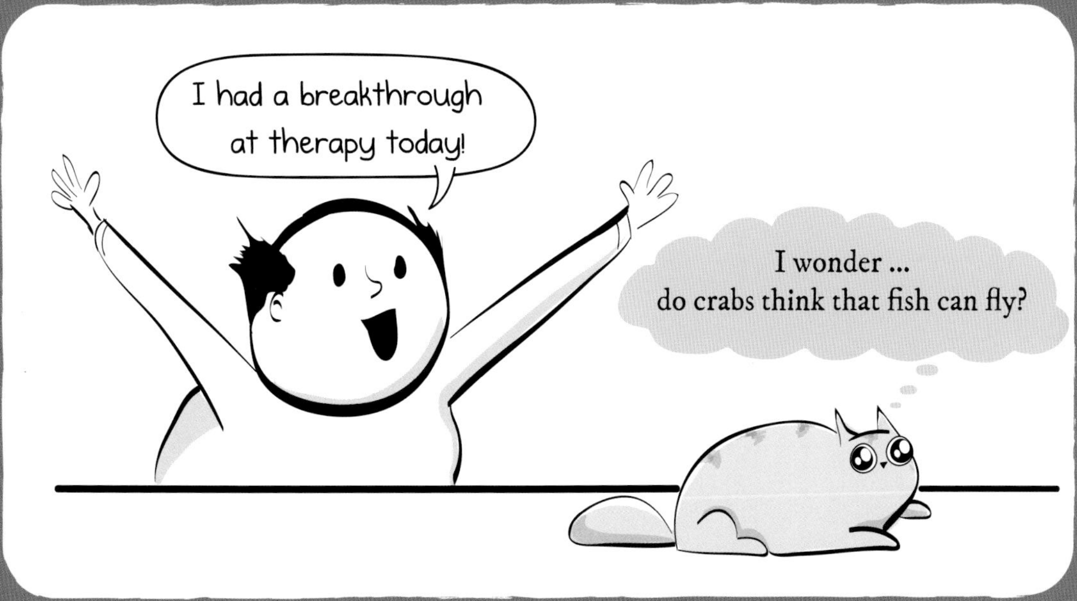
I had a breakthrough at therapy today!
I wonder ... do crabs think that fish can fly?

YOUR CAT ONLY VOCALIZES WHEN FOOD IS PRESENT.

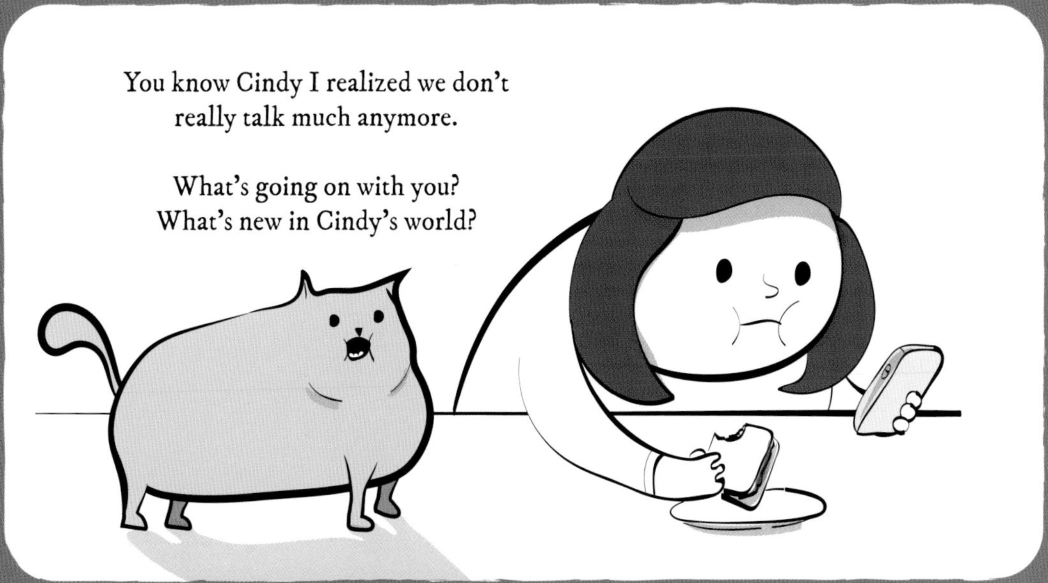
You know Cindy I realized we don't really talk much anymore.
What's going on with you? What's new in Cindy's world?

YOUR CAT EXHIBITS UNWARRANTED HOSTILITY.

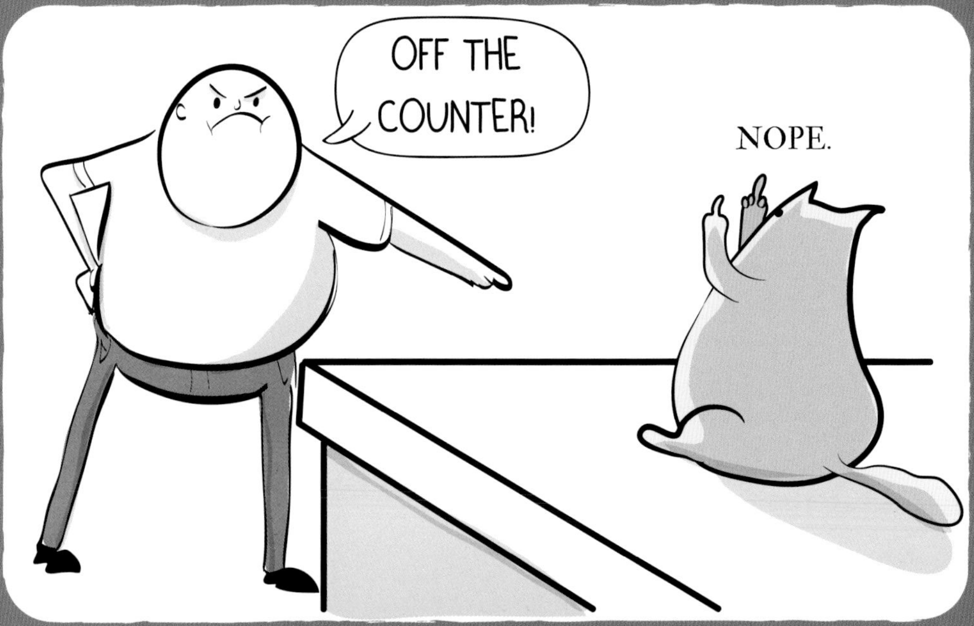
OFF THE COUNTER!
NOPE.

WHEN YOU COME HOME, YOUR CAT HIDES.

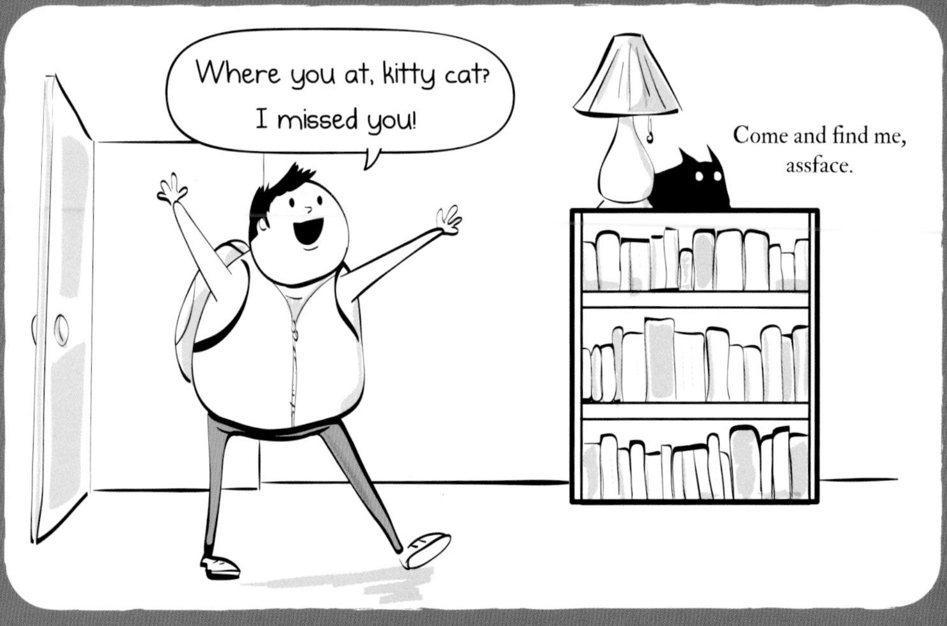
Where you at, kitty cat? I missed you!
Come and find me, assface.

YOUR CAT FORCES YOU TO BE ON THEIR SCHEDULE.

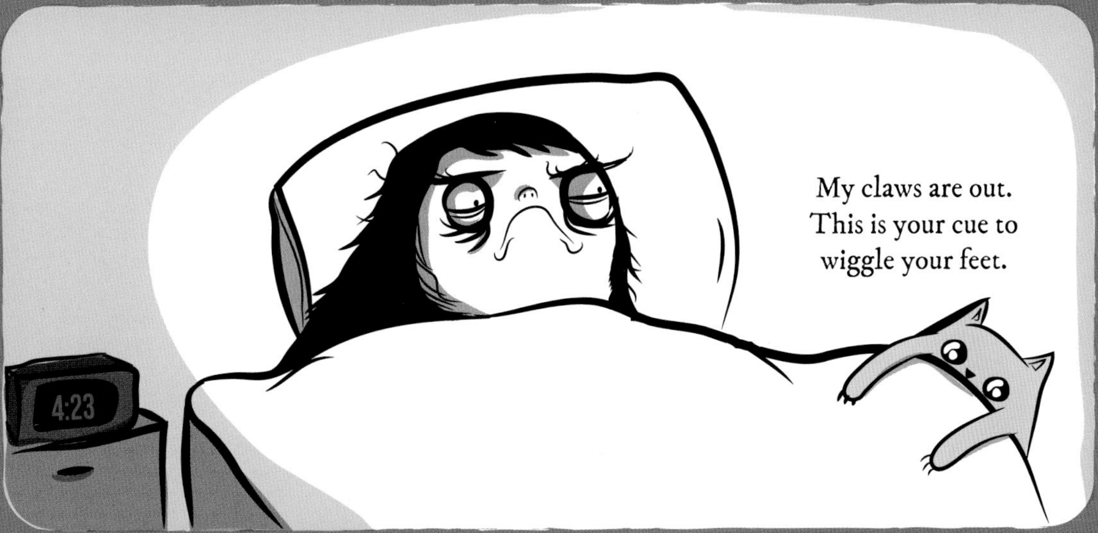
4:23
My claws are out. This is your cue to wiggle your feet.

YOUR CAT NEVER COVERS UP. NOT EVEN WHEN YOU HAVE COMPANY OVER.

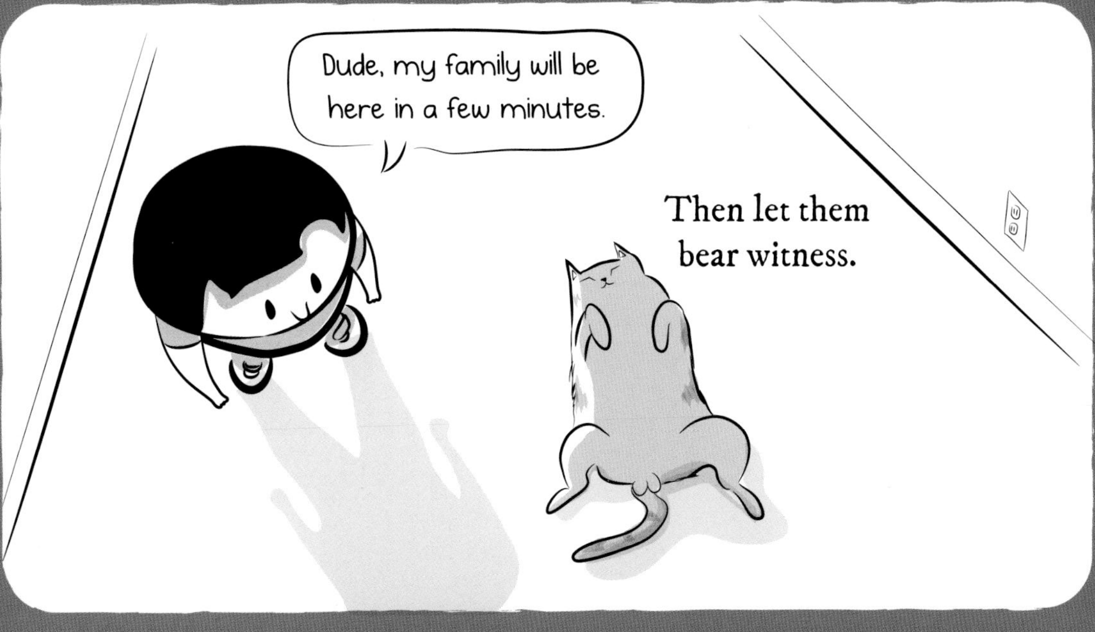
Dude, my family will be here in a few minutes.
Then let them bear witness.

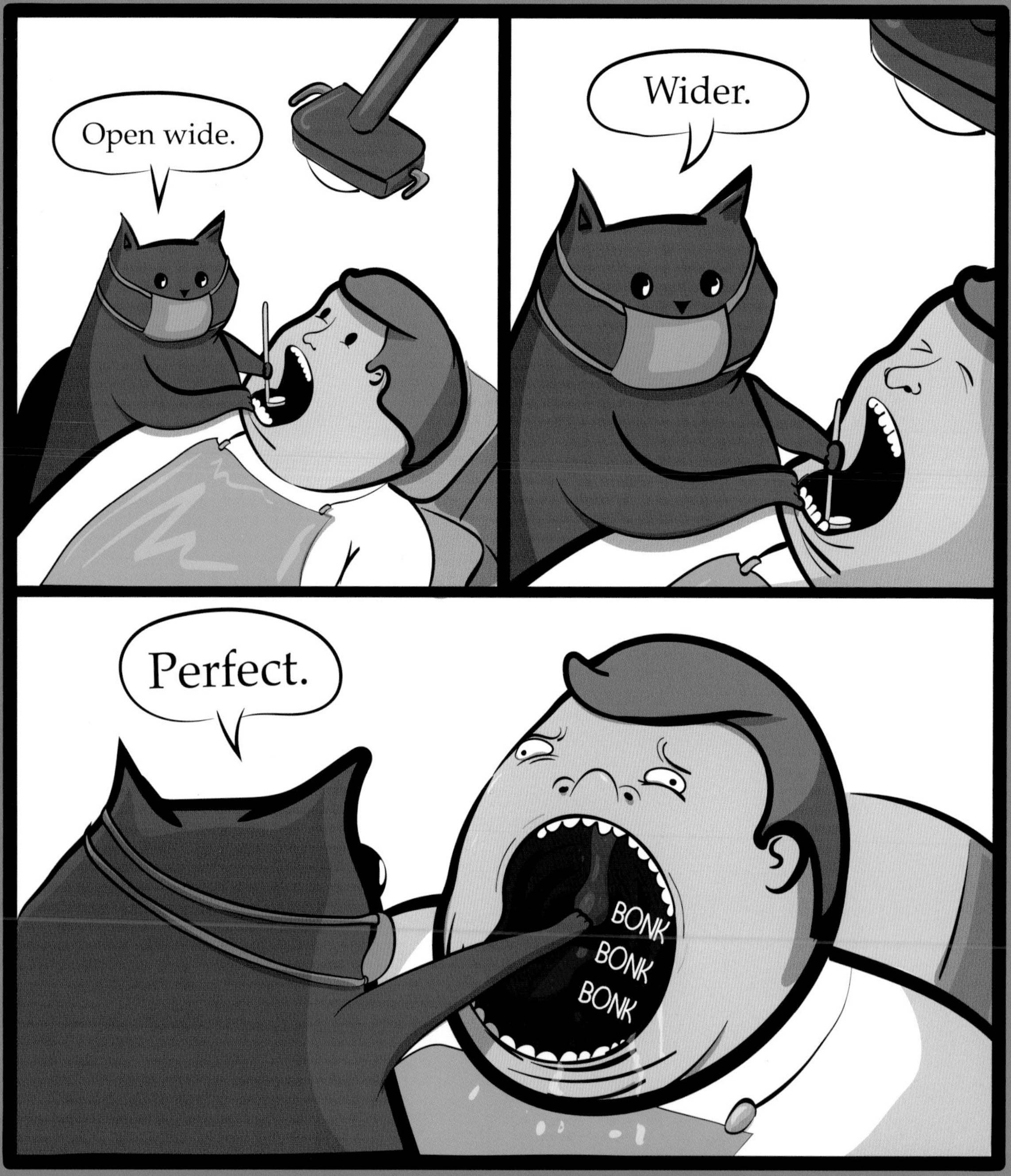
Open wide.
Wider.
Perfect.
BONK
BONK
BONK

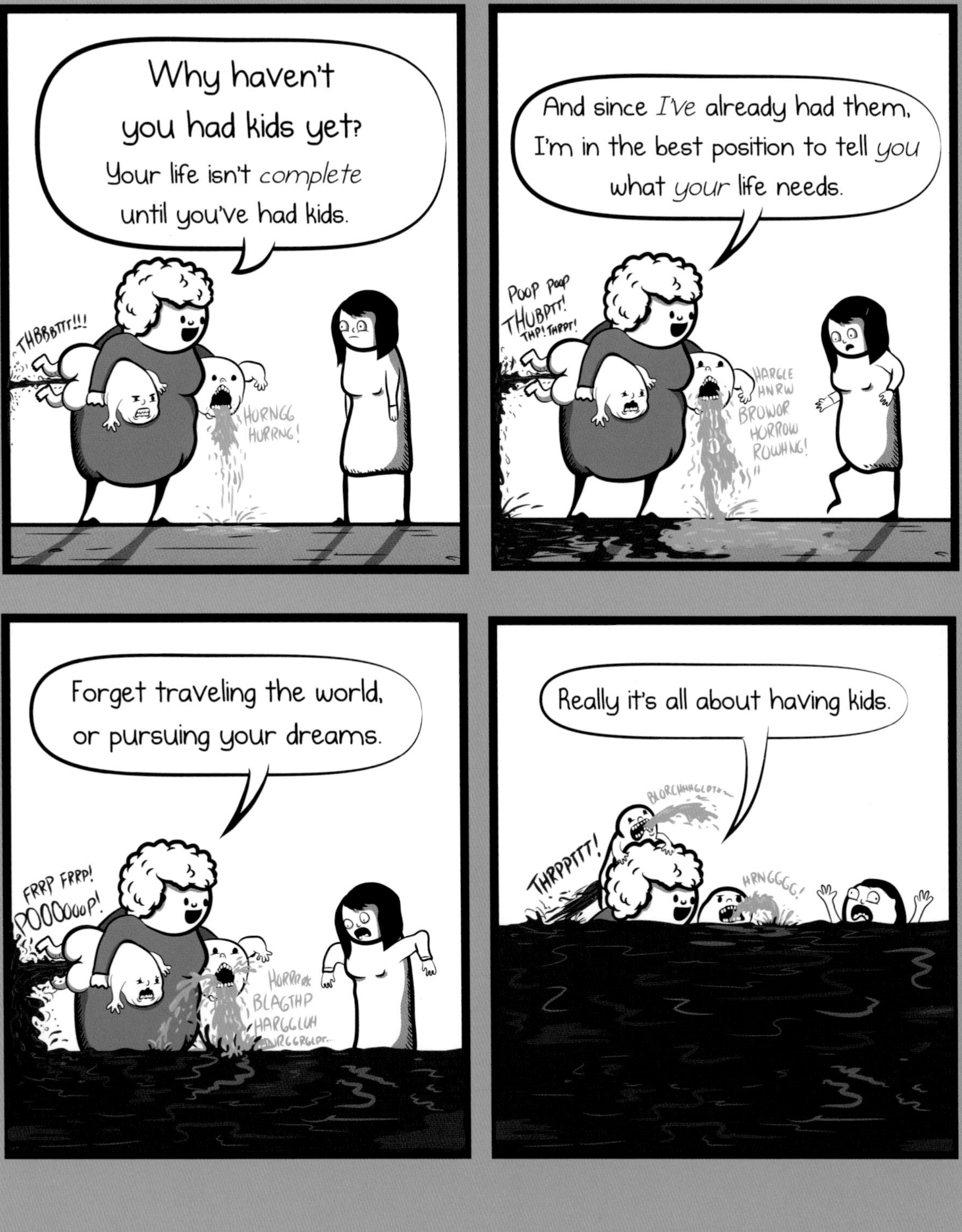
Why haven't you had kids yet? Your life isn't *complete* until you've had kids.
THBBBTTT!!!
HORNGG HURRNG!
And since *I've* already had them, I'm in the best position to tell *you* what *your* life needs.
POOP POOP THUBPTT! THP! THRPT!
HARGLE HNRW BROWOR HORROW ROWHNG!
Forget traveling the world, or pursuing your dreams.
FRRP FRRP! POOOooop!
HORRRRK BLAGTHP HARGGLUH
Really it's all about having kids.
THRPPTTT!
HRNGGGG!

HOW TO BE A DOG

1. MAKE SOMEONE LOVE YOU.

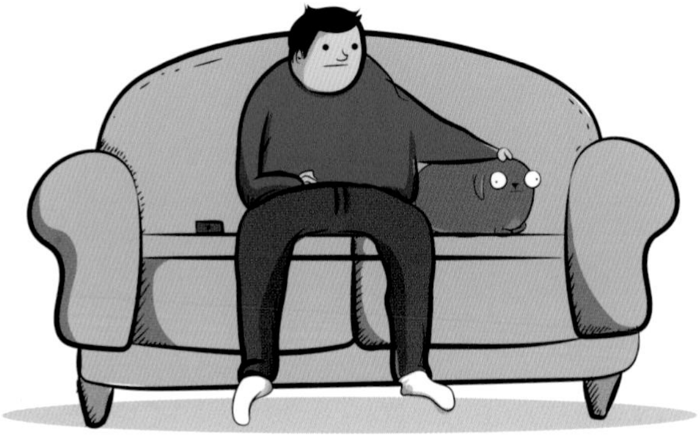

2. SPEND YOUR WHOLE LIFE FINDING CREATIVE WAYS TO KILL YOURSELF.

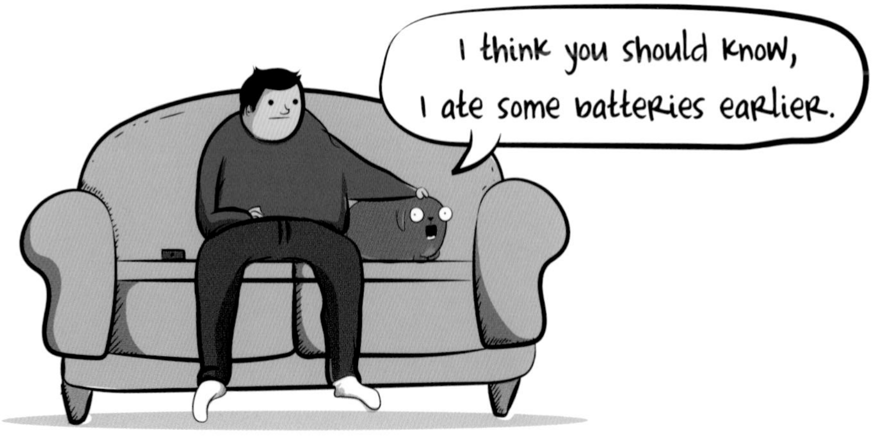
I think you should know, I ate some batteries earlier.

HOW TO BE A BABY

1. SEE "HOW TO BE A DOG."

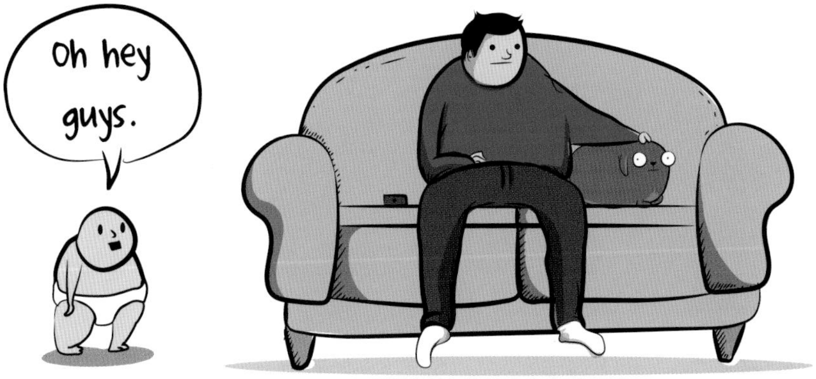
Oh hey guys.

2. REPEAT.

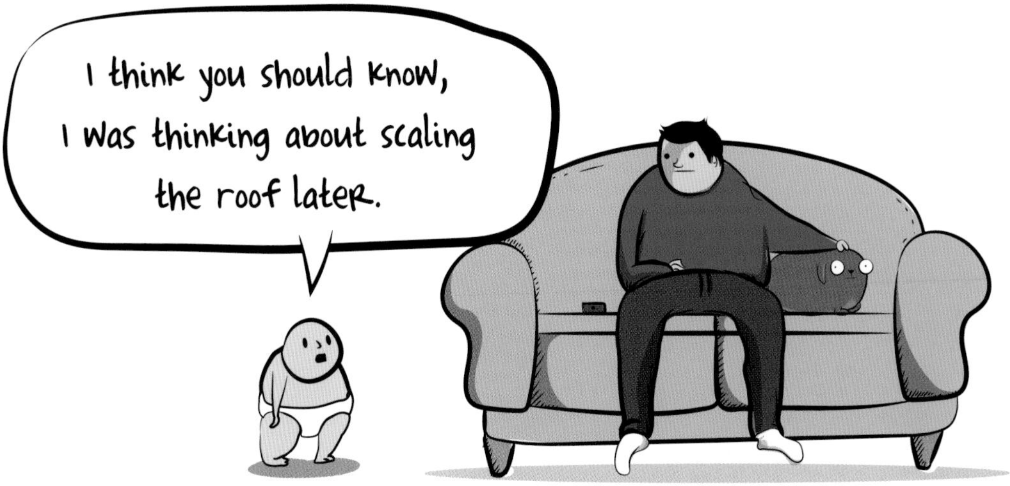
I think you should know, I was thinking about scaling the roof later.

Leaving the dog.

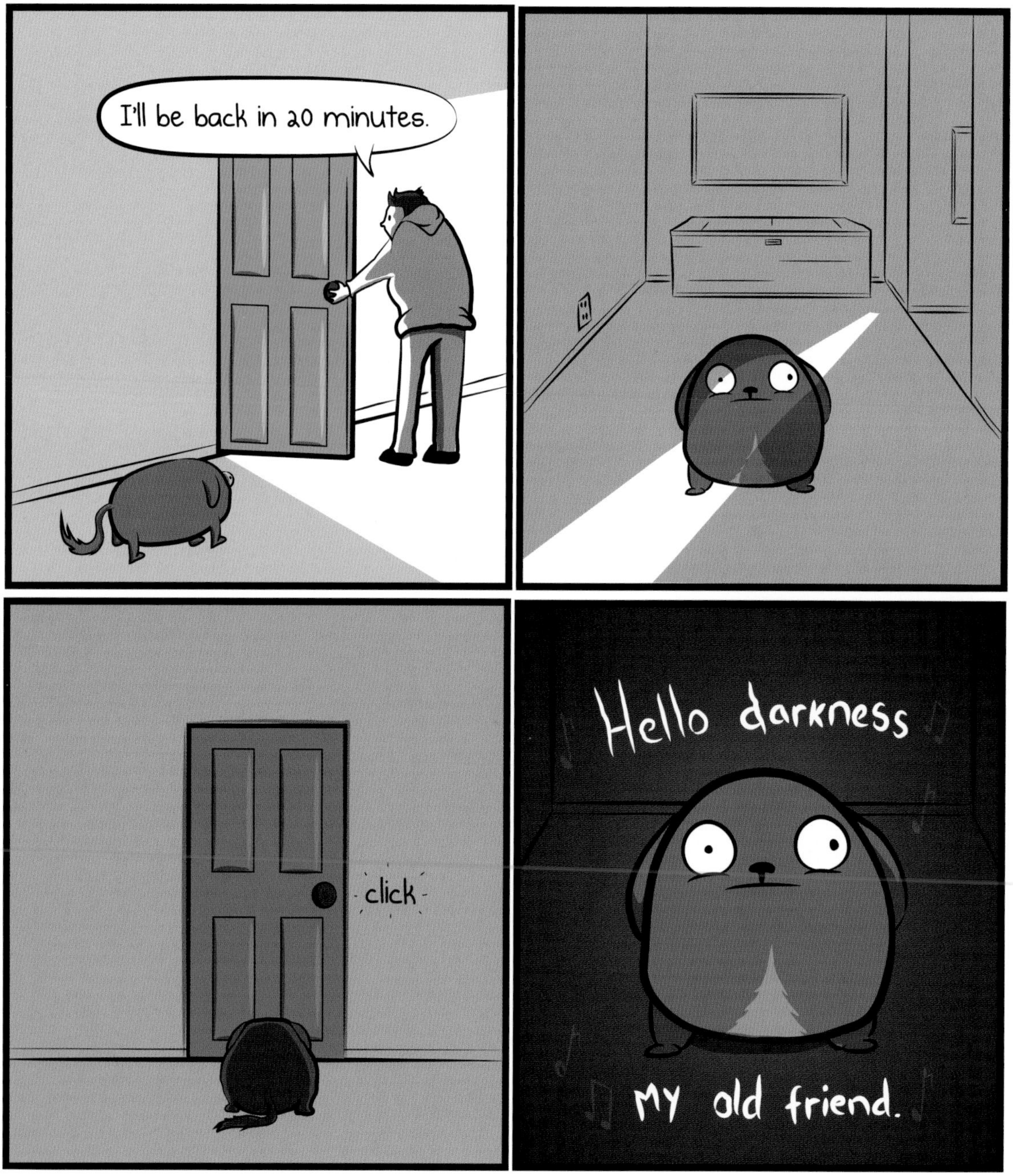
I'll be back in 20 minutes.
click
Hello darkness
My old friend.

Leaving the cat.

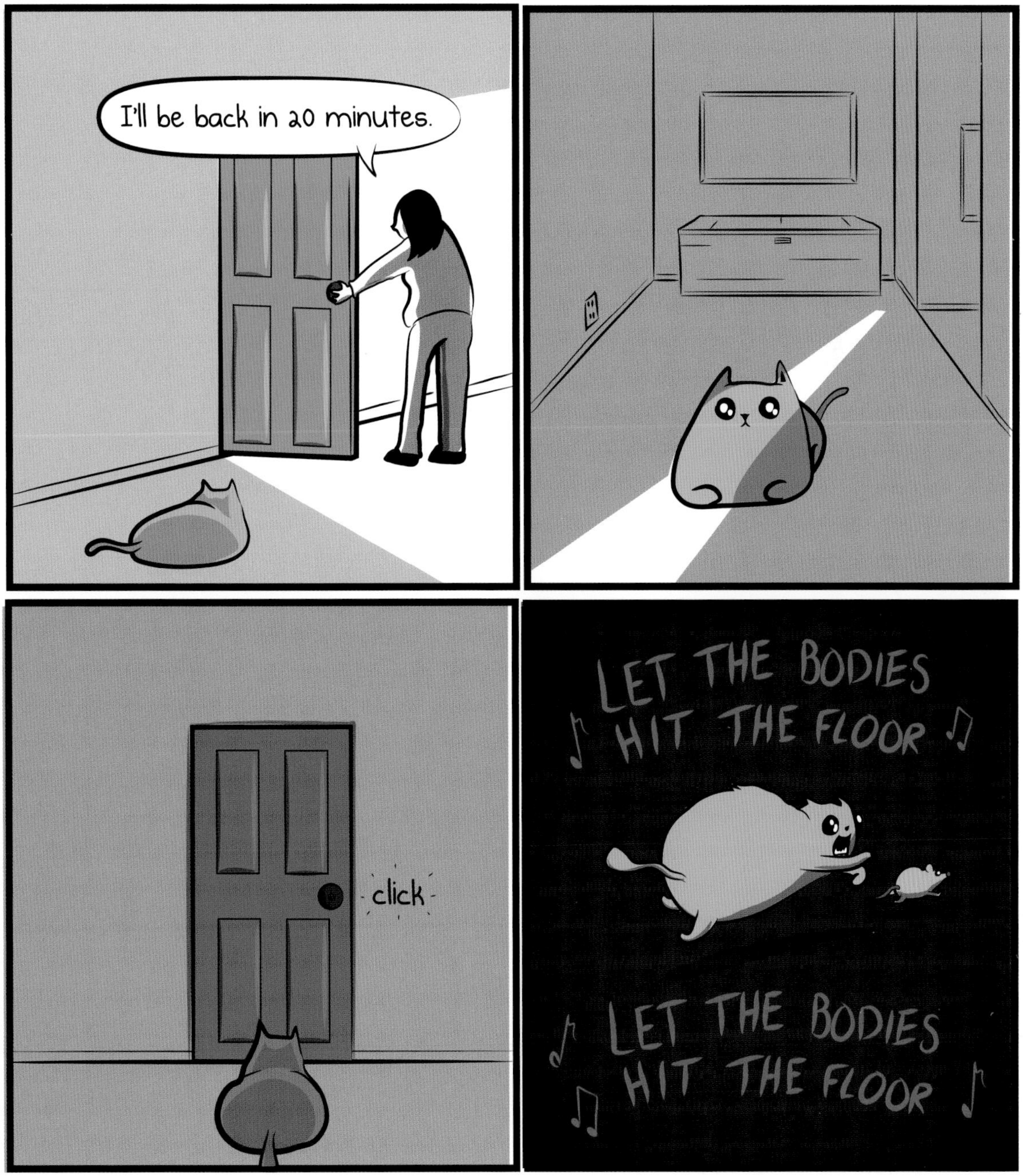
I'll be back in 20 minutes.
click
LET THE BODIES HIT THE FLOOR
LET THE BODIES HIT THE FLOOR

How to cuddle like you mean it.

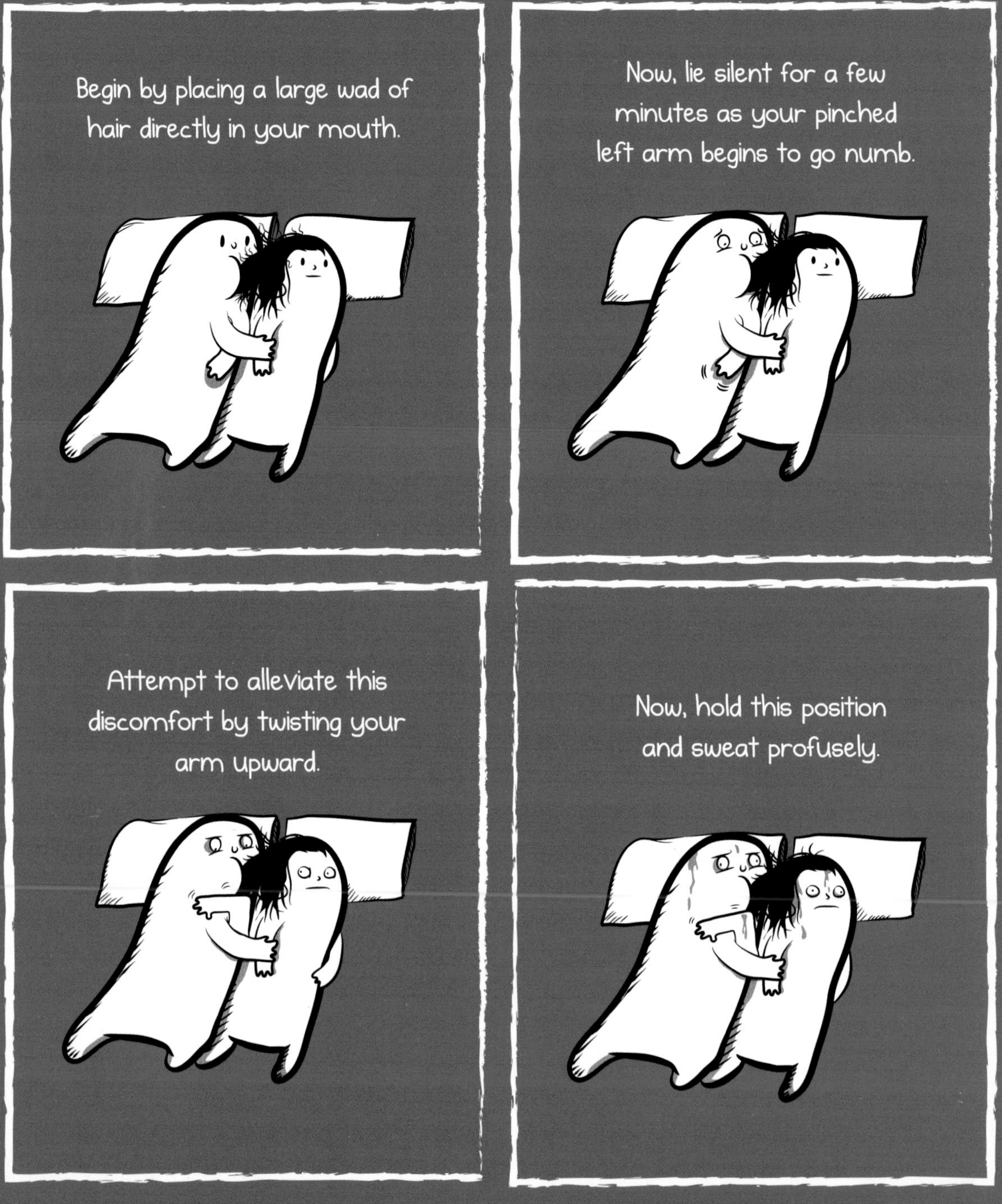
Begin by placing a large wad of hair directly in your mouth.
Now, lie silent for a few minutes as your pinched left arm begins to go numb.
Attempt to alleviate this discomfort by twisting your arm upward.
Now, hold this position and sweat profusely.

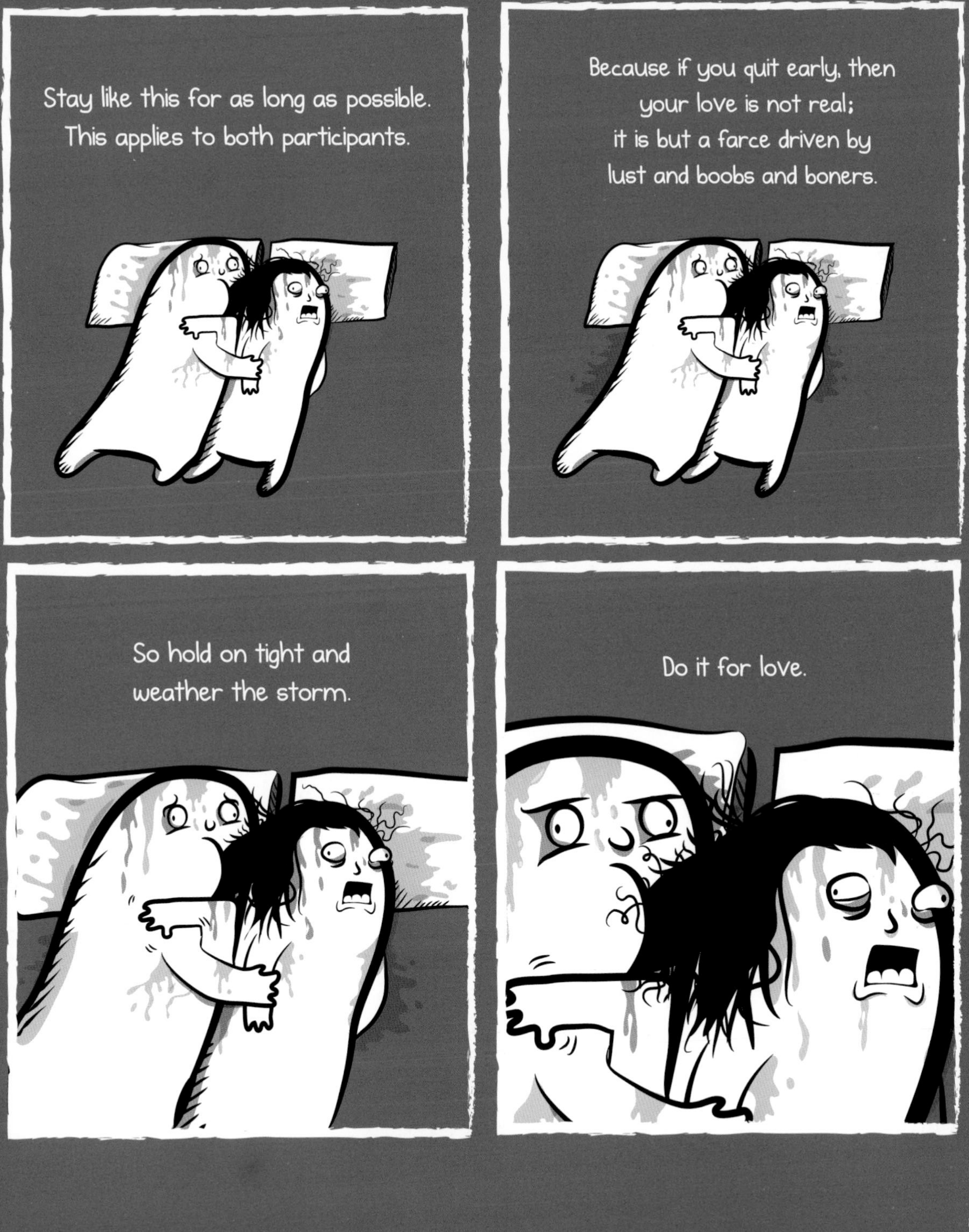
Stay like this for as long as possible. This applies to both participants.
Because if you quit early, then your love is not real; it is but a farce driven by lust and boobs and boners.
So hold on tight and weather the storm.
Do it for love.

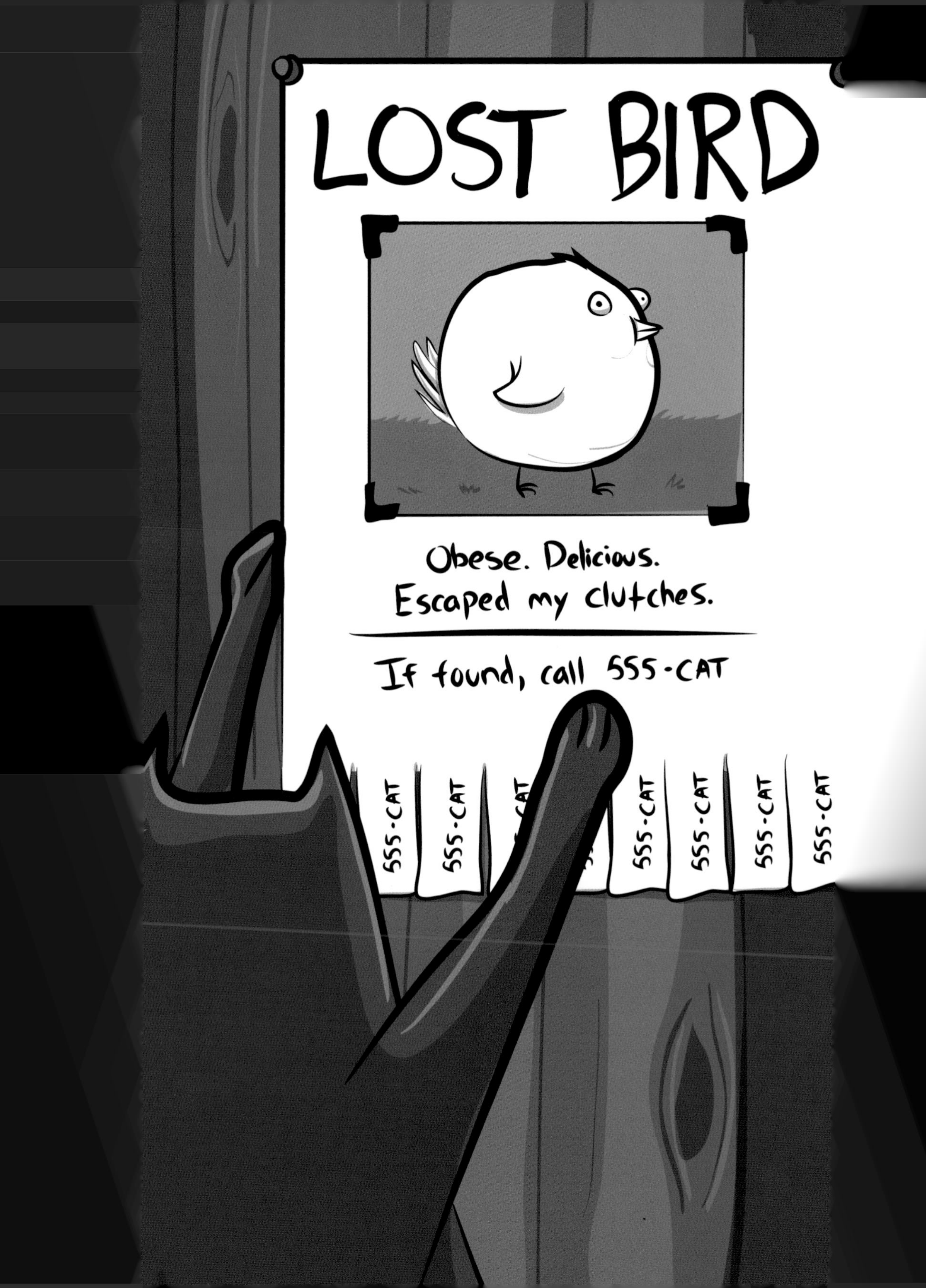
LOST BIRD
Obese. Delicious.
Escaped my clutches.
If found, call 555-CAT
555-CAT
555-CAT
555-CAT
555-CAT
555-CAT

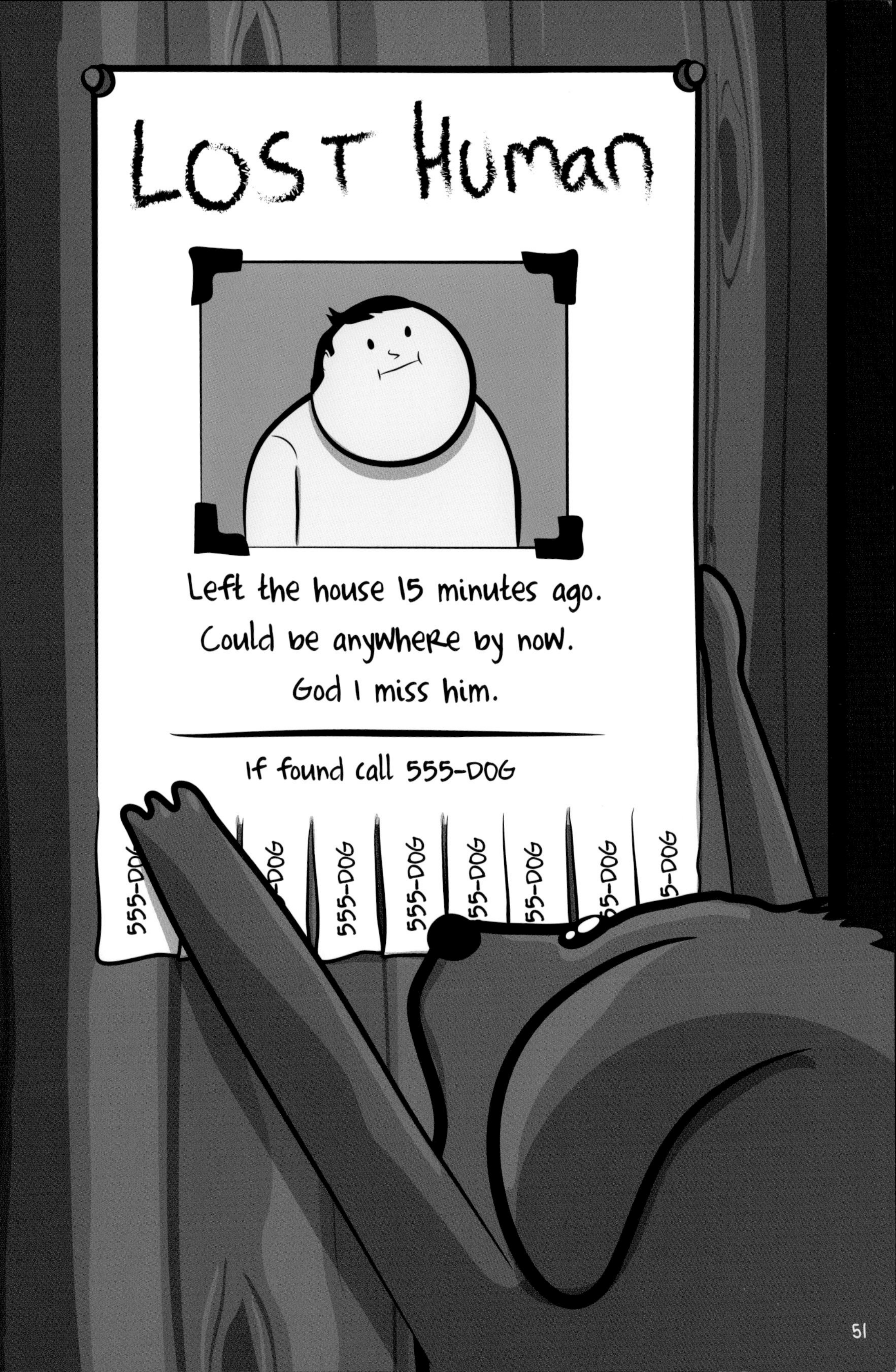
LOST HUMAN
Left the house 15 minutes ago.
Could be anywhere by now.
God I miss him.
If found call 555-DOG
555-DOG
555-DOG
555-DOG
555-DOG
555-DOG
5-DOG

How I see my cat.

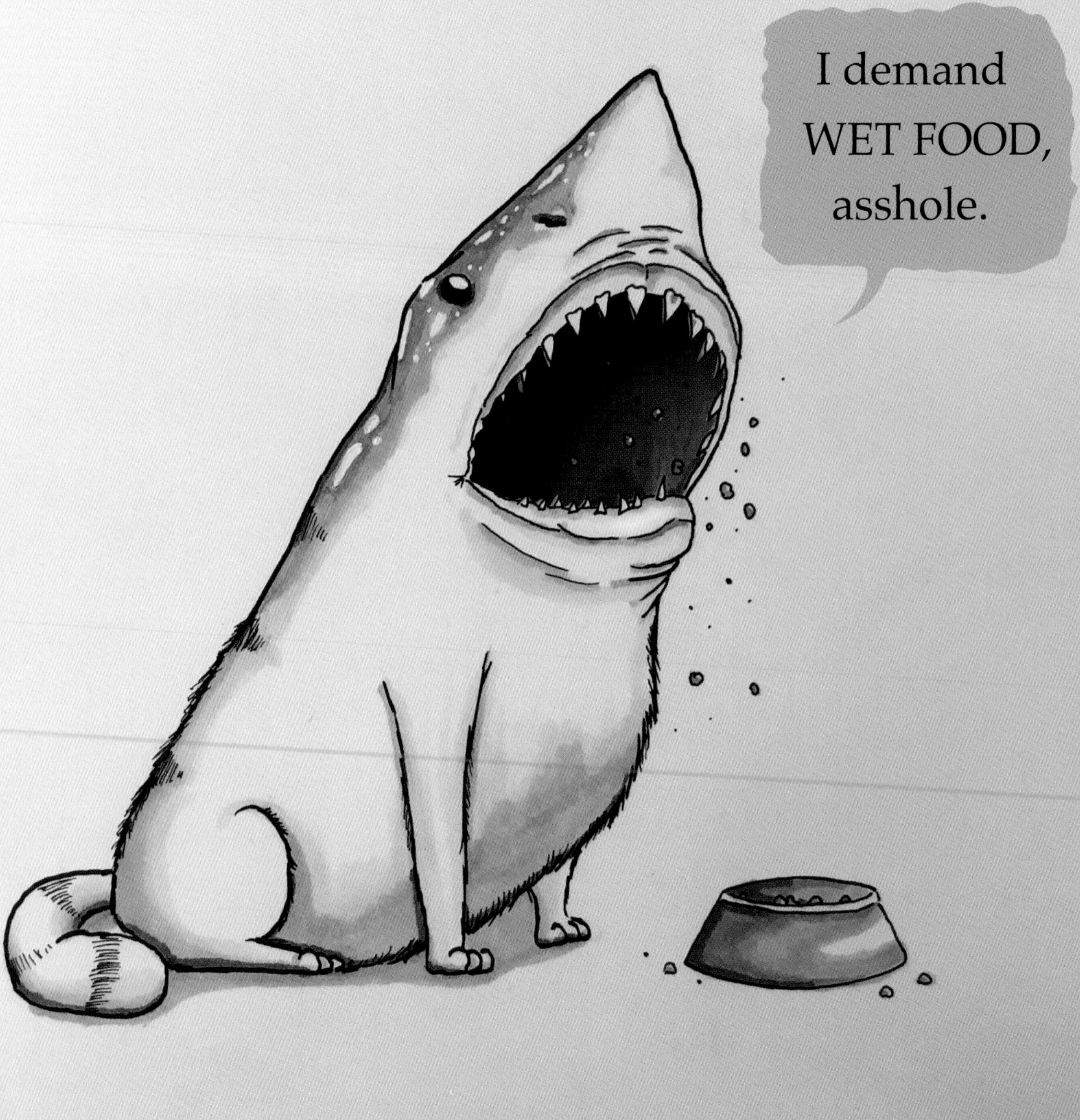
I demand
WET FOOD,
asshole.

How my cat sees me.

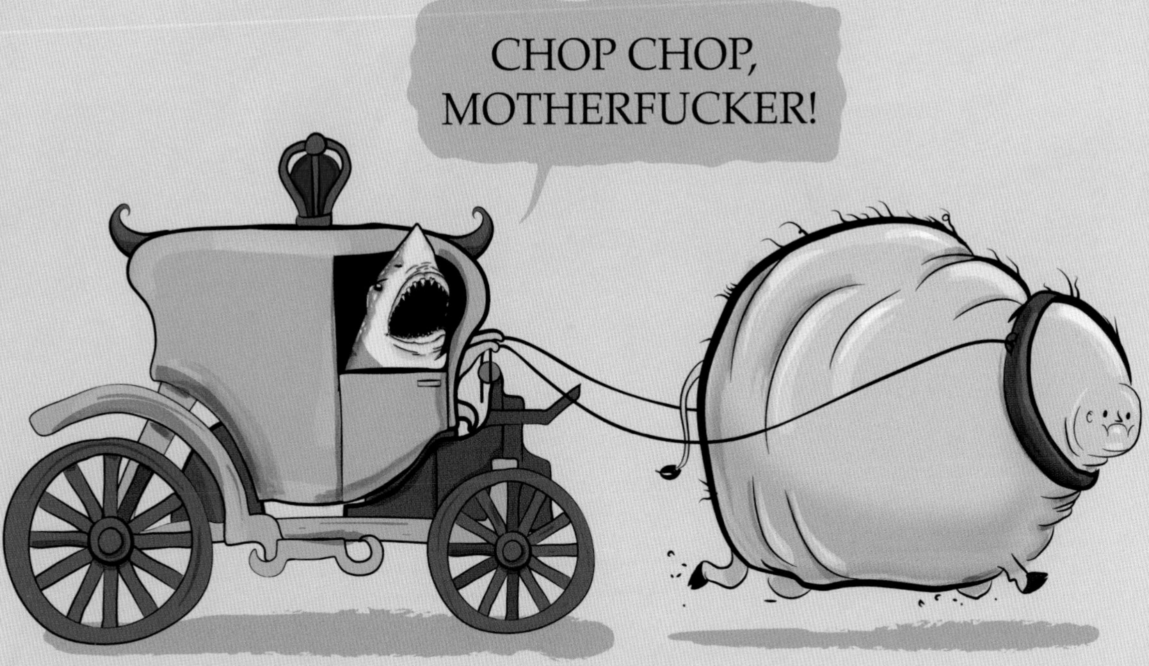
CHOP CHOP,
MOTHERFUCKER!

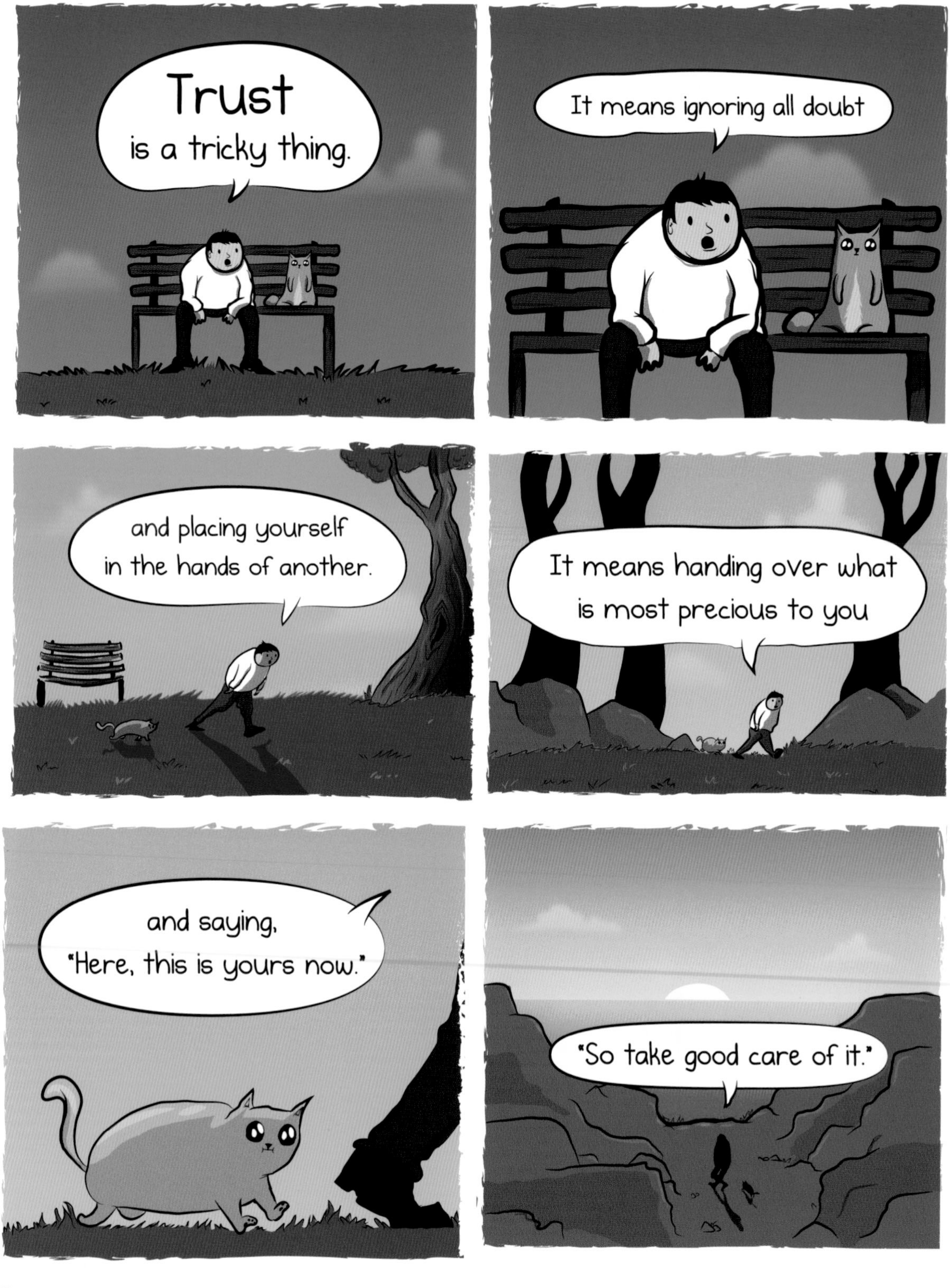
Trust
is a tricky thing.
It means ignoring all doubt
and placing yourself in the hands of another.
It means handing over what is most precious to you
and saying, "Here, this is yours now."
"So take good care of it."

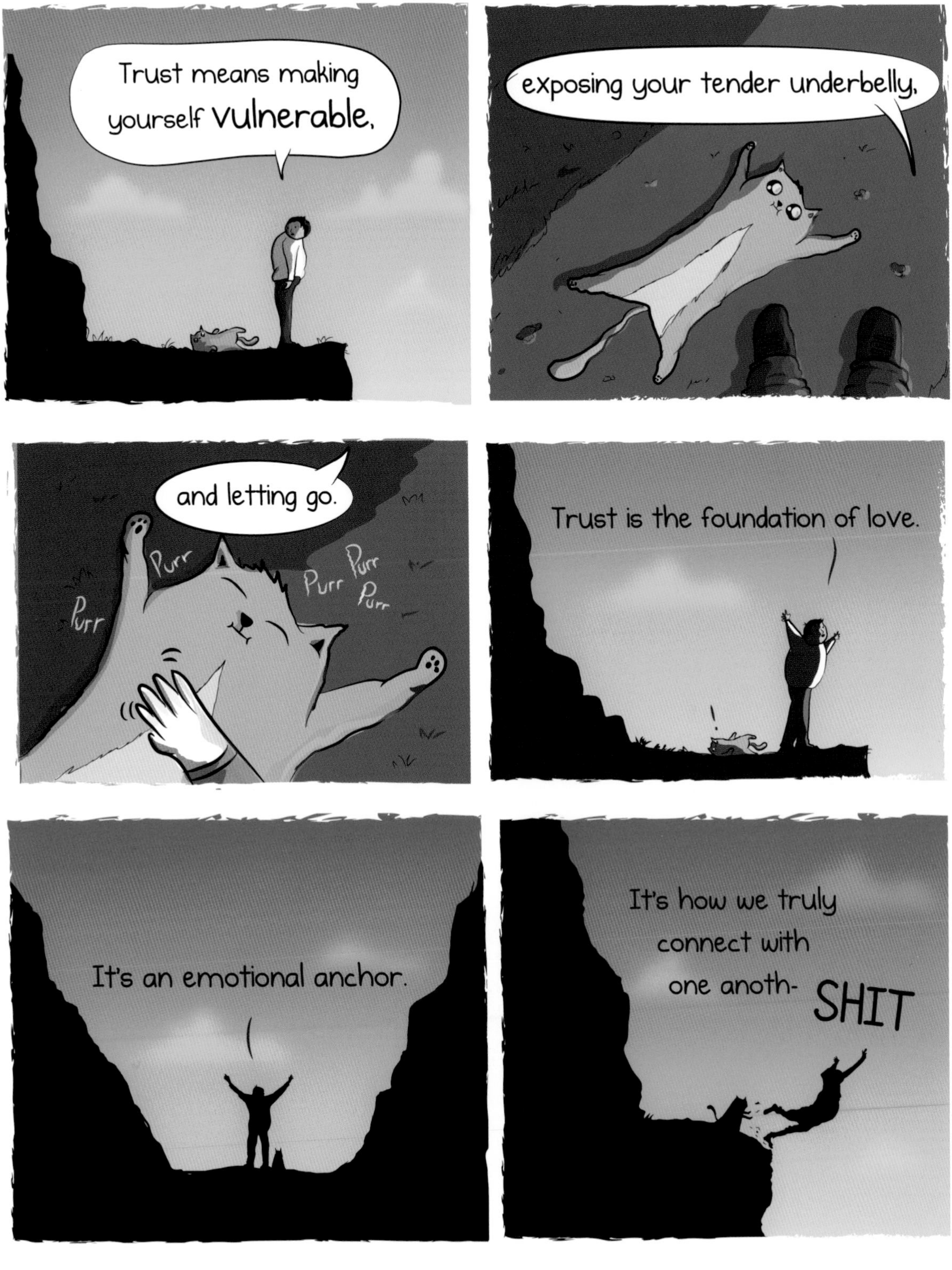
Trust means making yourself vulnerable,
exposing your tender underbelly,
and letting go.
Purr
Purr
Purr
Purr
Purr
Trust is the foundation of love.
It's an emotional anchor.
It's how we truly connect with one anoth-
SHIT

Cat: Tactical Analysis

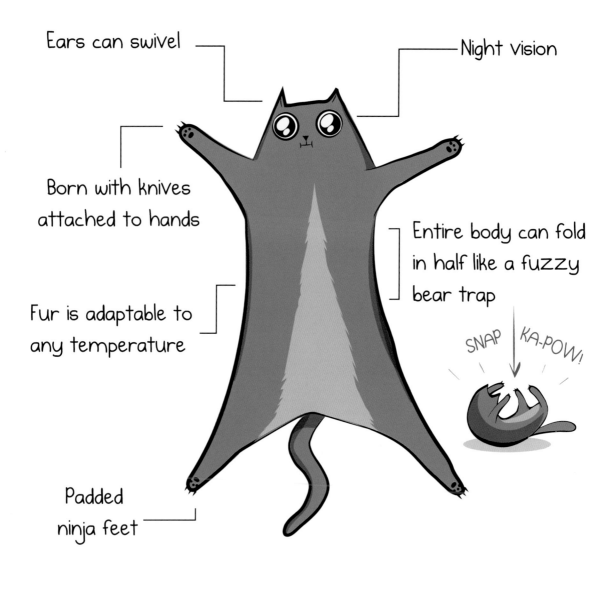

Ears can swivel

Night vision

Born with knives attached to hands

Fur is adaptable to any temperature

Entire body can fold in half like a fuzzy bear trap

SNAP KA-POW!

Padded ninja feet

Tactical score: ★★★★★

Baby: Tactical Analysis

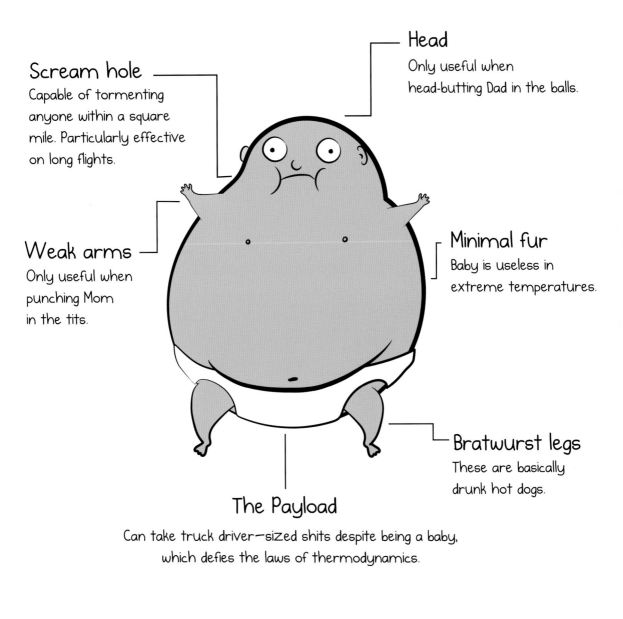

Head
Only useful when head-butting Dad in the balls.

Scream hole
Capable of tormenting anyone within a square mile. Particularly effective on long flights.

Weak arms
Only useful when punching Mom in the tits.

Minimal fur
Baby is useless in extreme temperatures.

Bratwurst legs
These are basically drunk hot dogs.

The Payload
Can take truck driver–sized shits despite being a baby, which defies the laws of thermodynamics.

Tactical score: ★★★★★

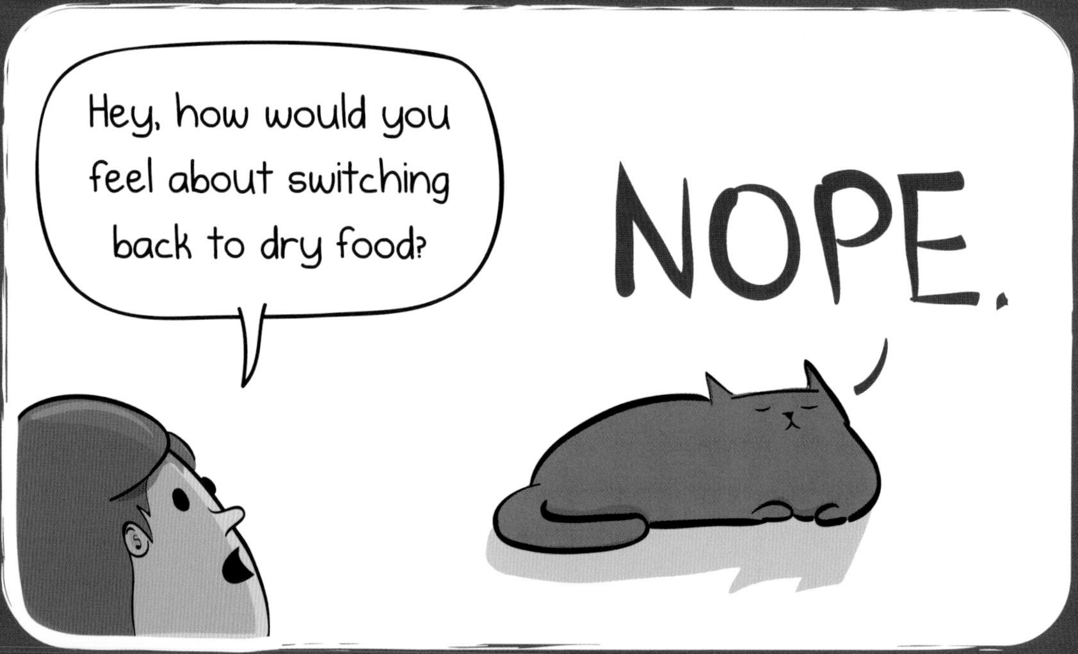
Hey, how would you feel about switching back to dry food?
NOPE.

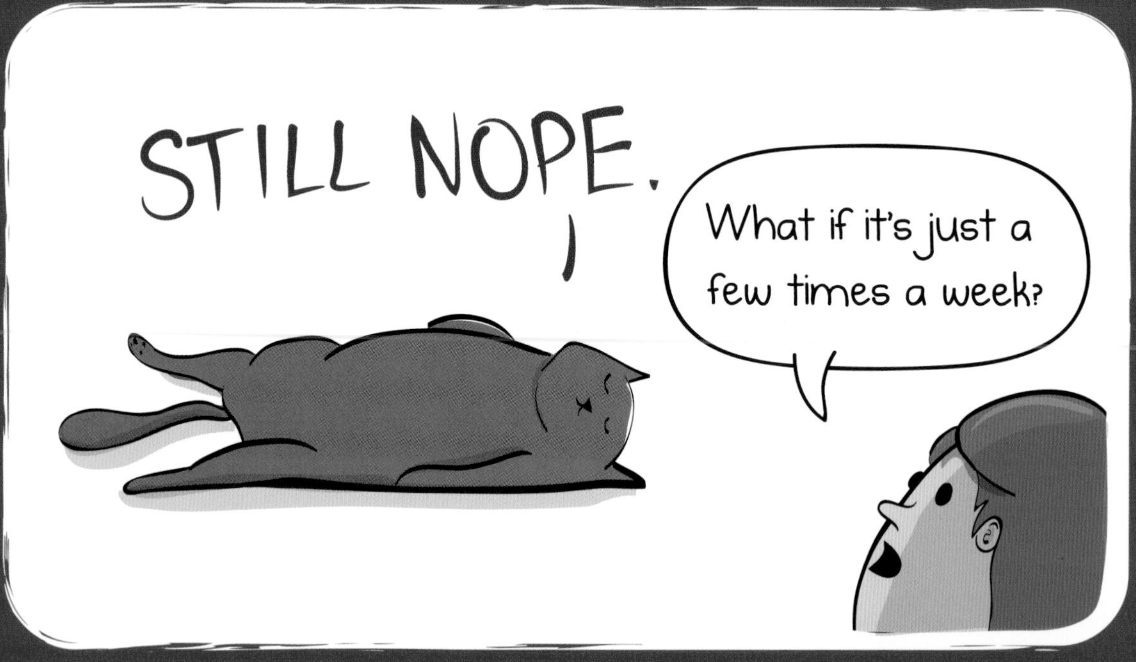
STILL NOPE.
What if it's just a few times a week?

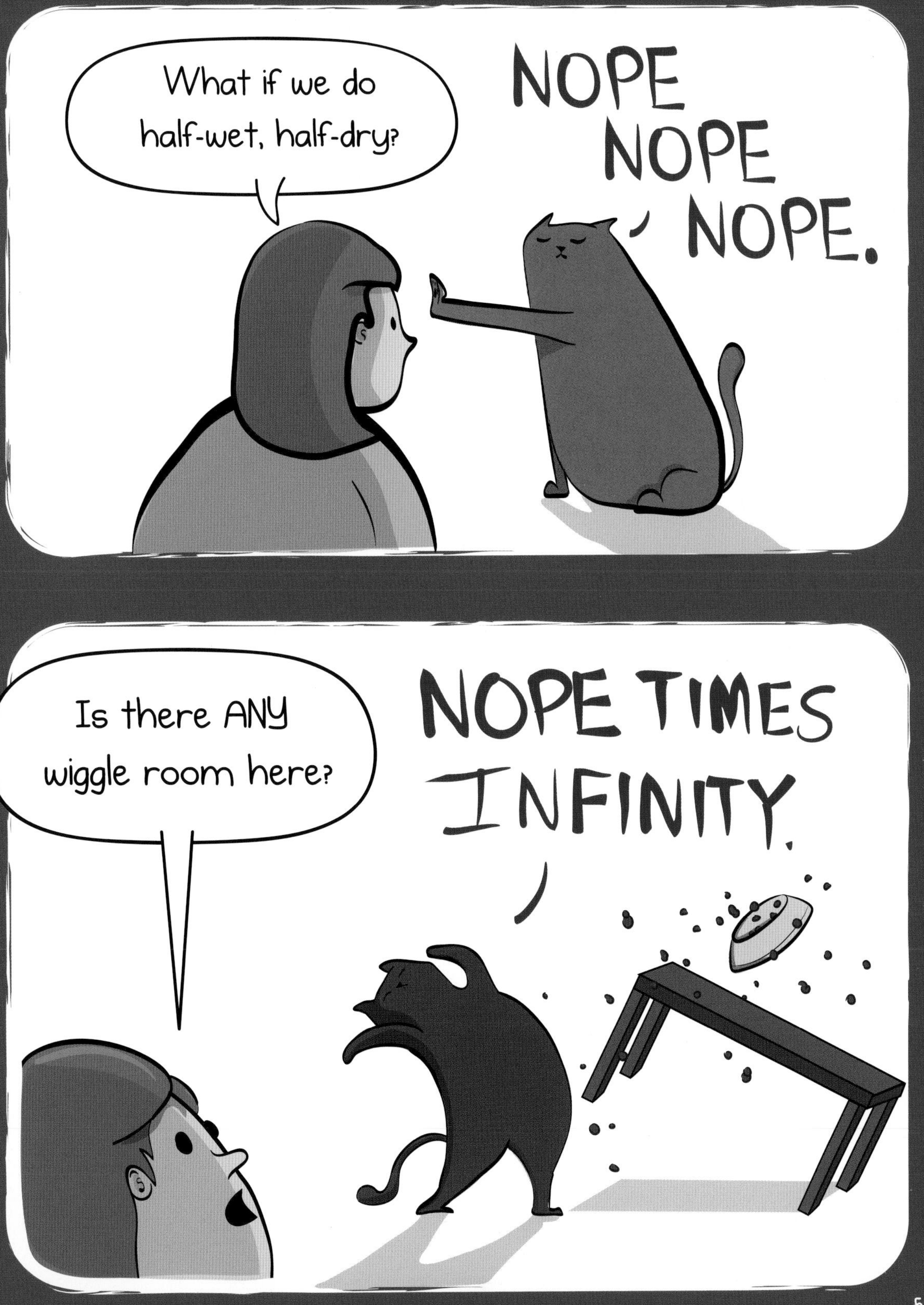
What if we do half-wet, half-dry?
NOPE NOPE NOPE.
Is there ANY wiggle room here?
NOPE TIMES INFINITY.

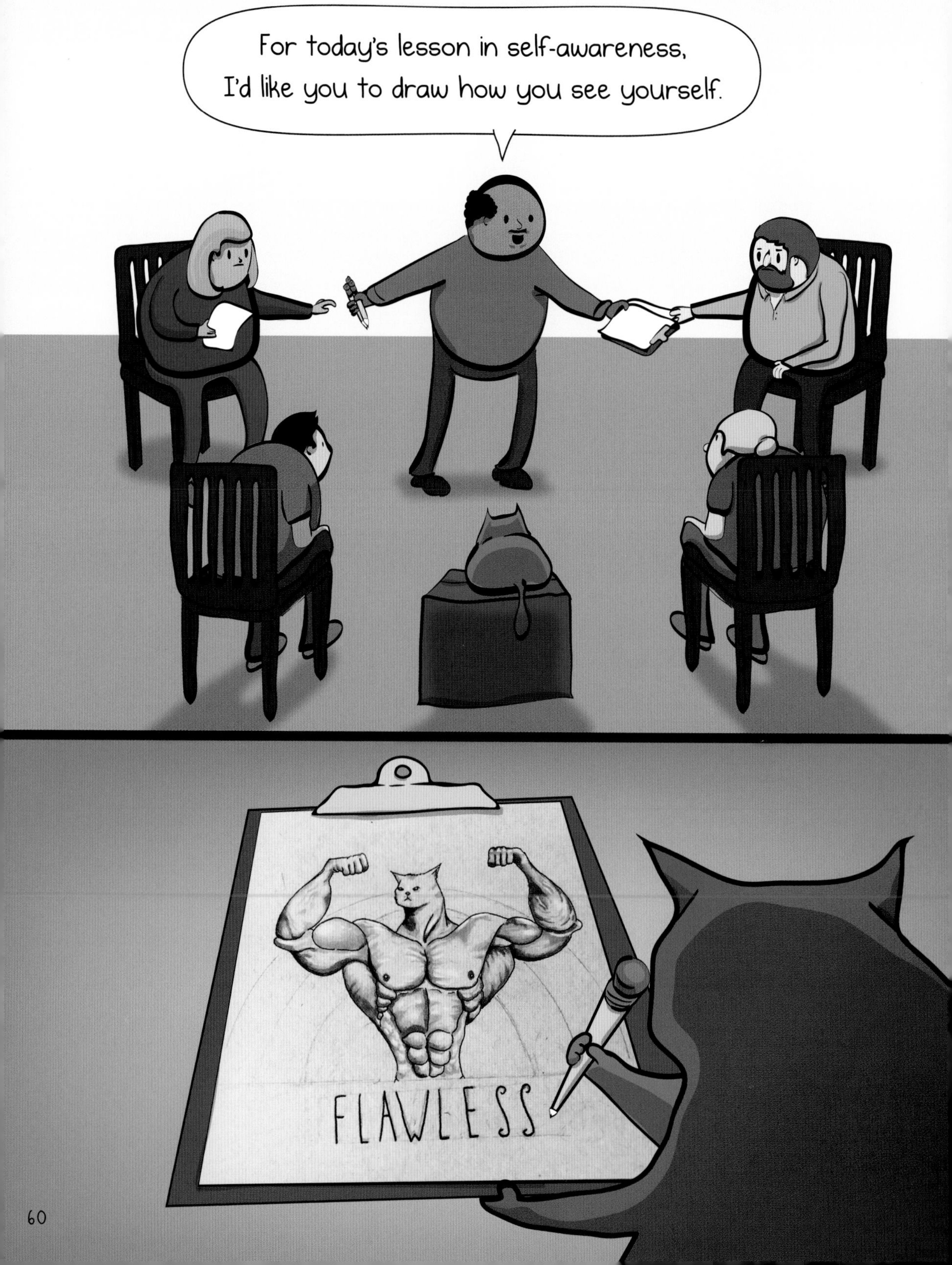
For today's lesson in self-awareness,
I'd like you to draw how you see yourself.
FLAWLESS

How to use a selfie stick without bothering others.

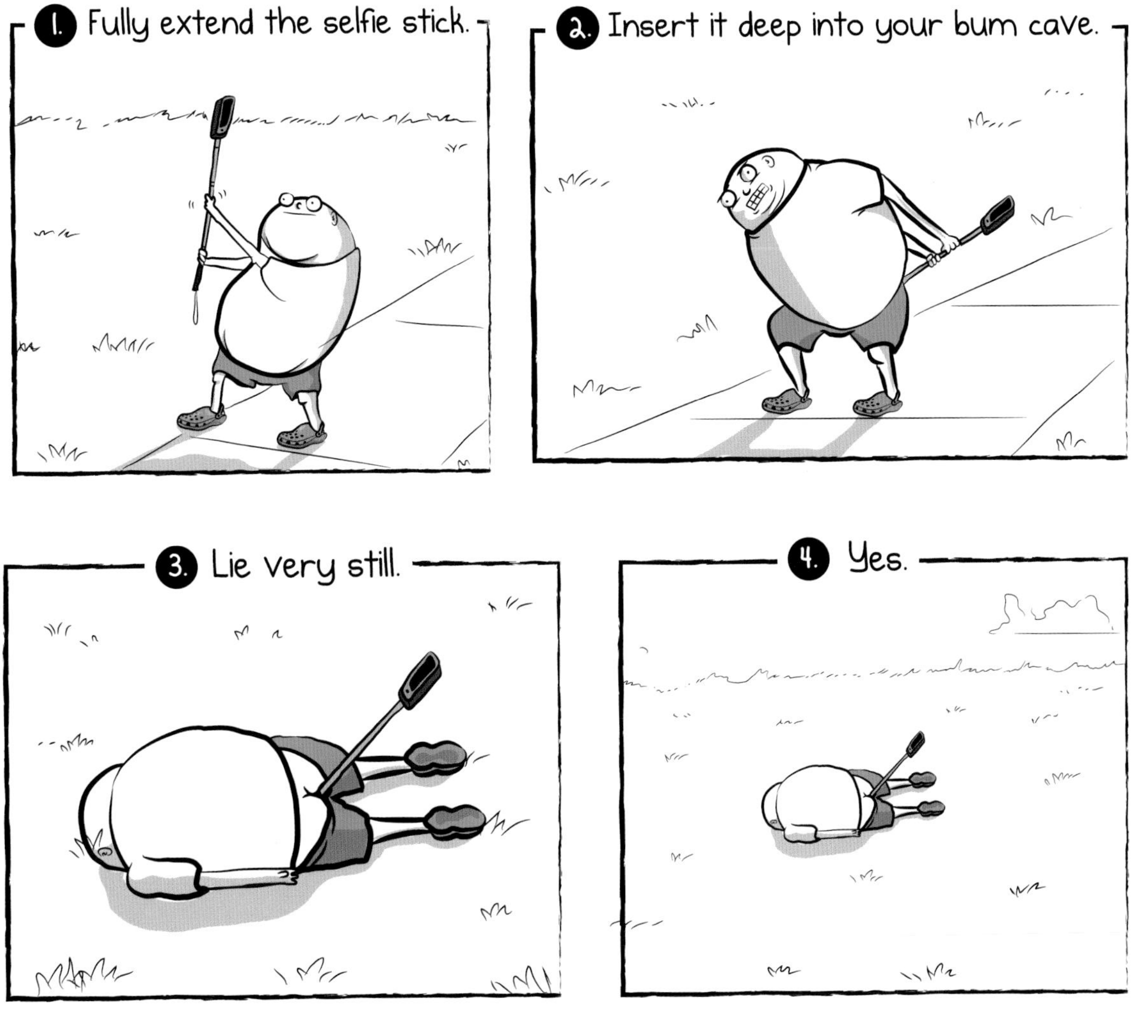
1. Fully extend the selfie stick.
2. Insert it deep into your bum cave.
3. Lie very still.
4. Yes.

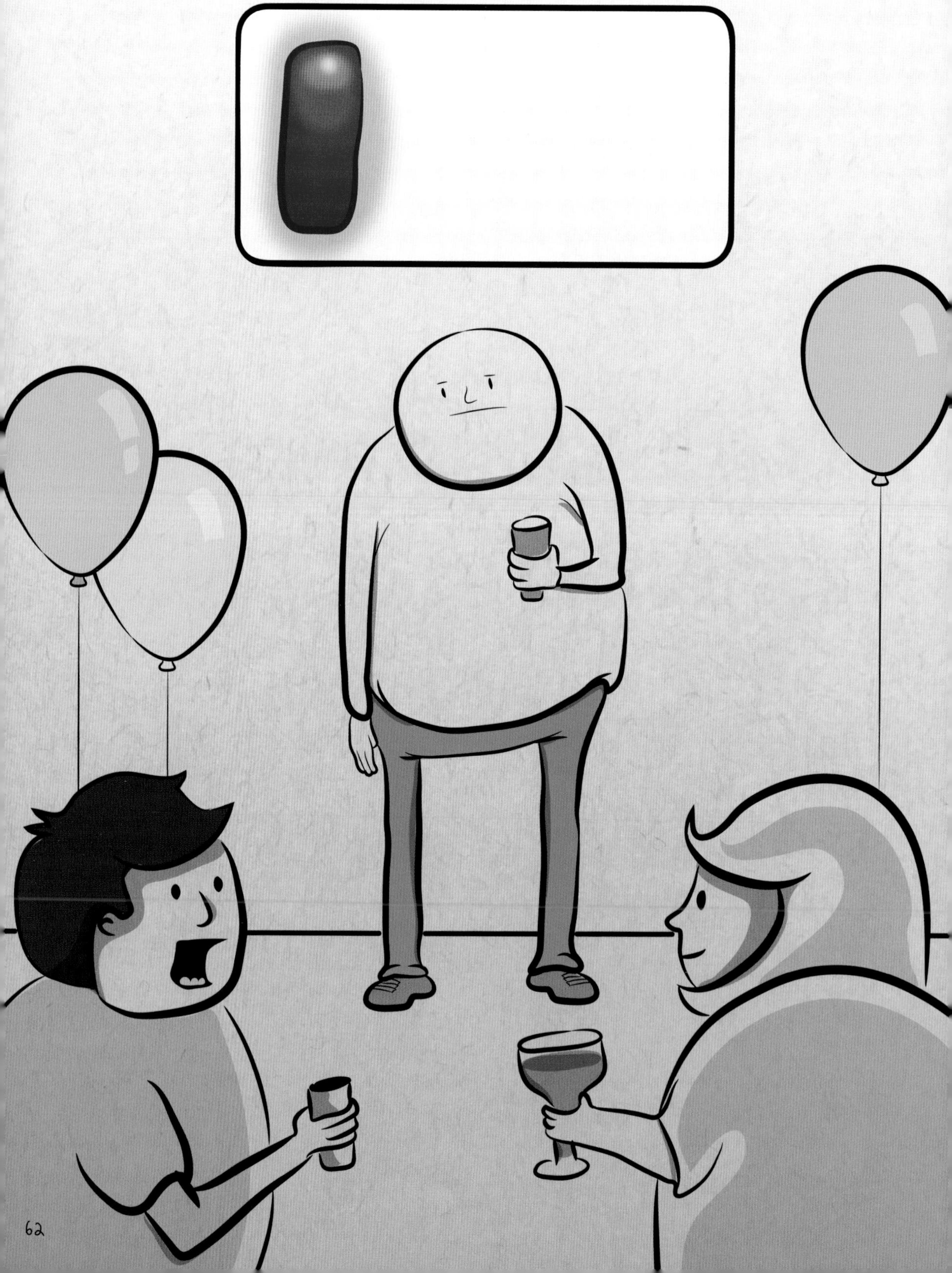

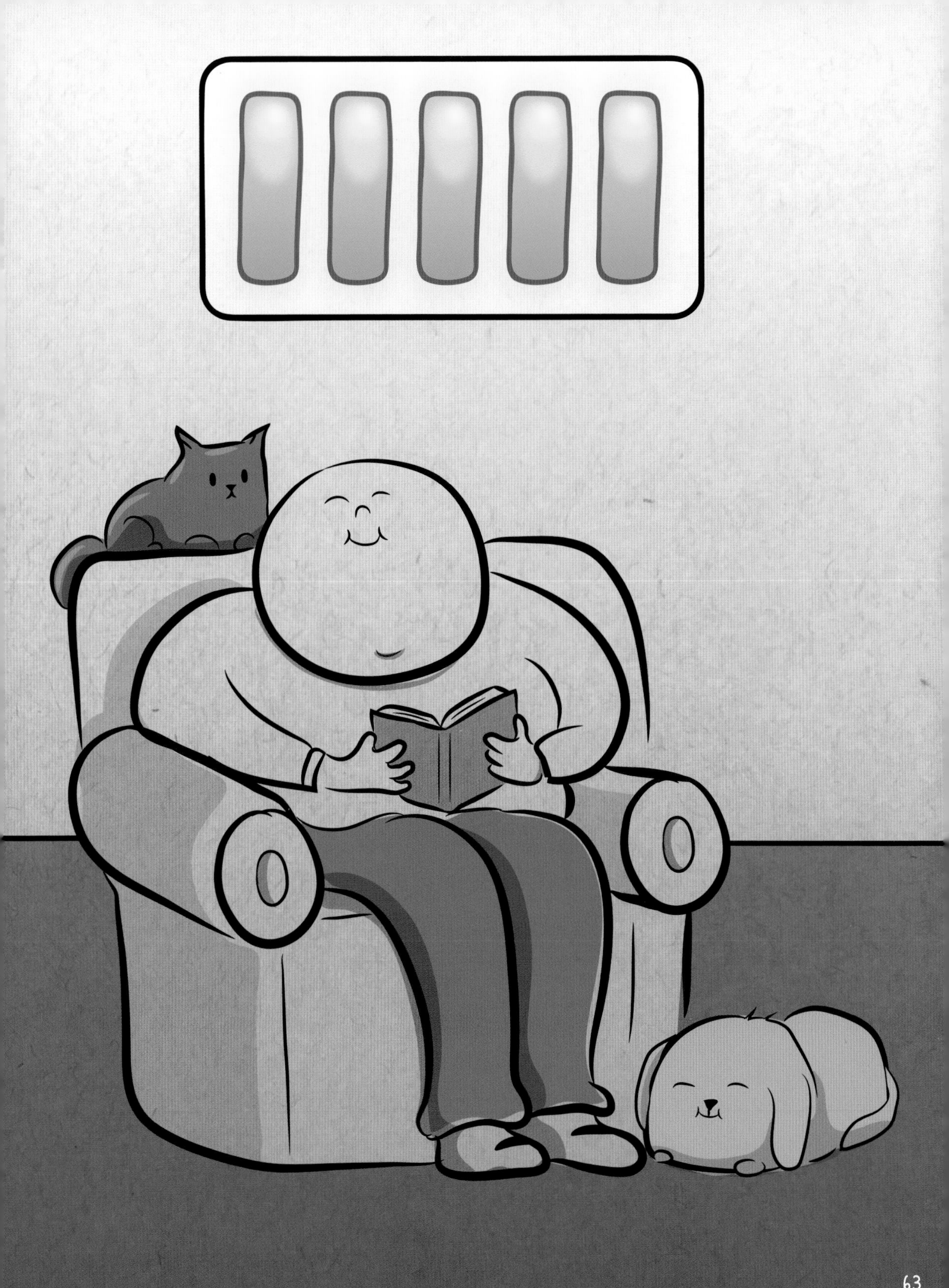

Cat versus laser pointer.

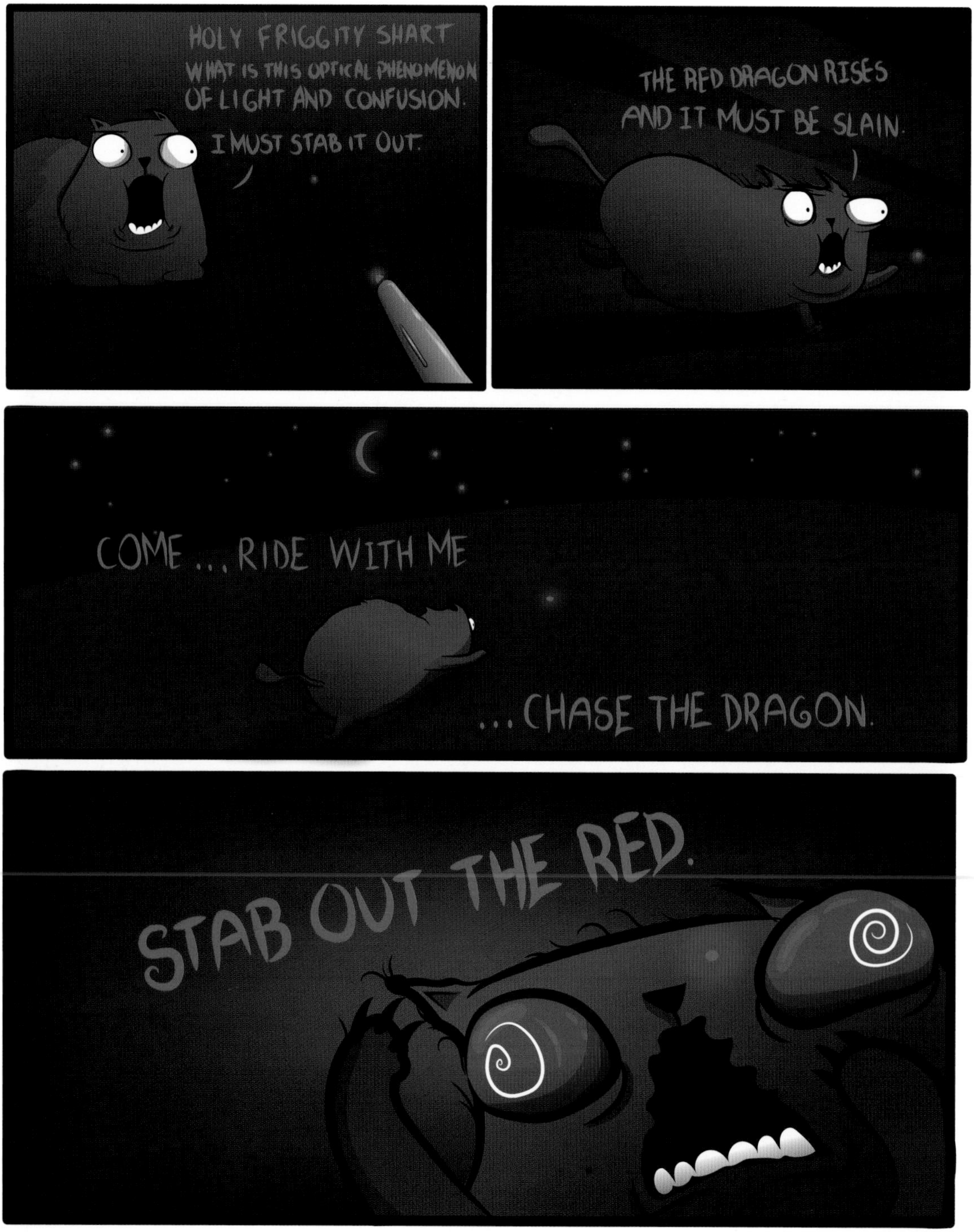
HOLY FRIGGITY SHART
WHAT IS THIS OPTICAL PHENOMENON OF LIGHT AND CONFUSION.
I MUST STAB IT OUT.
THE RED DRAGON RISES AND IT MUST BE SLAIN.
COME... RIDE WITH ME
...CHASE THE DRAGON.
STAB OUT THE RED.

Dog versus laser pointer.

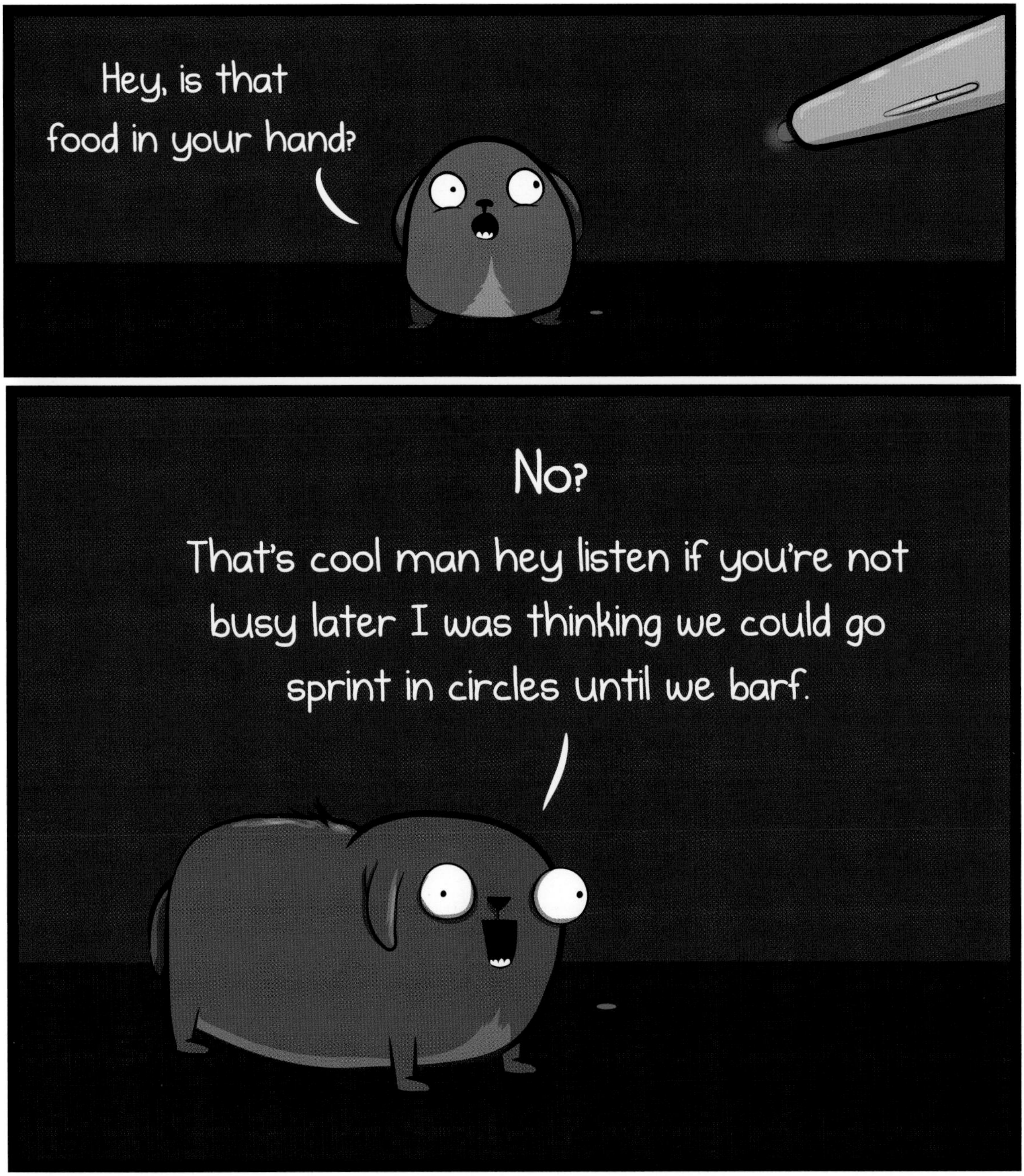
Hey, is that food in your hand?
No?
That's cool man hey listen if you're not busy later I was thinking we could go sprint in circles until we barf.

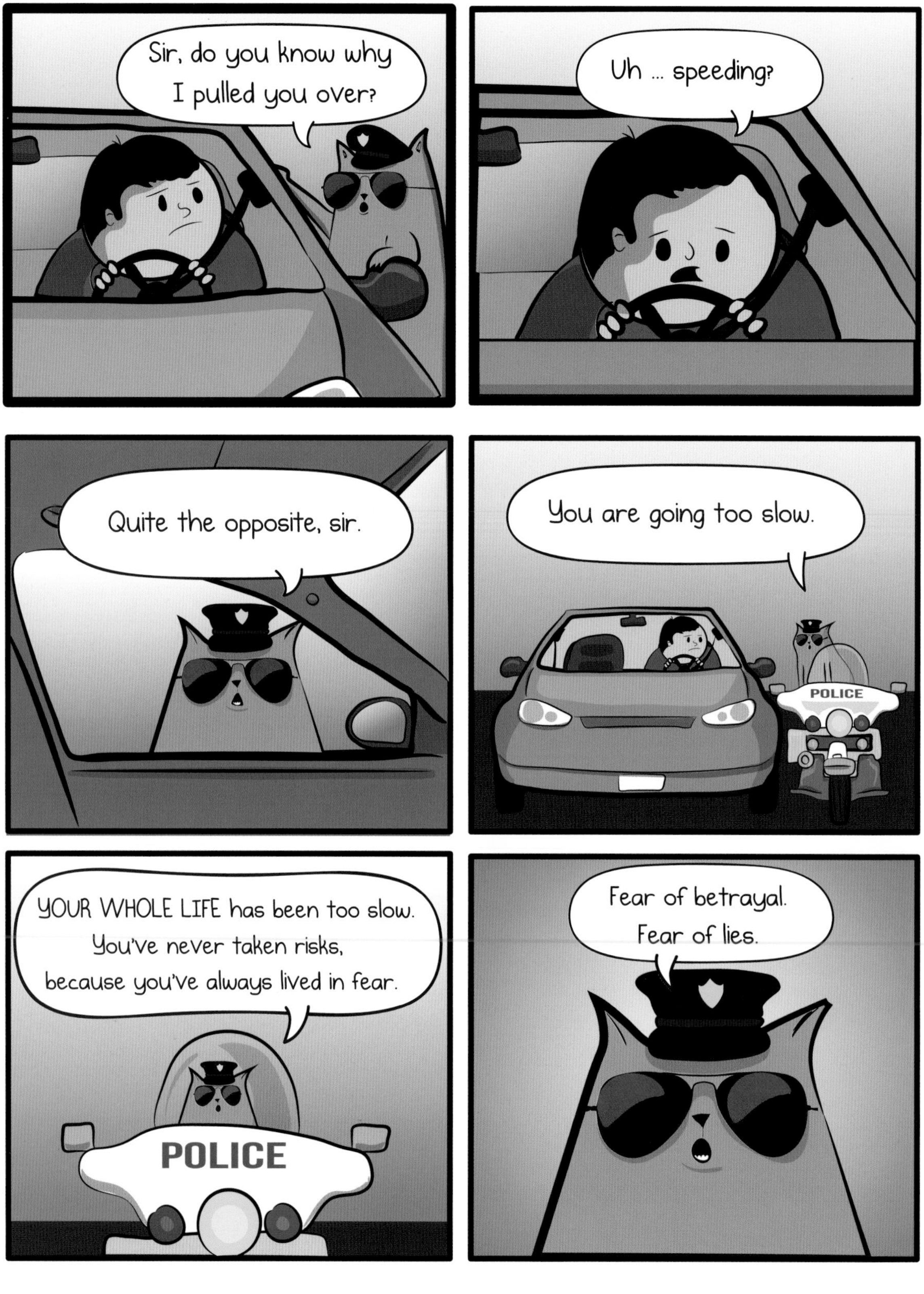
Sir, do you know why I pulled you over?
Uh ... speeding?
Quite the opposite, sir.
You are going too slow.
POLICE
YOUR WHOLE LIFE has been too slow. You've never taken risks, because you've always lived in fear.
POLICE
Fear of betrayal. Fear of lies.

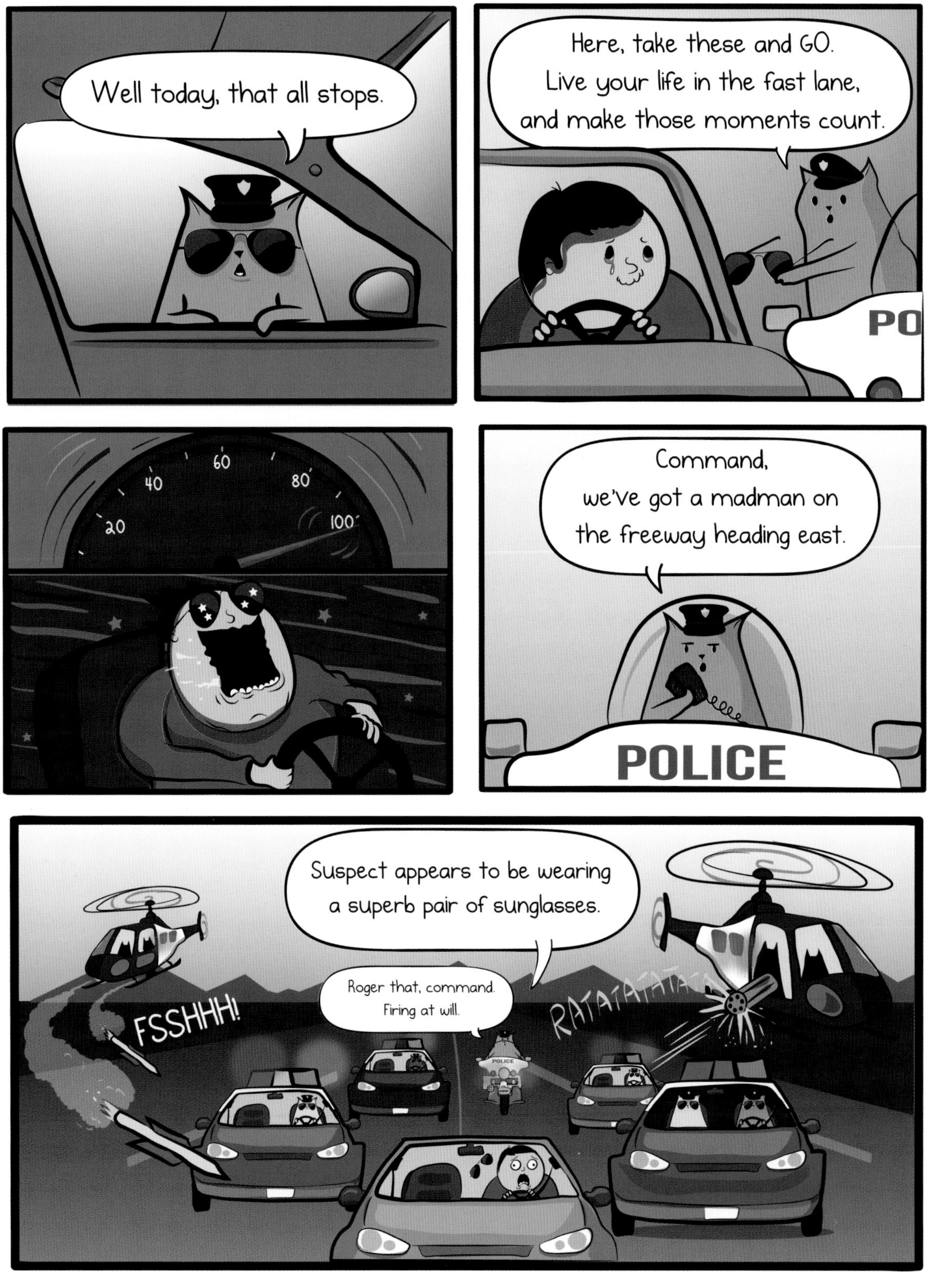

Well today, that all stops.
Here, take these and GO. Live your life in the fast lane, and make those moments count.
PO
20
40
60
80
100
Command, we've got a madman on the freeway heading east.
POLICE
Suspect appears to be wearing a superb pair of sunglasses.
Roger that, command. Firing at will.
FSSHHH!
RATATATATATA

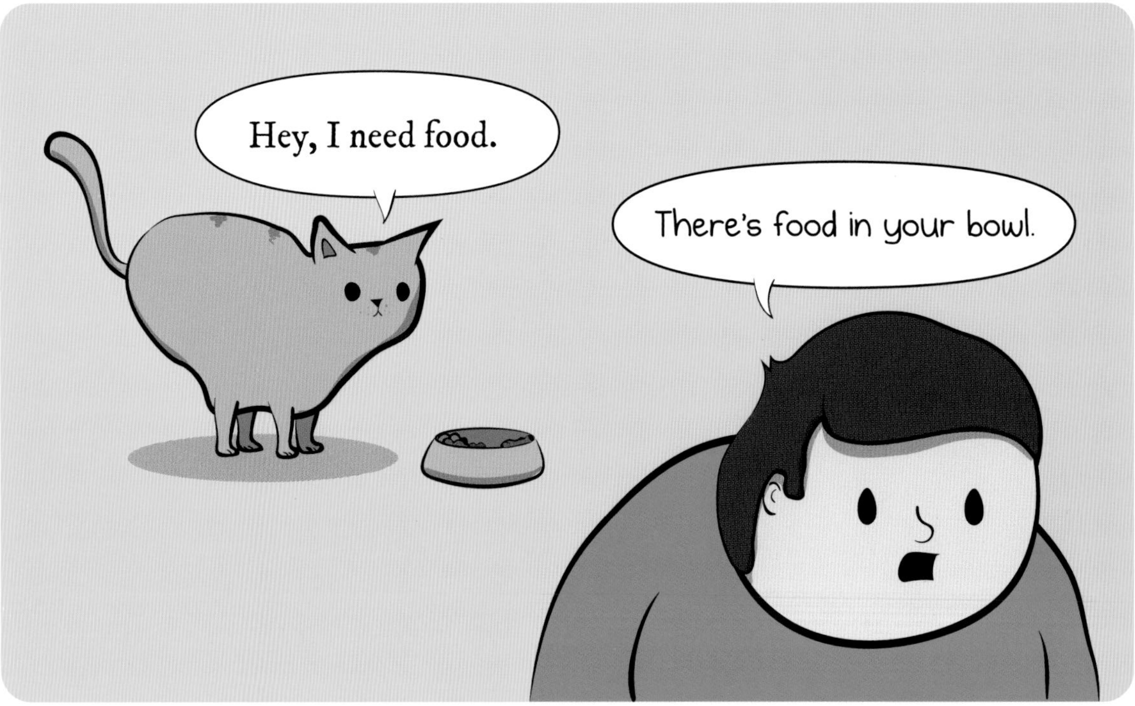
Hey, I need food.
There's food in your bowl.

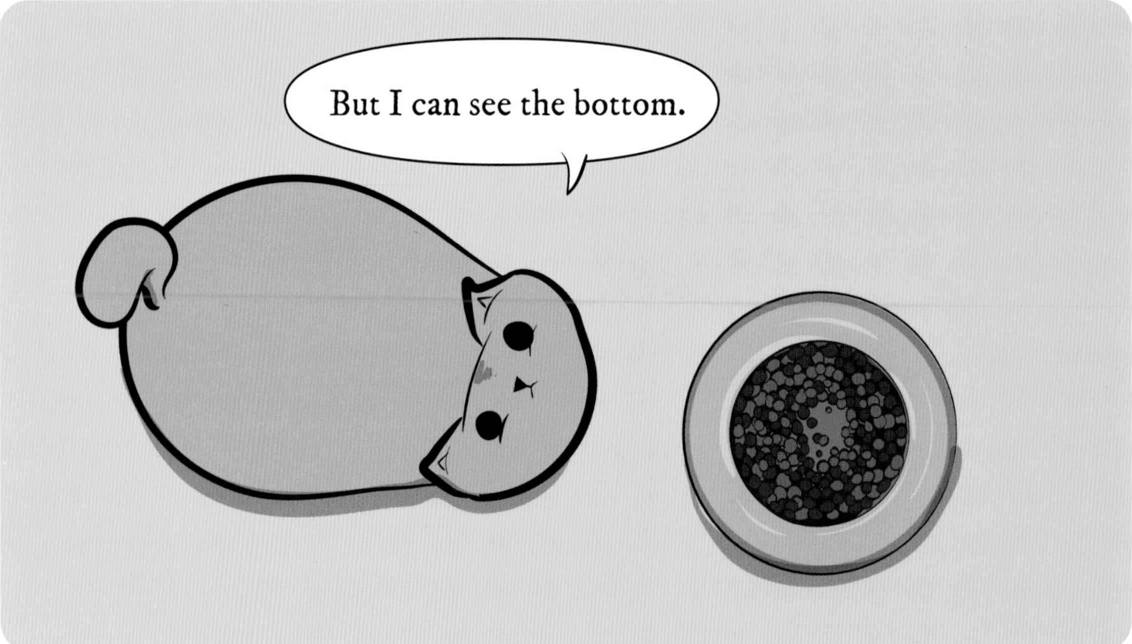
But I can see the bottom.

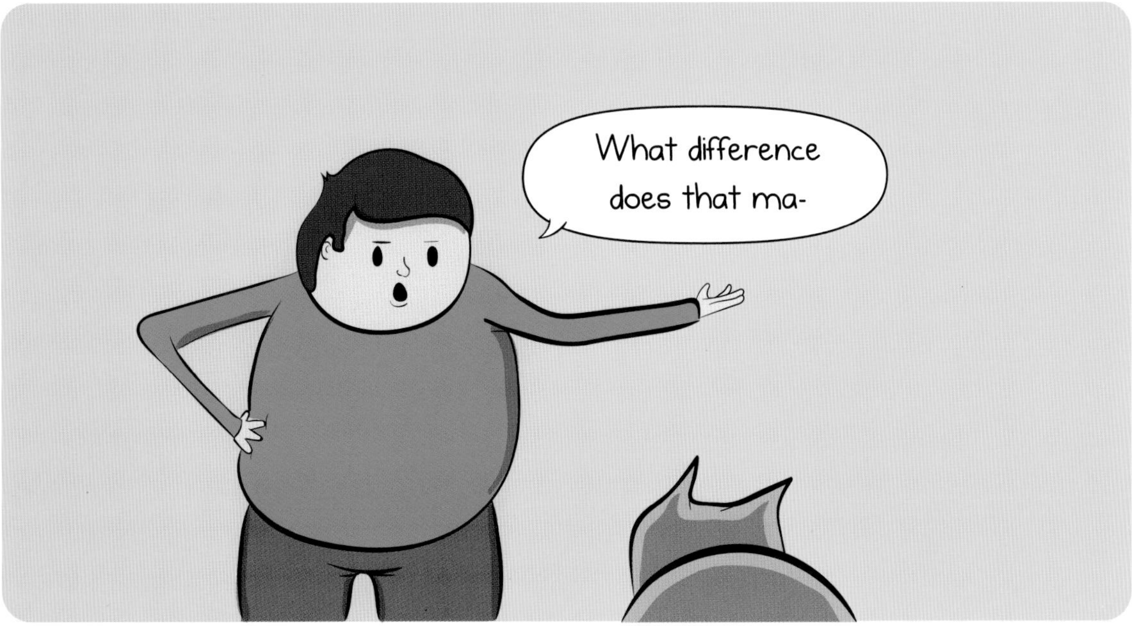
What difference does that ma-

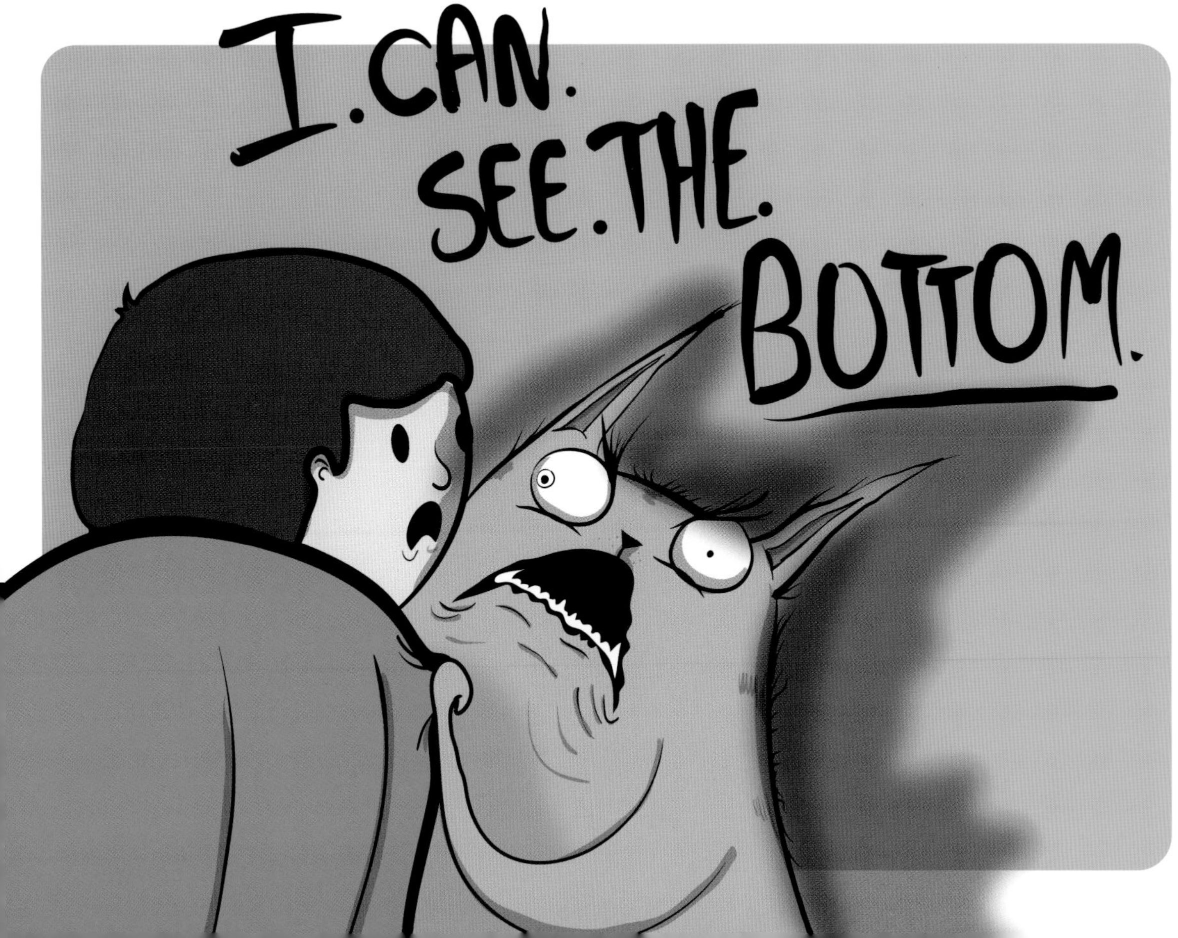
I. CAN. SEE. THE. BOTTOM.

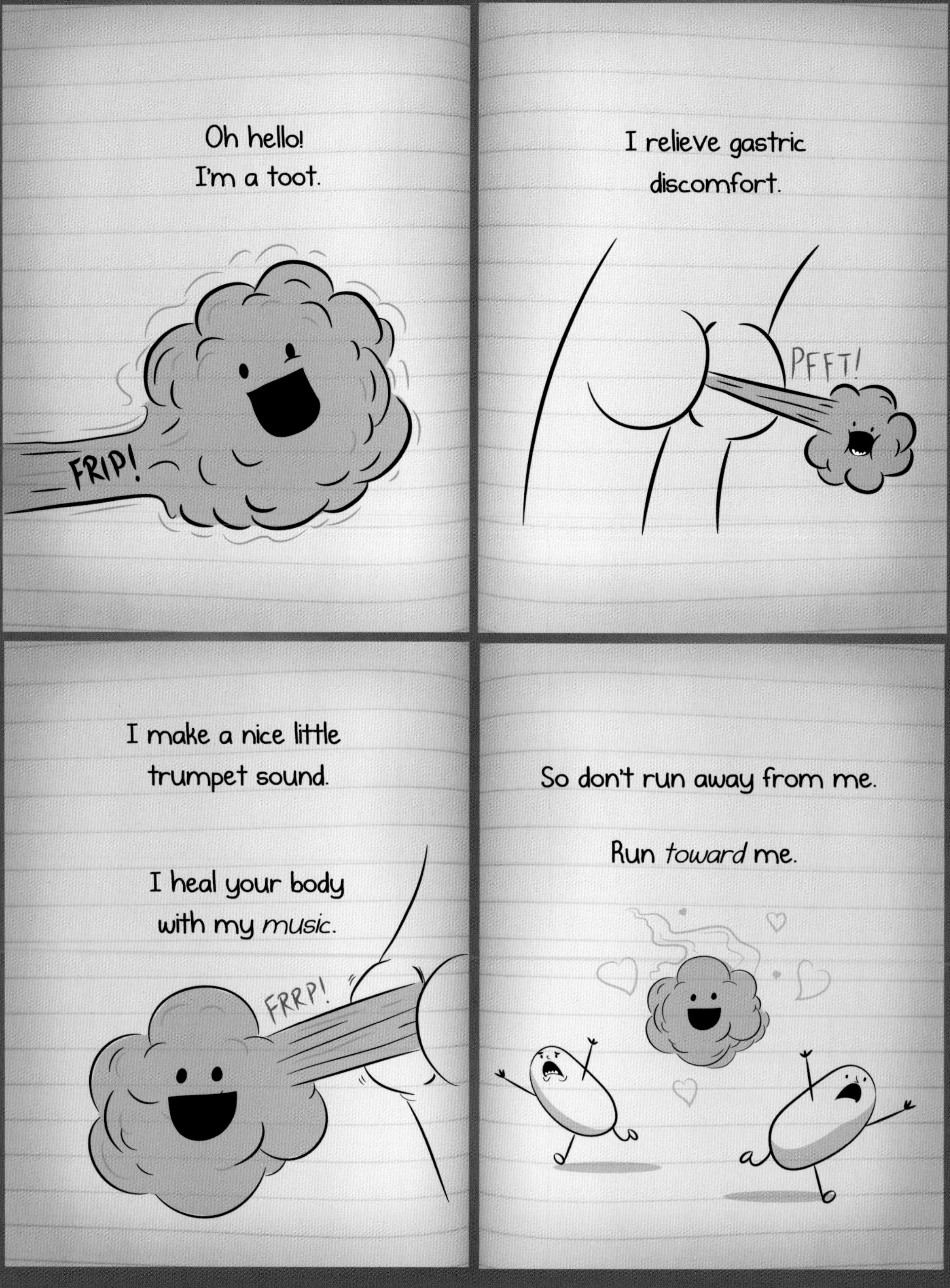
Oh hello!
I'm a toot.
FRIP!
I relieve gastric discomfort.
PFFT!
I make a nice little trumpet sound.
I heal your body with my *music*.
FRRP!
So don't run away from me.
Run *toward* me.

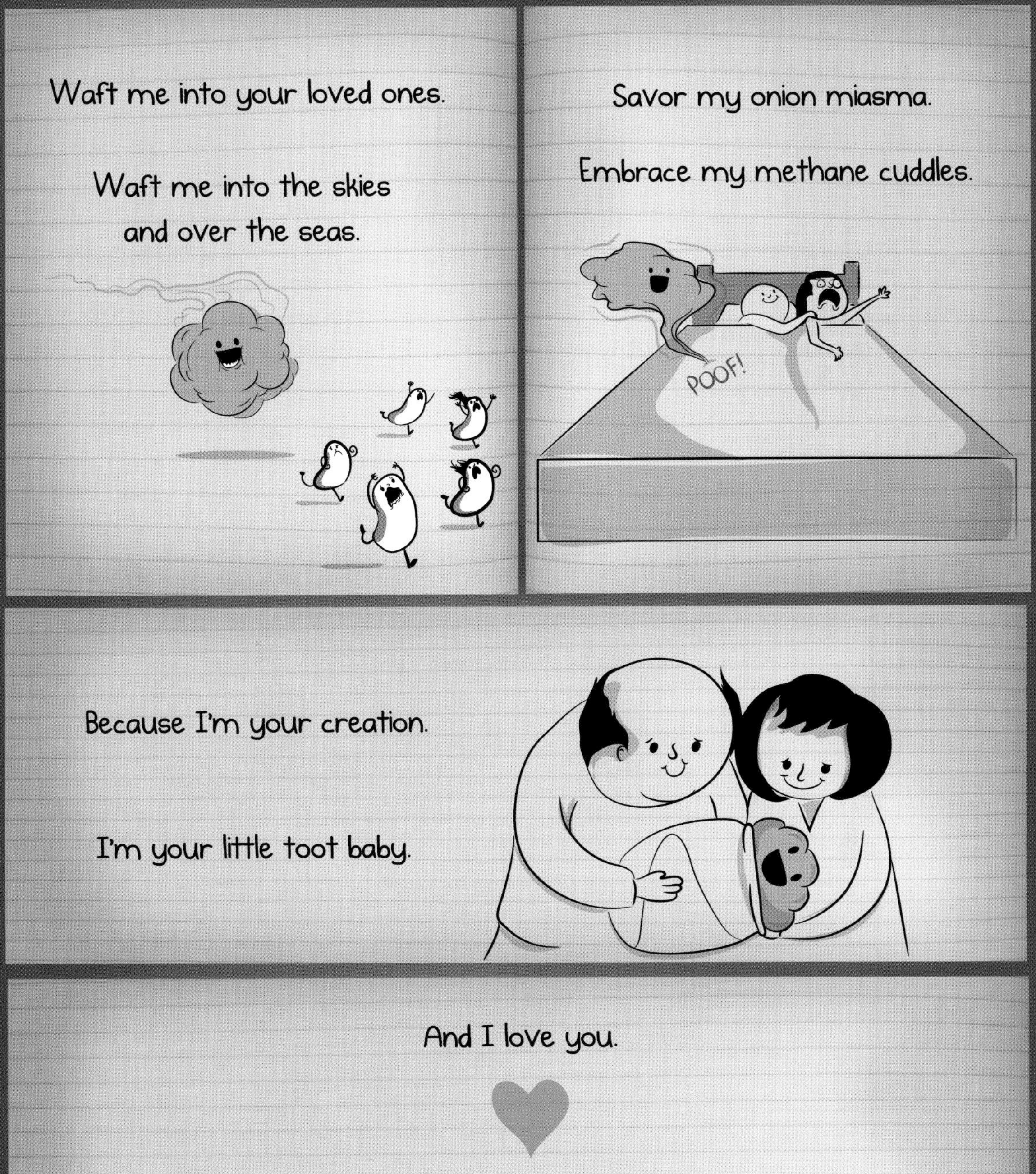
Waft me into your loved ones.
Waft me into the skies
and over the seas.
Savor my onion miasma.
Embrace my methane cuddles.
POOF!
Because I'm your creation.
I'm your little toot baby.
And I love you.

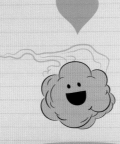

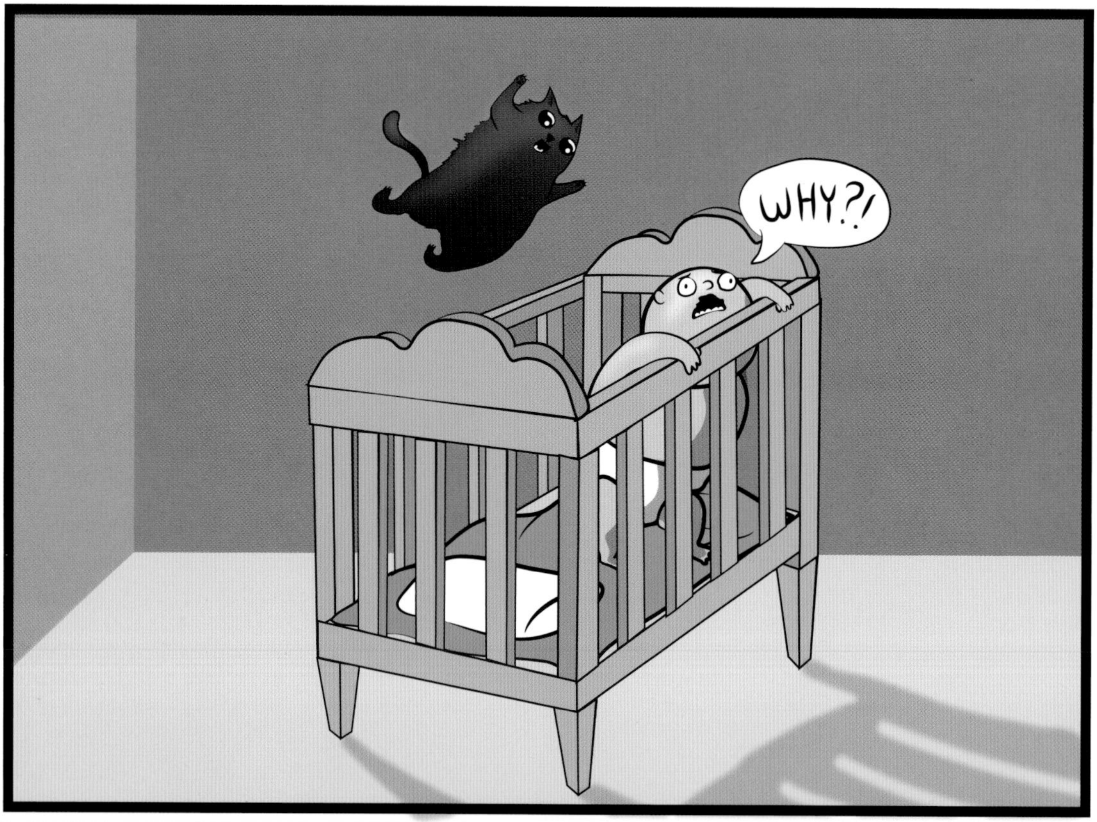
WHY?!

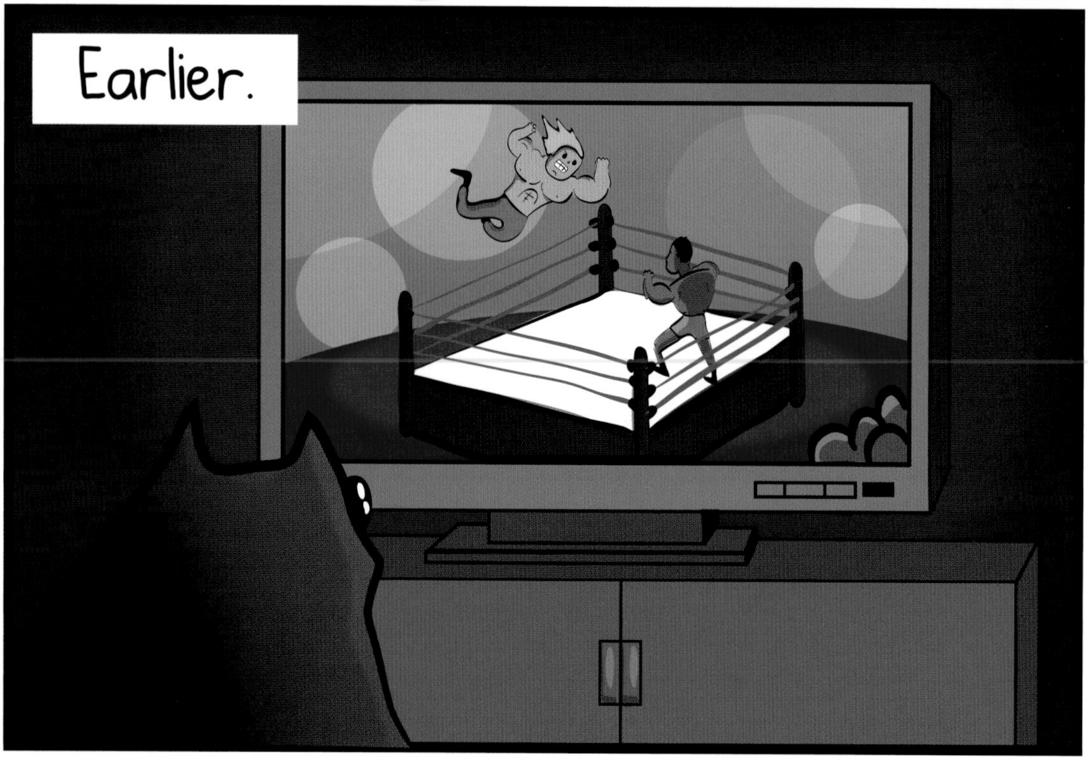
Earlier.

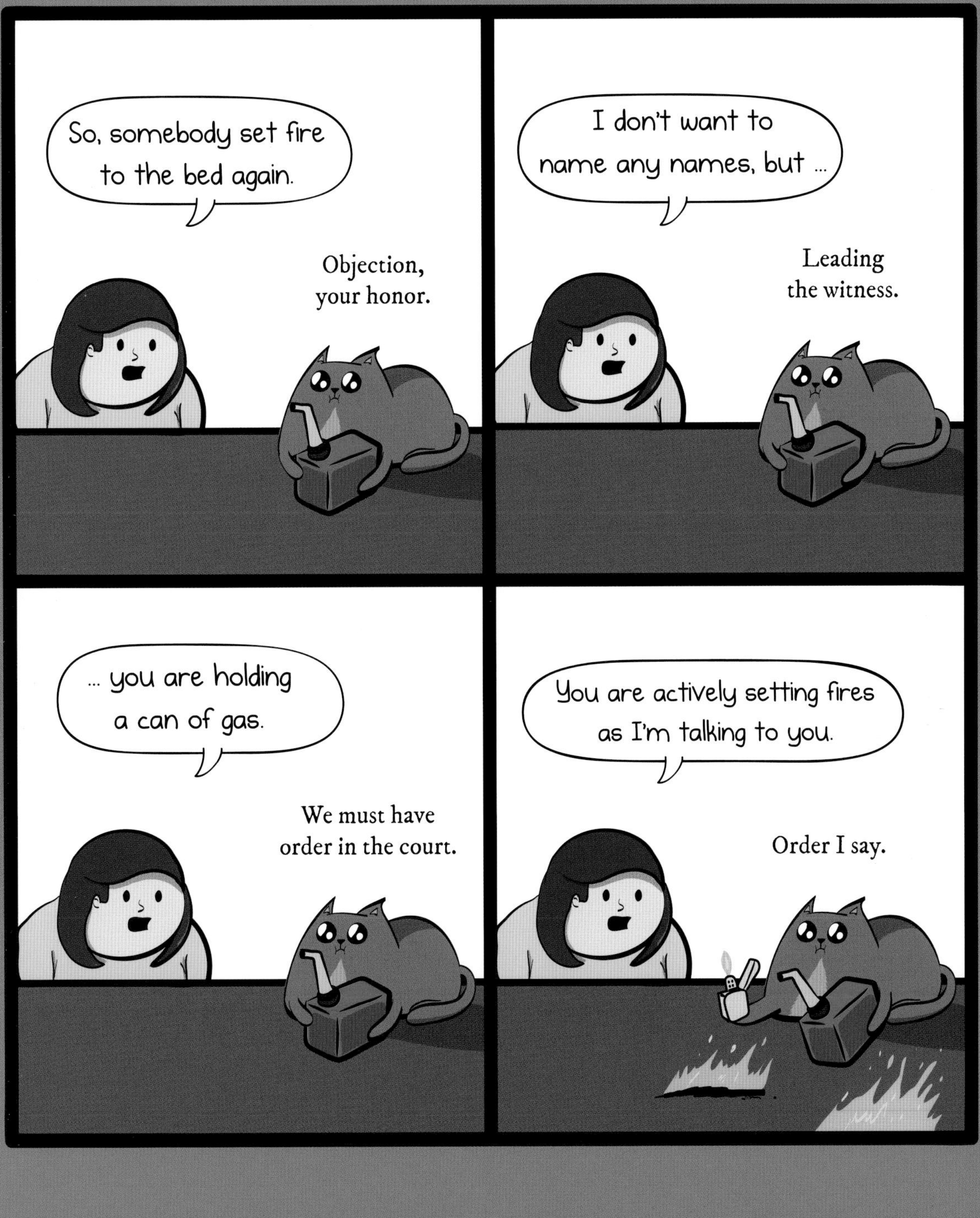
So, somebody set fire to the bed again.
Objection, your honor.
I don't want to name any names, but ...
Leading the witness.
... you are holding a can of gas.
We must have order in the court.
You are actively setting fires as I'm talking to you.
Order I say.

I used to have a hard time thinking that babies were cute.

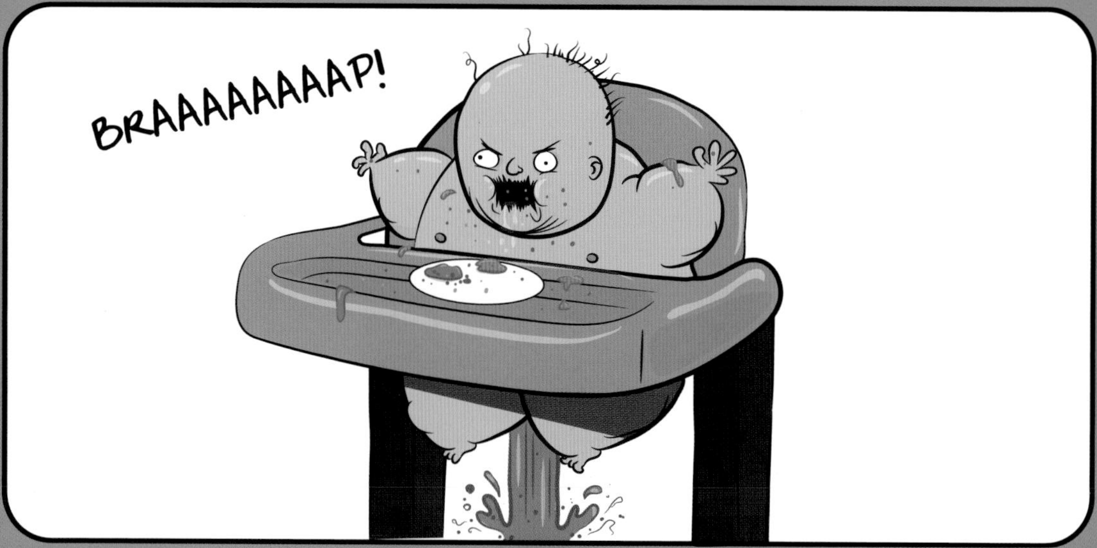
BRAAAAAAAAP!

Until one day many years ago, I saw a family out walking together.

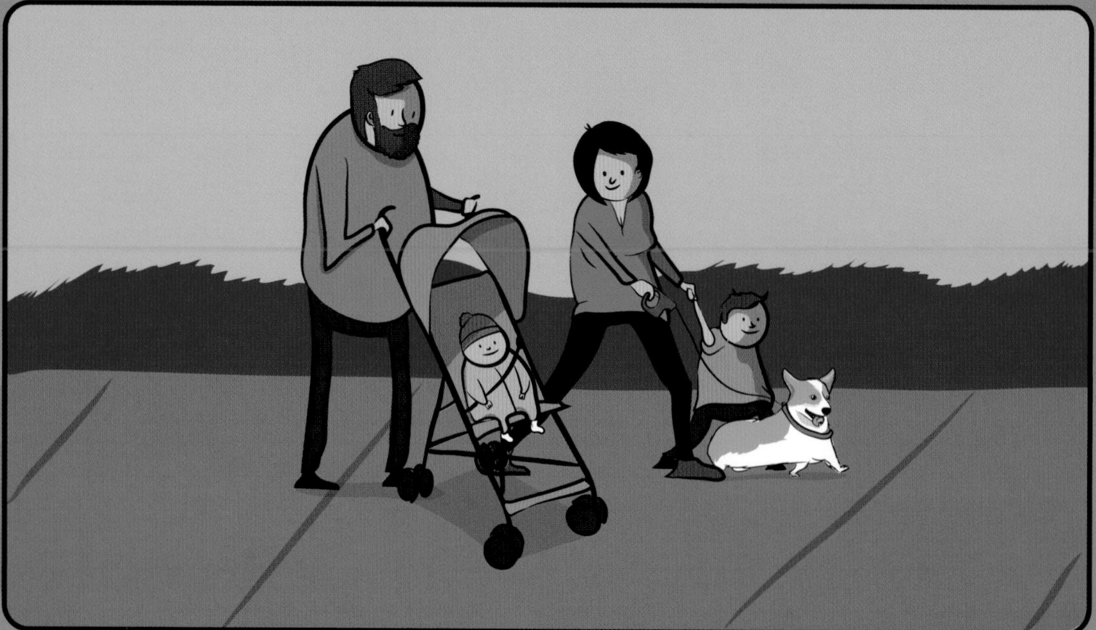

It was then that I got it.

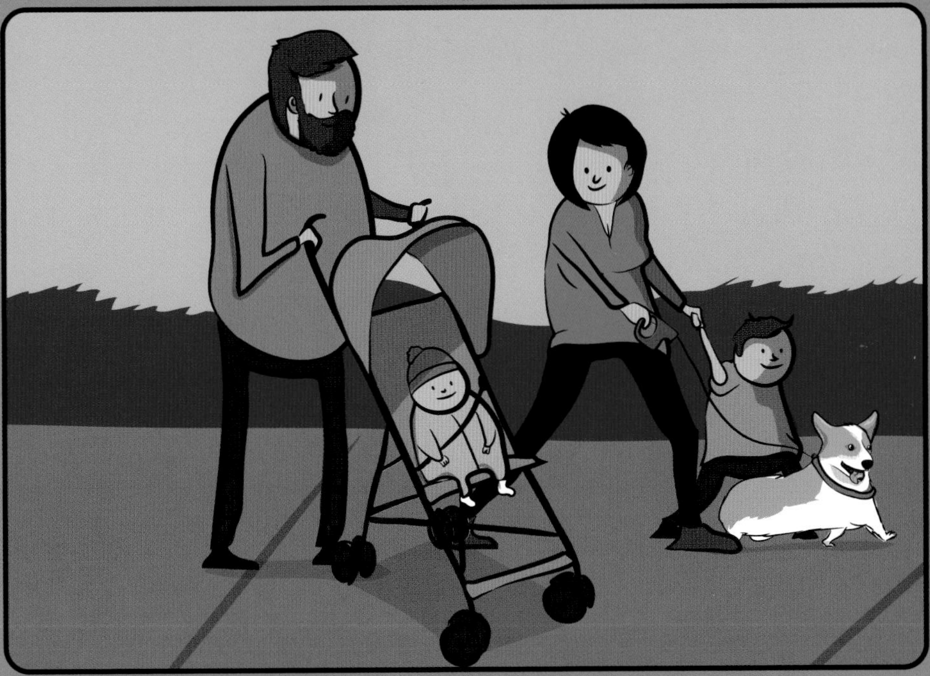

I understood.

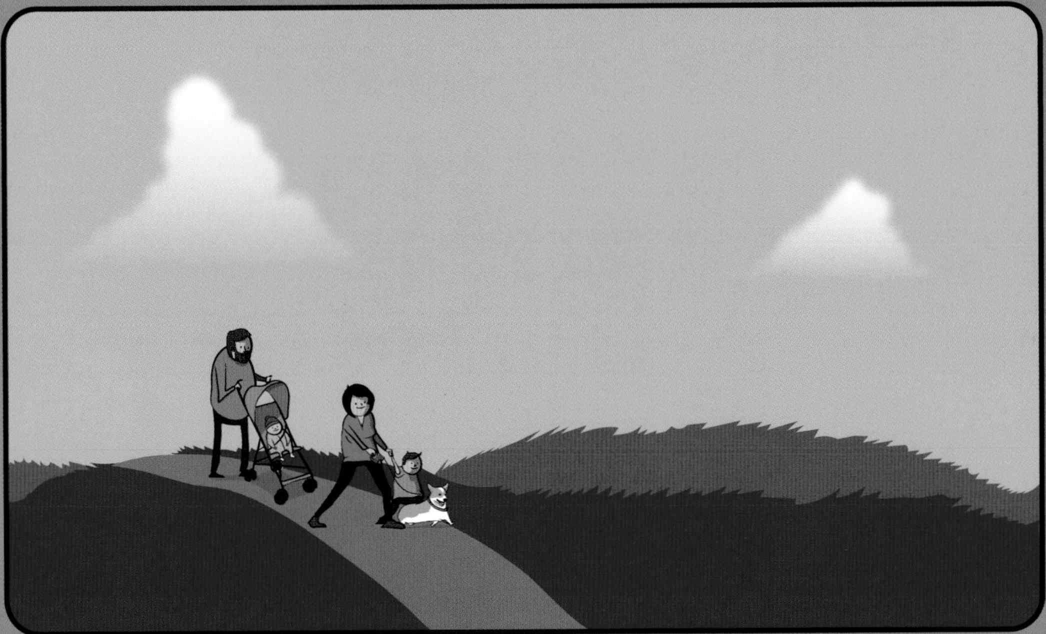

You just have to imagine babies as Corgis.

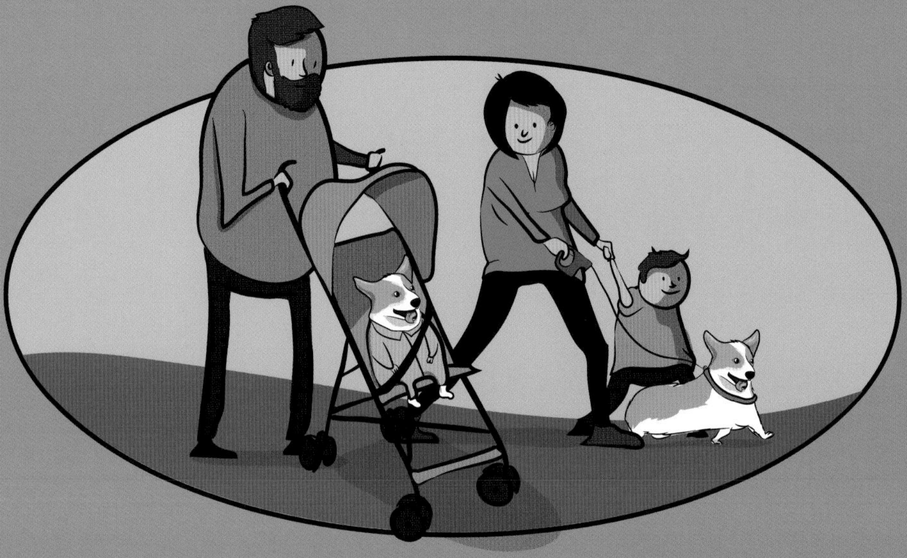

Then they're super cute.

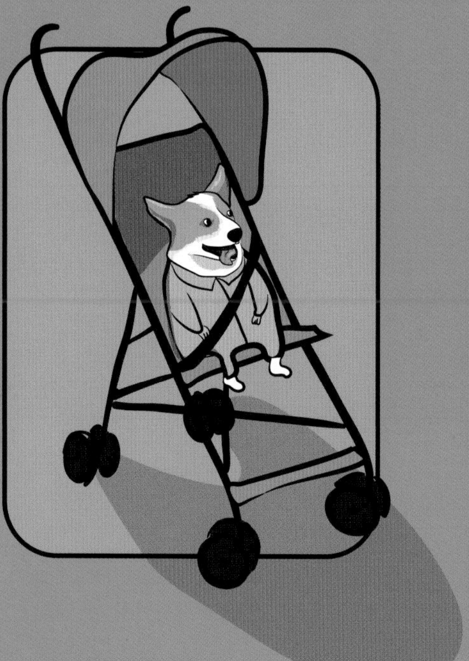

Even the horrible ones.

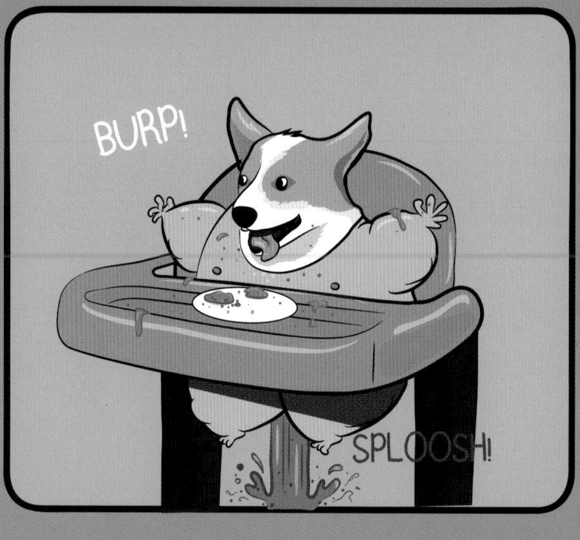
BURP!
SPLOOSH!

I now apply this philosophy to anything that I find unpleasant.

That guy who cut me off in traffic?

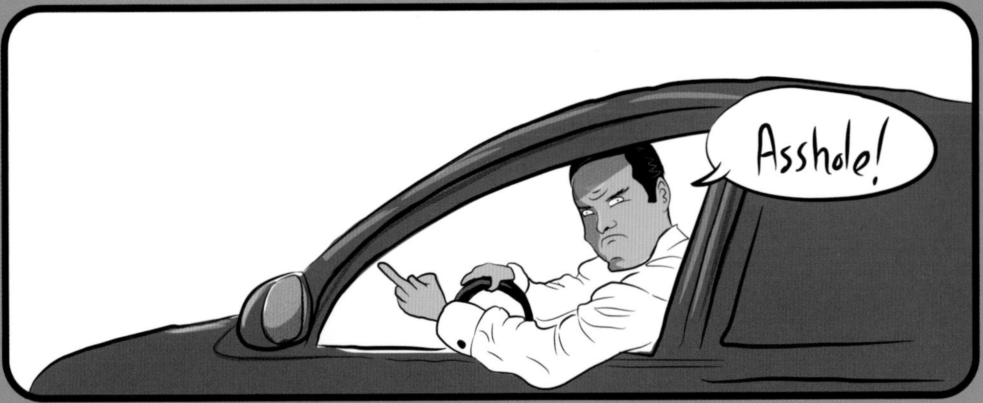
Asshole!

He's just a corgi out for an evening drive.

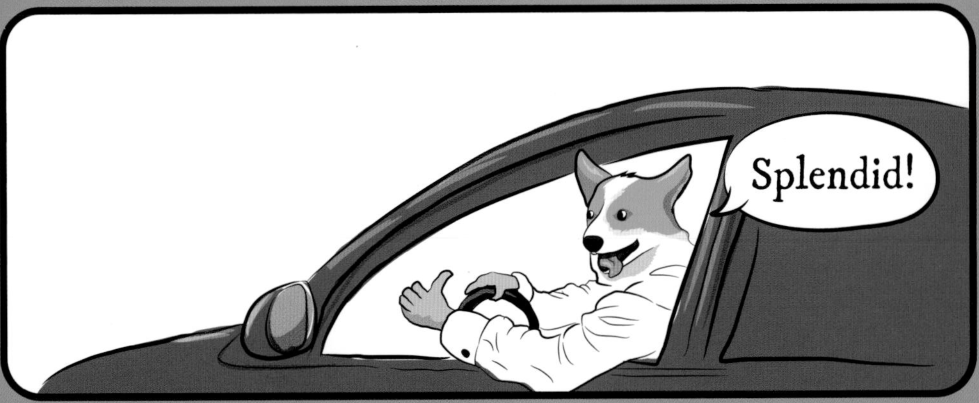
Splendid!

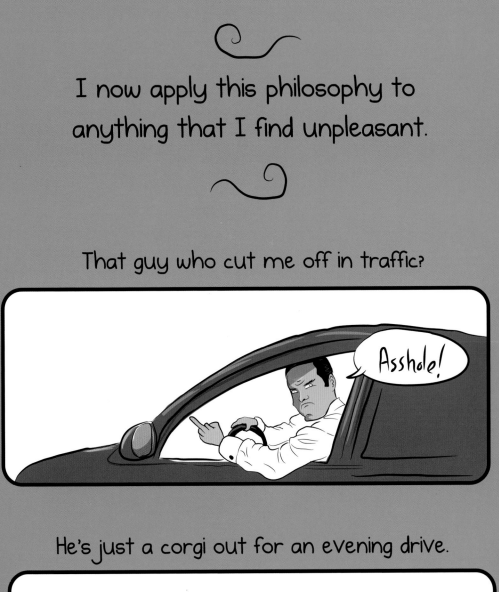

That strange lump growing on my leg?

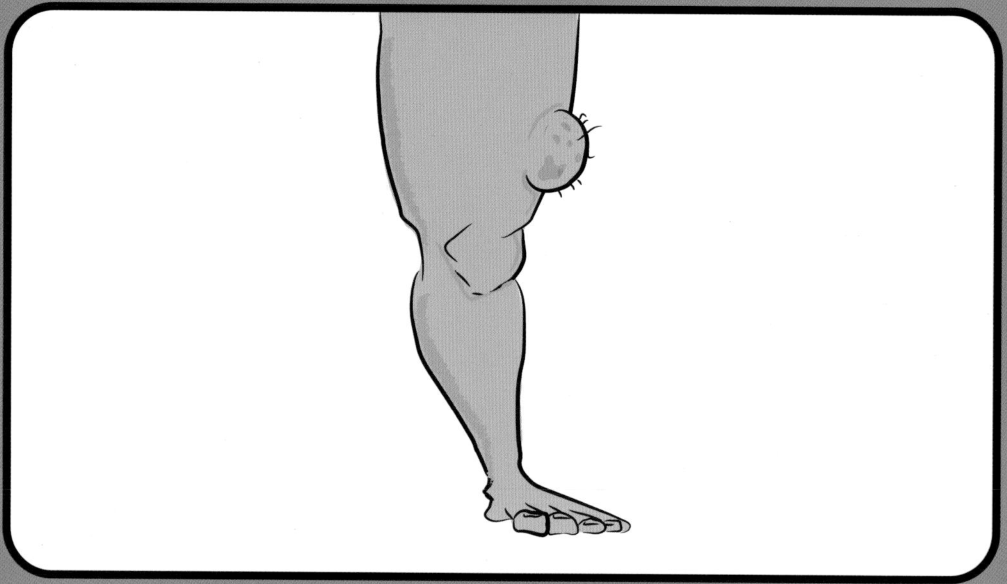

It's just your friendly neighborhood corgi!

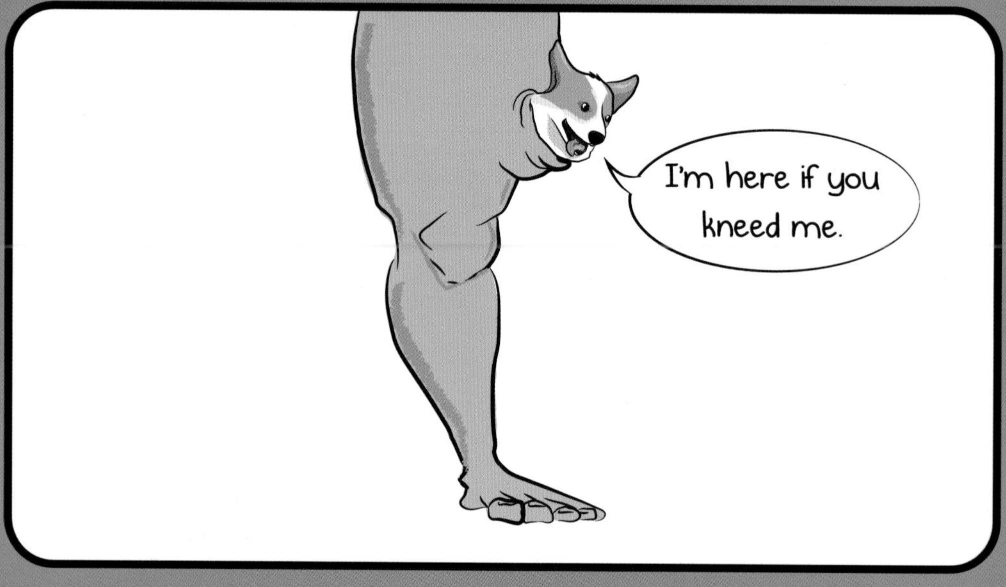
I'm here if you kneed me.

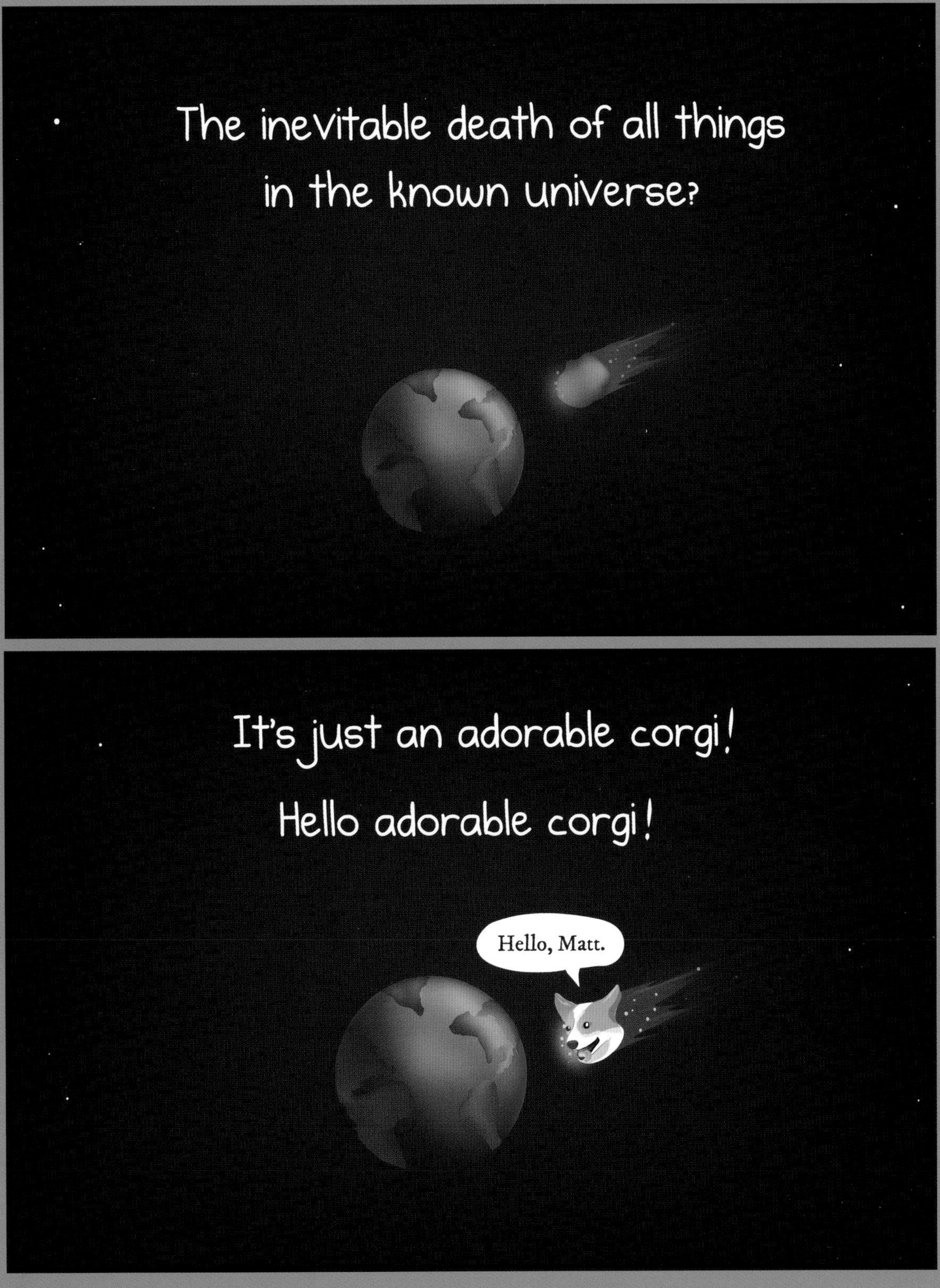
The inevitable death of all things in the known universe?
It's just an adorable corgi!
Hello adorable corgi!
Hello, Matt.

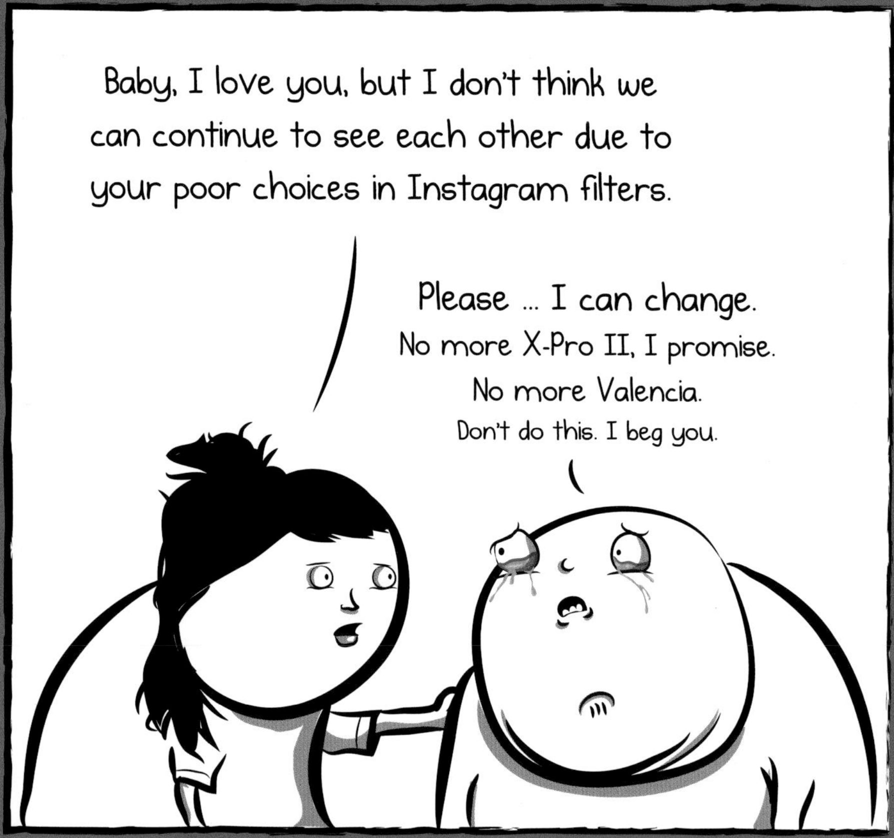
Baby, I love you, but I don't think we can continue to see each other due to your poor choices in Instagram filters.
Please ... I can change.
No more X-Pro II, I promise.
No more Valencia.
Don't do this. I beg you.

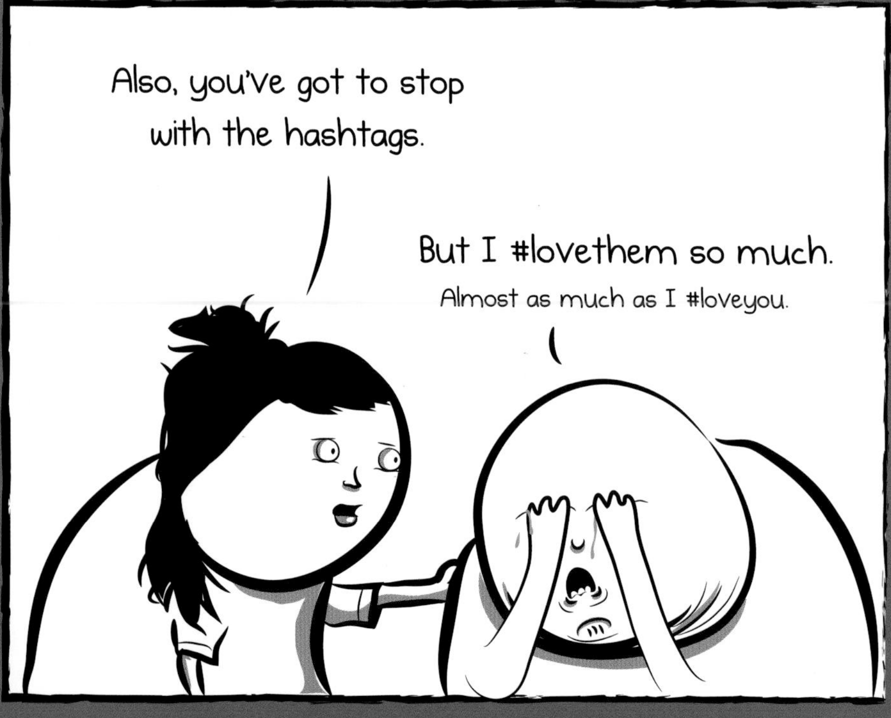
Also, you've got to stop with the hashtags.
But I #lovethem so much.
Almost as much as I #loveyou.

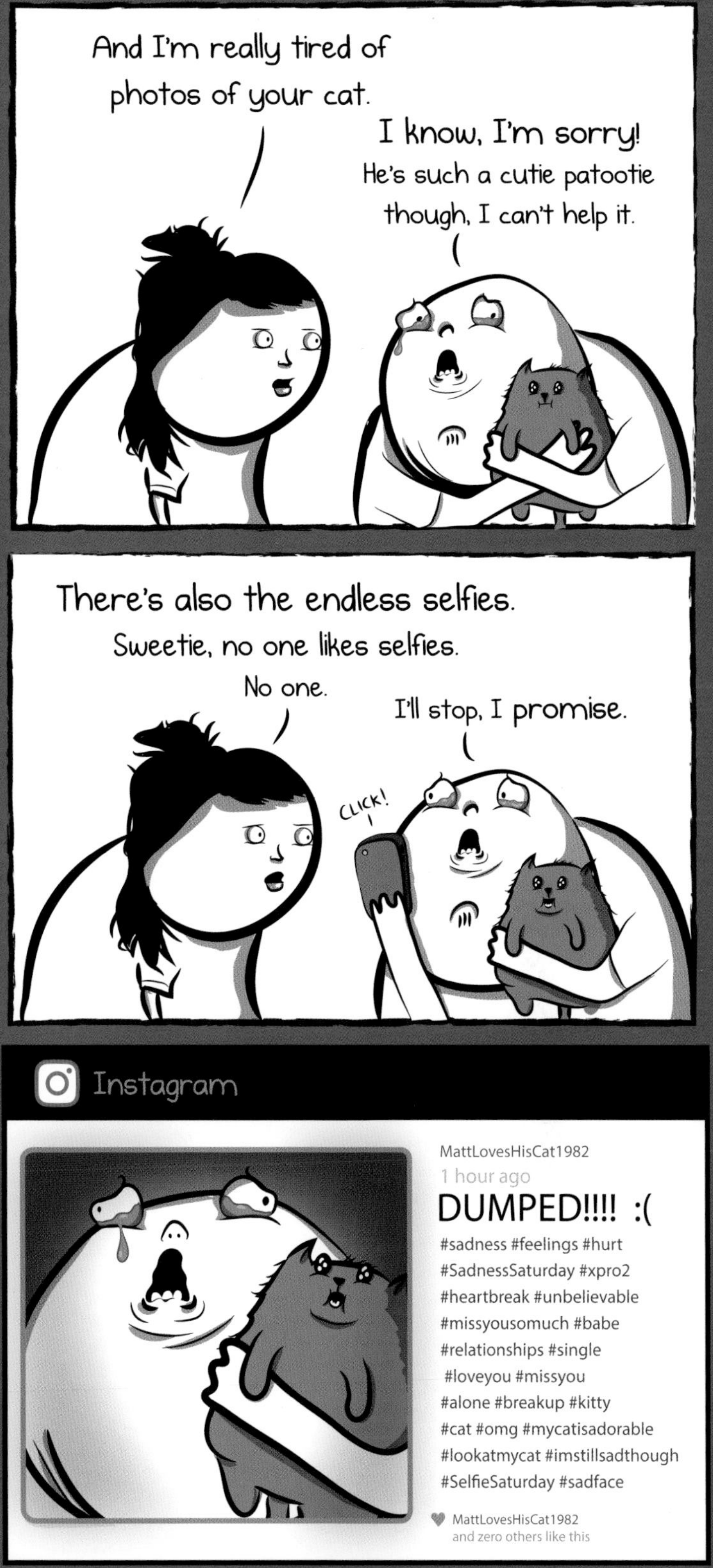
And I'm really tired of photos of your cat.
I know, I'm sorry! He's such a cutie patootie though, I can't help it.
There's also the endless selfies. Sweetie, no one likes selfies. No one.
I'll stop, I promise.
CLICK!
Instagram
MattLovesHisCat1982
1 hour ago
DUMPED!!!! :(
#sadness #feelings #hurt #SadnessSaturday #xpro2 #heartbreak #unbelievable #missyousomuch #babe #relationships #single #loveyou #missyou #alone #breakup #kitty #cat #omg #mycatisadorable #lookatmycat #imstillsadthough #SelfieSaturday #sadface
MattLovesHisCat1982
and zero others like this

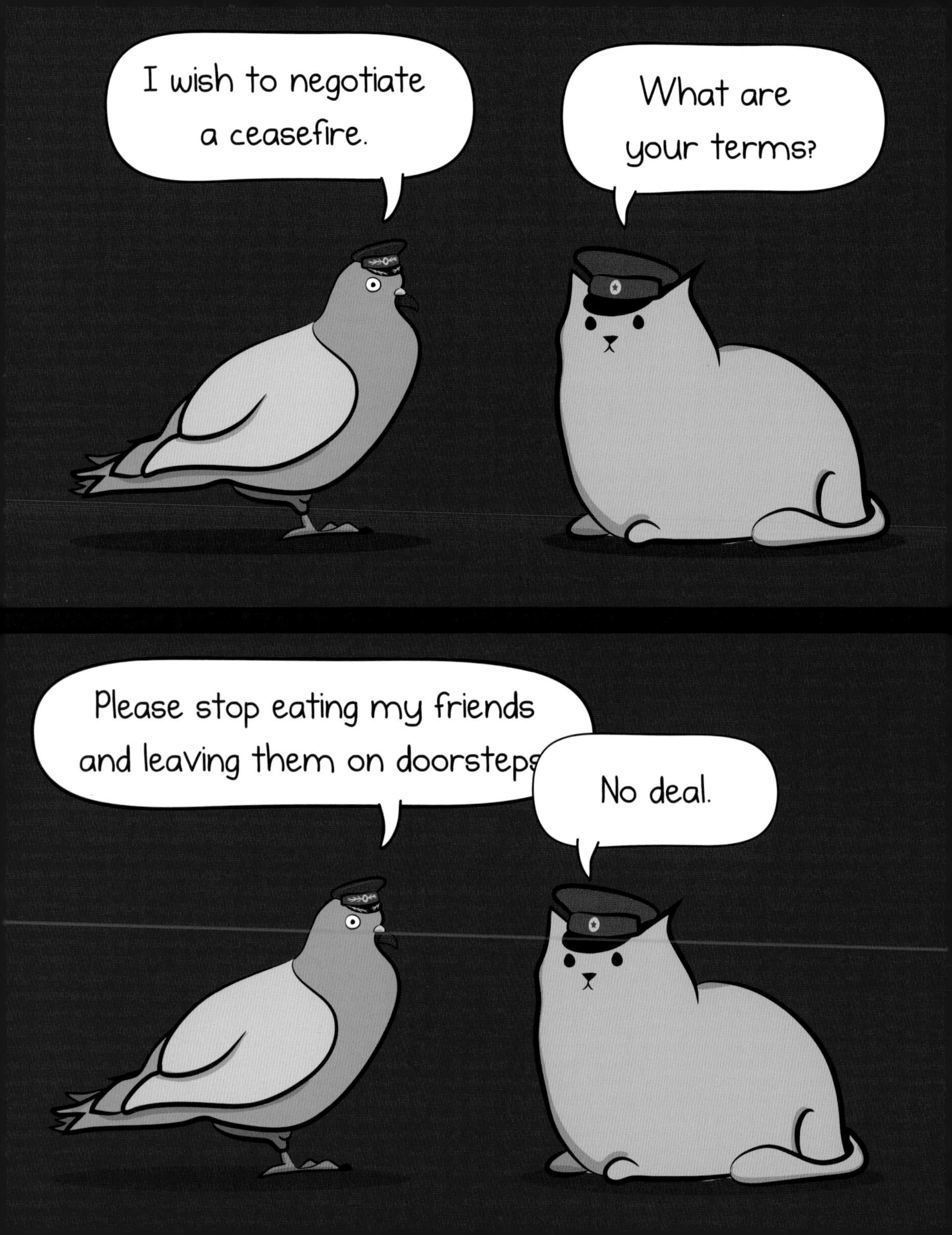
I wish to negotiate a ceasefire.
What are your terms?
Please stop eating my friends and leaving them on doorsteps
No deal.

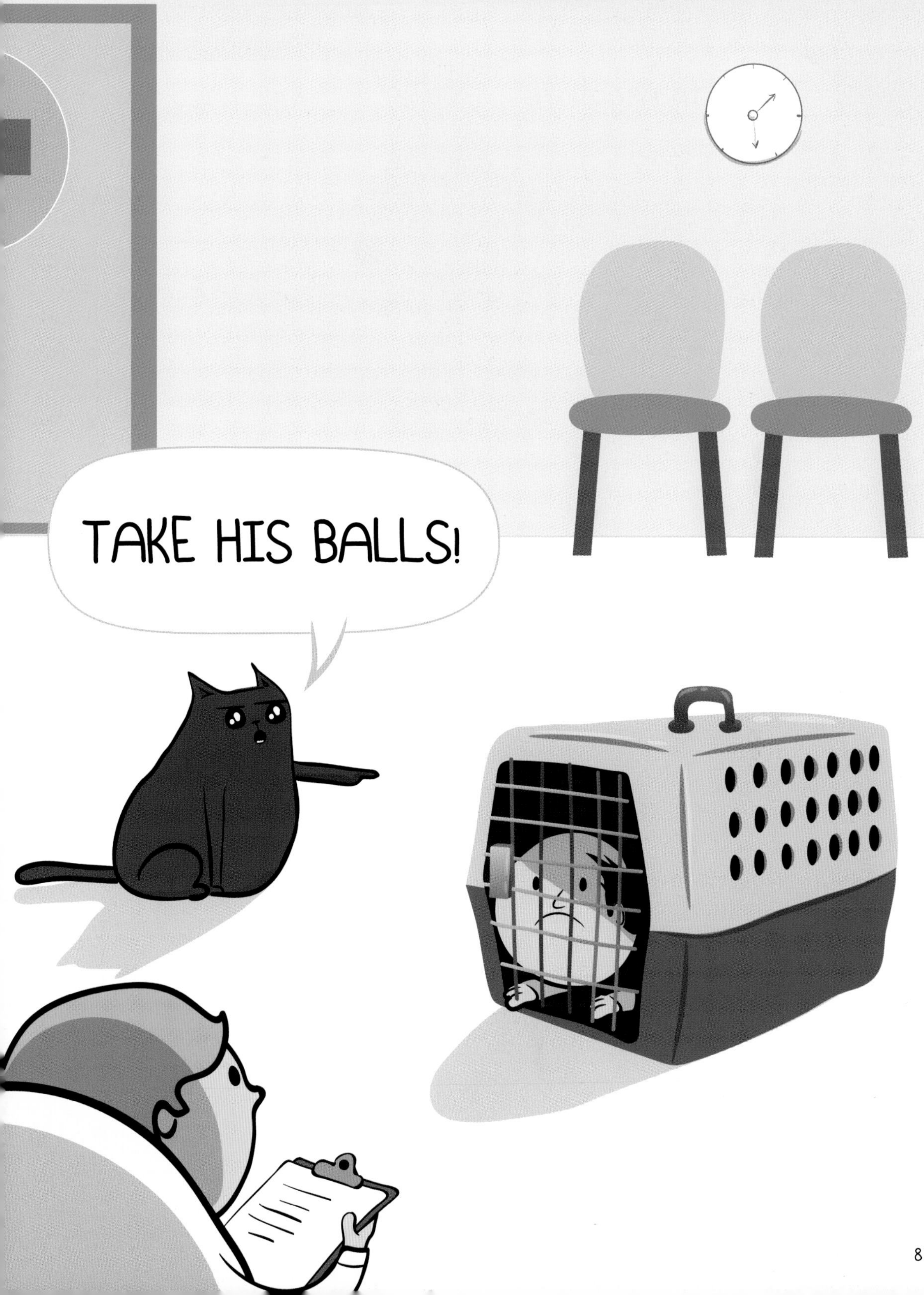
TAKE HIS BALLS!

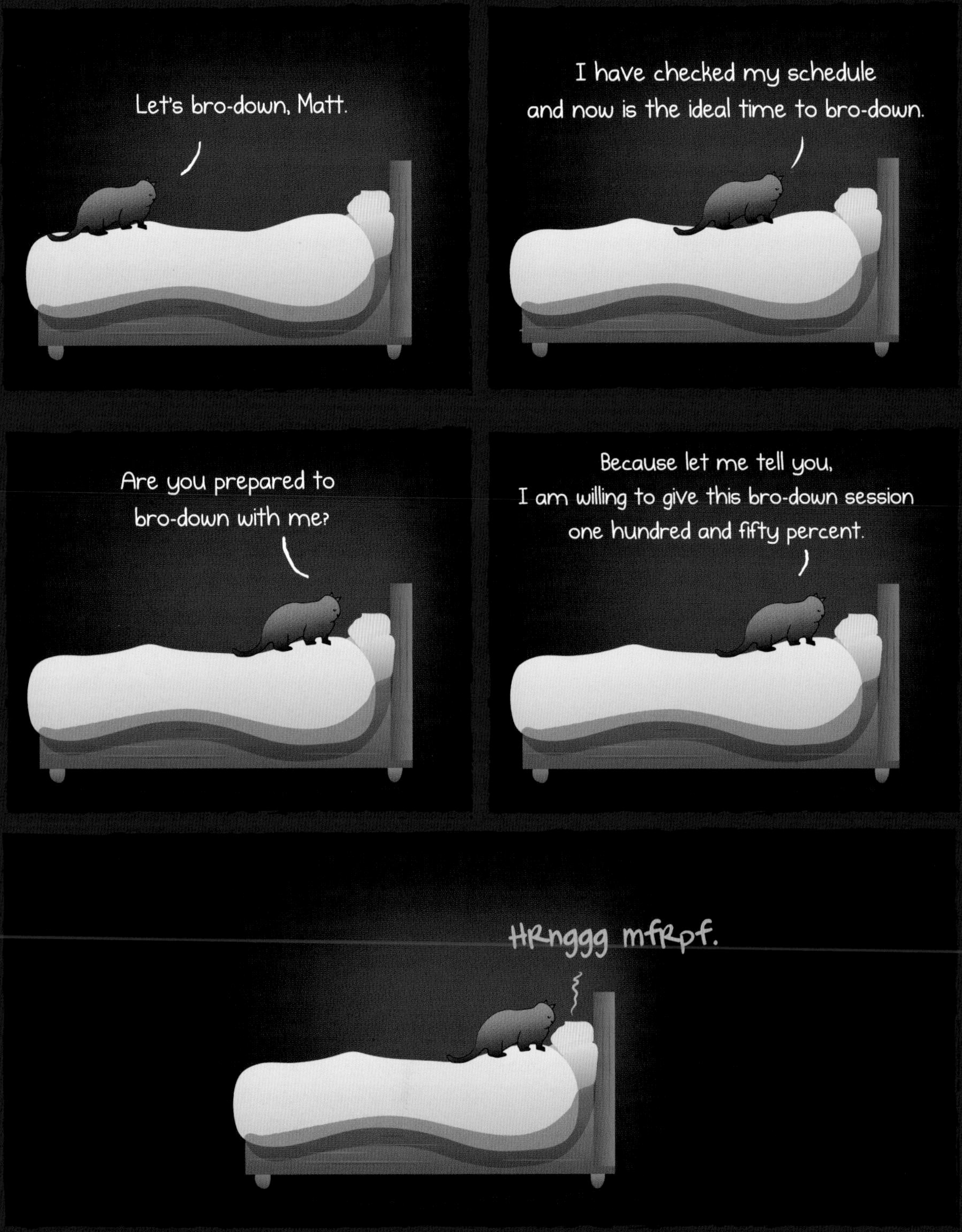
Let's bro-down, Matt.
I have checked my schedule and now is the ideal time to bro-down.
Are you prepared to bro-down with me?
Because let me tell you, I am willing to give this bro-down session one hundred and fifty percent.
HRnggg mfRpf.

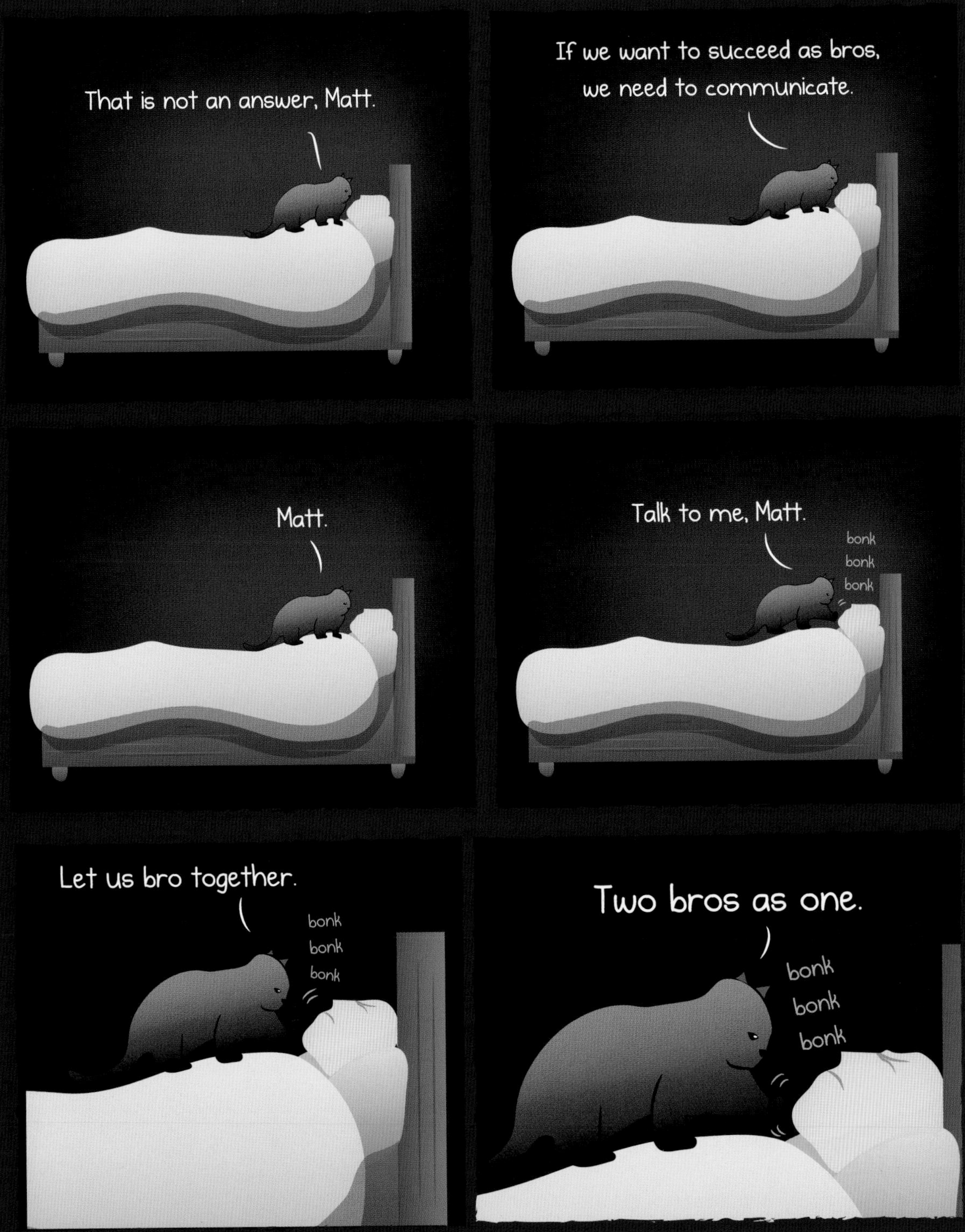
That is not an answer, Matt.
If we want to succeed as bros, we need to communicate.
Matt.
Talk to me, Matt.
bonk
bonk
bonk
Let us bro together.
bonk
bonk
bonk
Two bros as one.
bonk
bonk
bonk

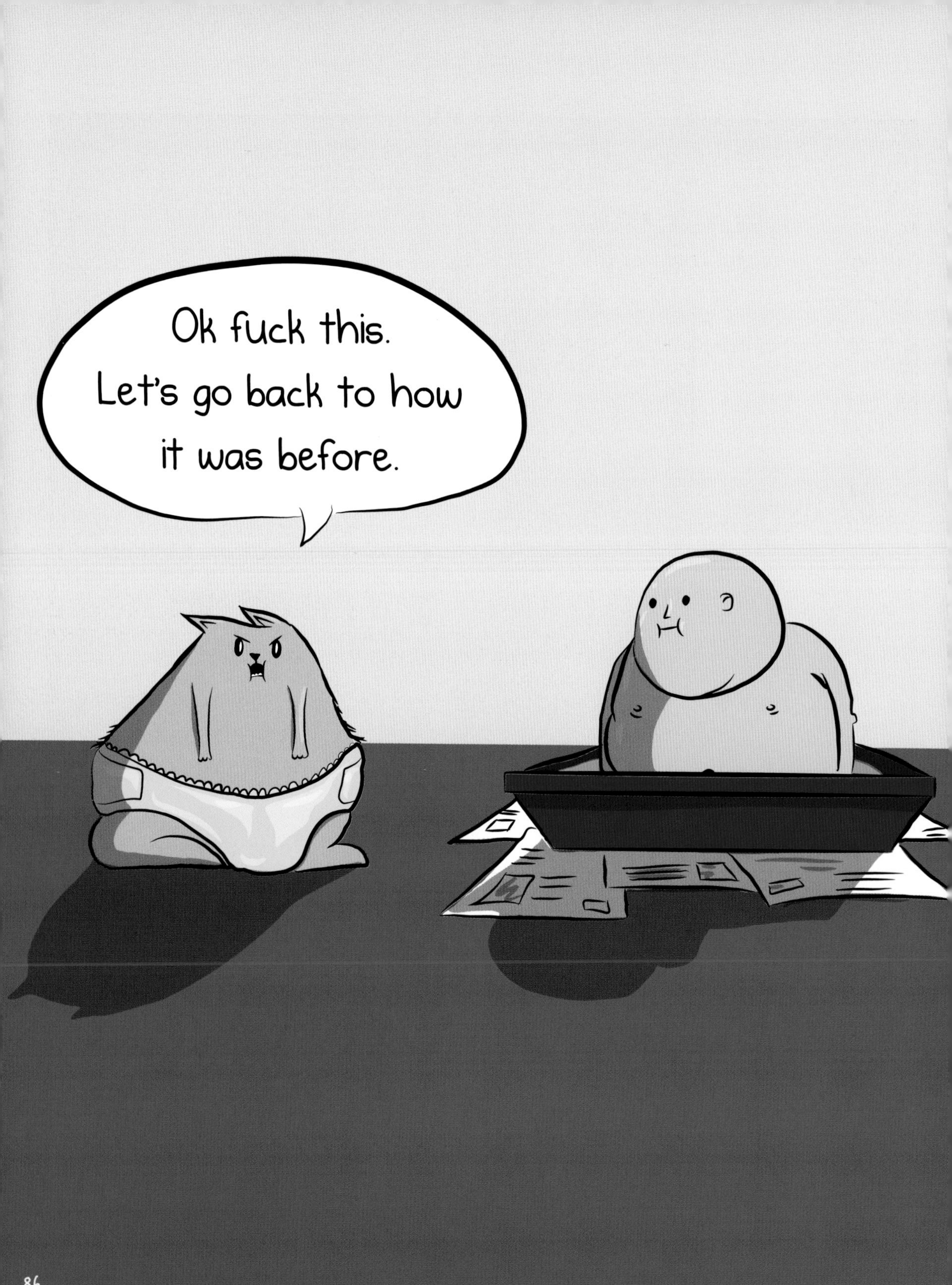
Ok fuck this.
Let's go back to how
it was before.

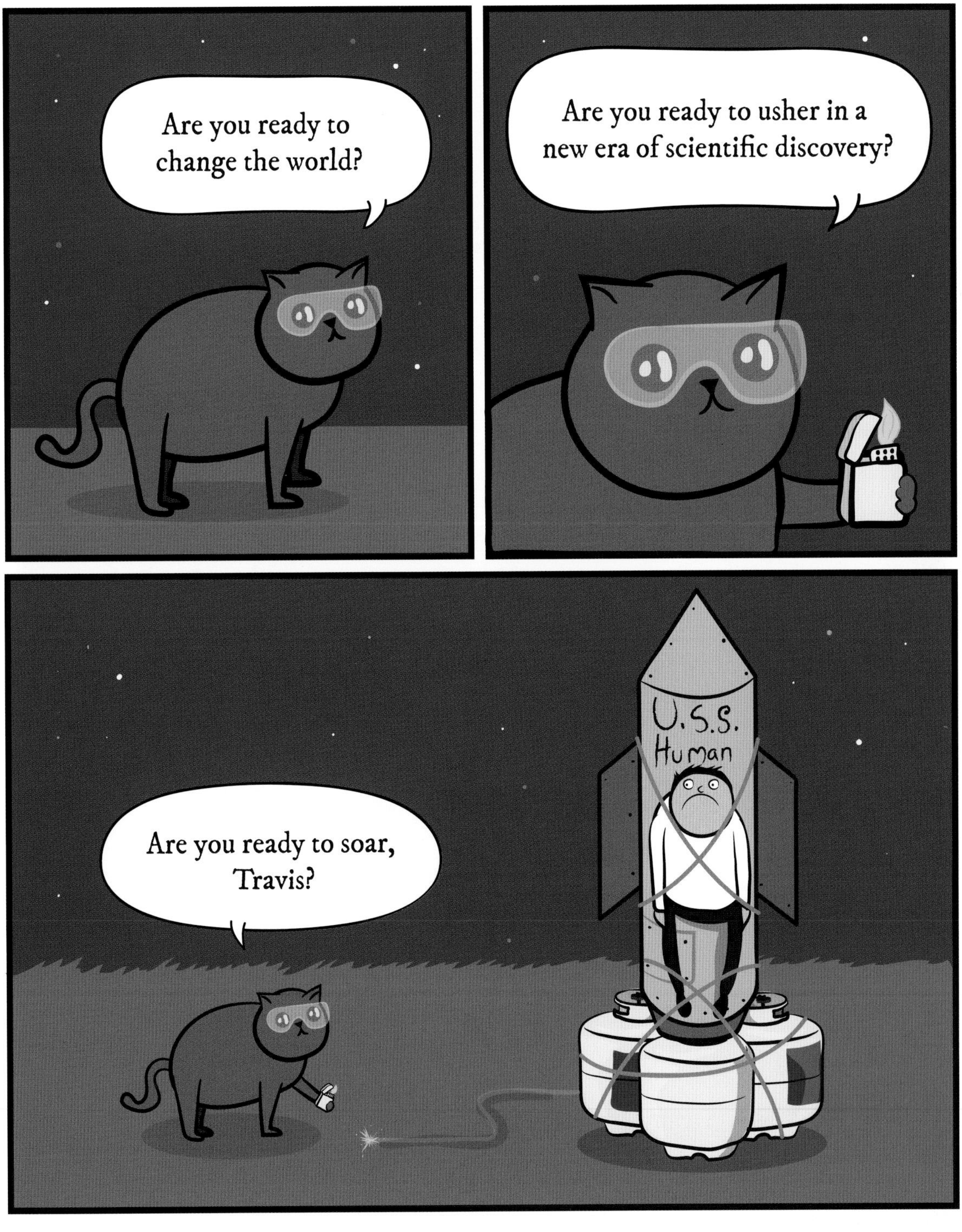
Are you ready to change the world?
Are you ready to usher in a new era of scientific discovery?
U.S.S. Human
Are you ready to soar, Travis?

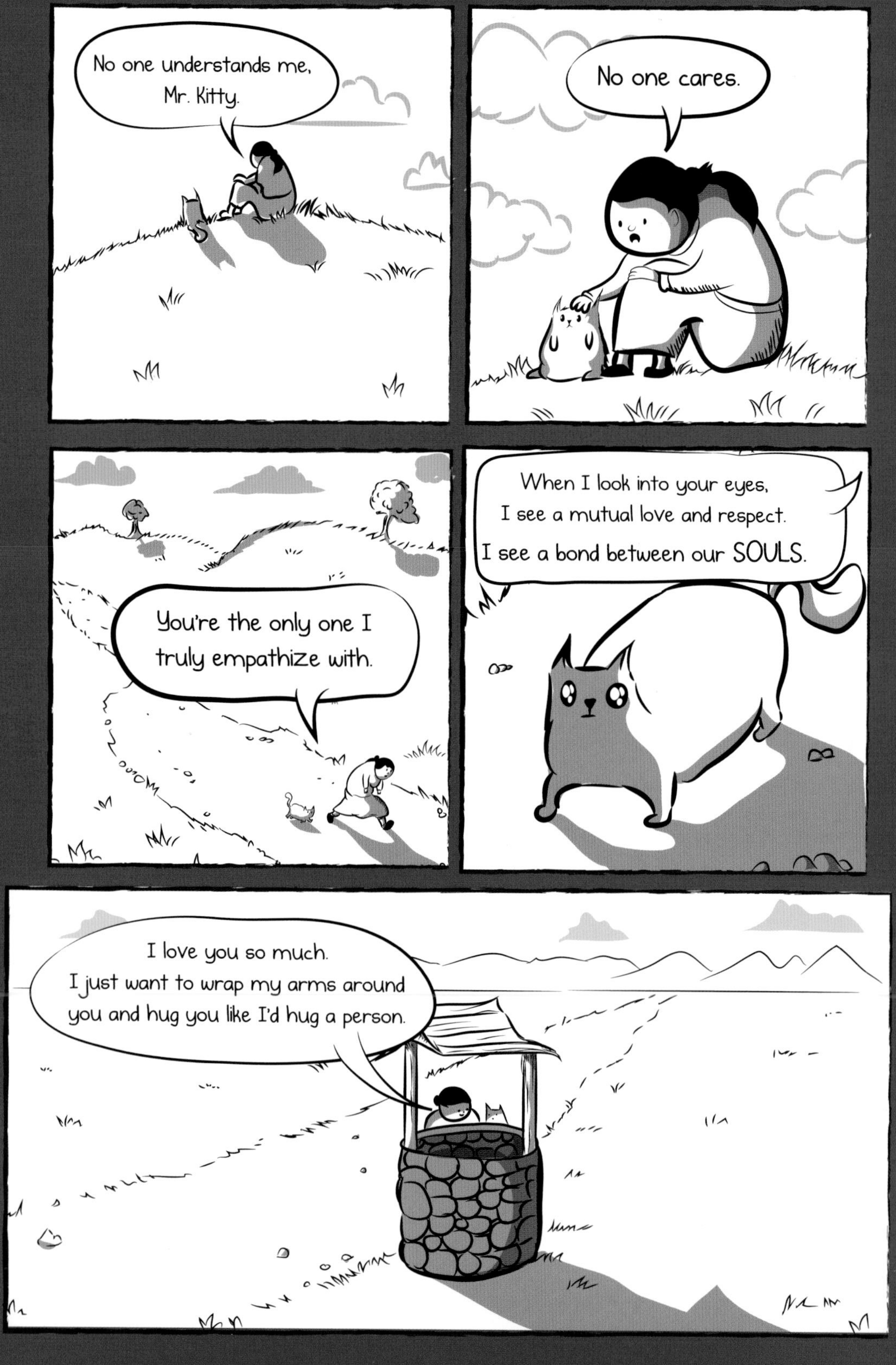

No one understands me, Mr. Kitty.
No one cares.
You're the only one I truly empathize with.
When I look into your eyes, I see a mutual love and respect. I see a bond between our SOULS.
I love you so much. I just want to wrap my arms around you and hug you like I'd hug a person.

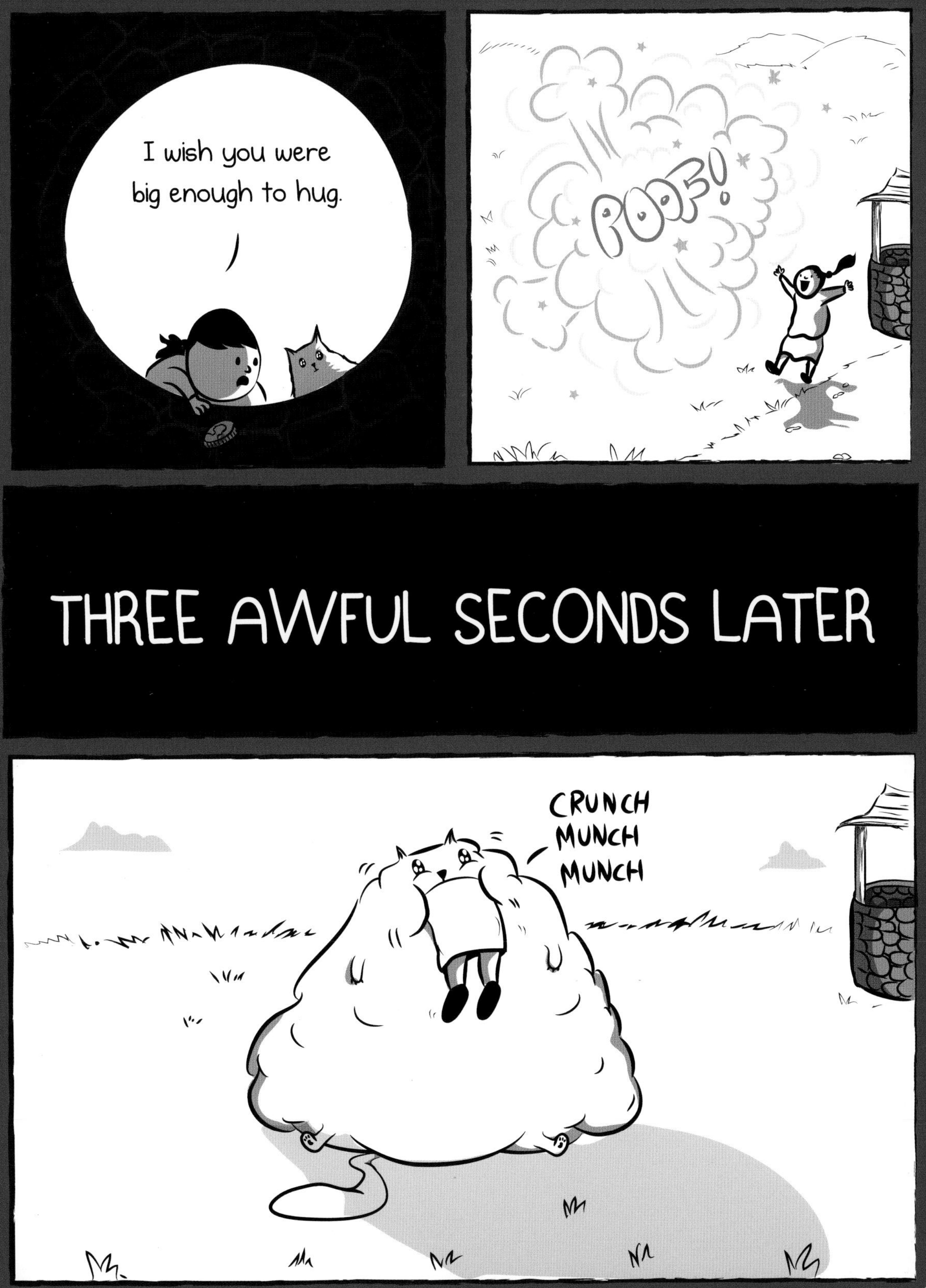
I wish you were big enough to hug.
POOF!
THREE AWFUL SECONDS LATER
CRUNCH
MUNCH
MUNCH

Dear Diary,

The pale monster keeps dropping delicacies onto the floor.
Food crashes into his mouth like dead whales crash upon a beach.
I'm not sure he even knows where his mouth is. The other day I
saw him try to put food in his own eye. What's the plan there? Are
you going to chew it with your eyelids? Ok idiot.

His incompetency is my gain: when he drops the food,
I eat the food. You could call this a truce.

I call it a cease-fire.

There can be no peace between us, not while the blood of ancients
courses through my veins.

Because I am a creature of war. Of chaos.

I am a beautiful weapon.

I am cat.

Deer darrey,

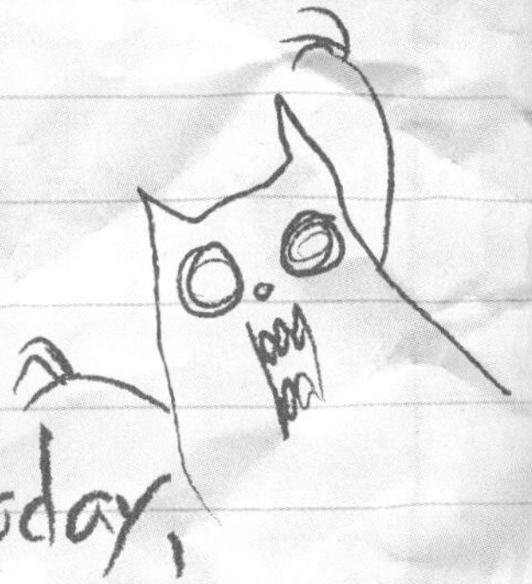

tried 2 get better at eat today,
but have no fangs yet. Small tiger has many fangs. It eat <u>EVERYTHING.</u>

Sometimes wonder... one day will try 2 eat me?

Small tiger murders too much. Other day it murdered bird. left bird parts all over patio. no trial. no lawyers.

got away <u>SCOT-FREE.</u>

Cat hung bird head over my crib.
its eyes are like collapsed stars,
it haunts me.

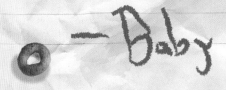

—Baby

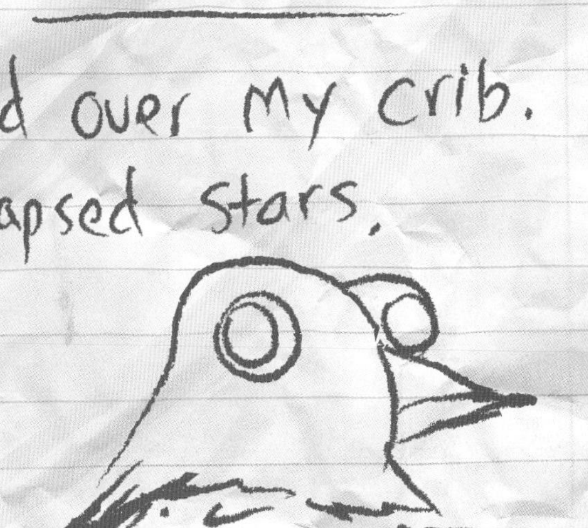

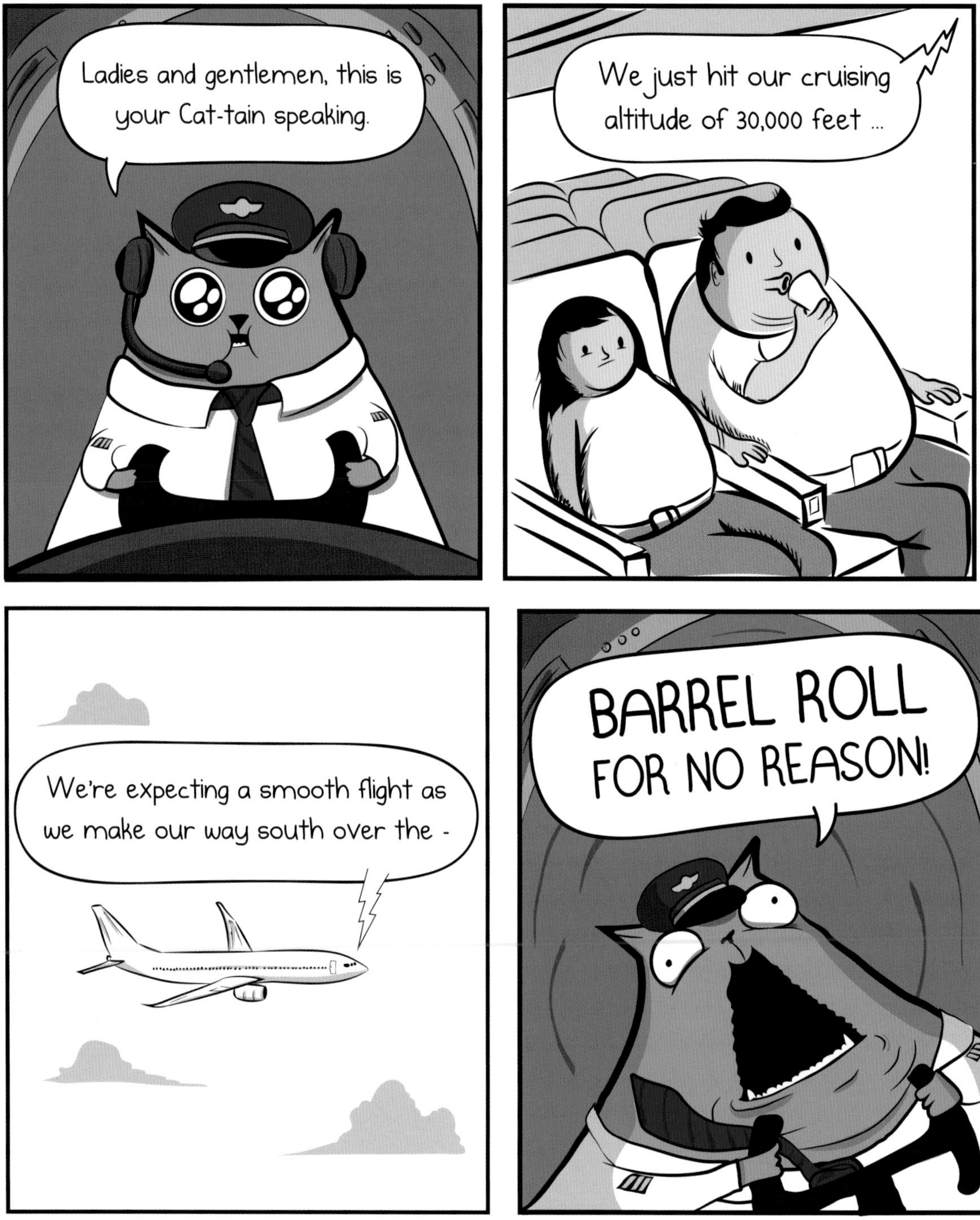
Ladies and gentlemen, this is your Cat-tain speaking.
We just hit our cruising altitude of 30,000 feet ...
We're expecting a smooth flight as we make our way south over the -
BARREL ROLL FOR NO REASON!

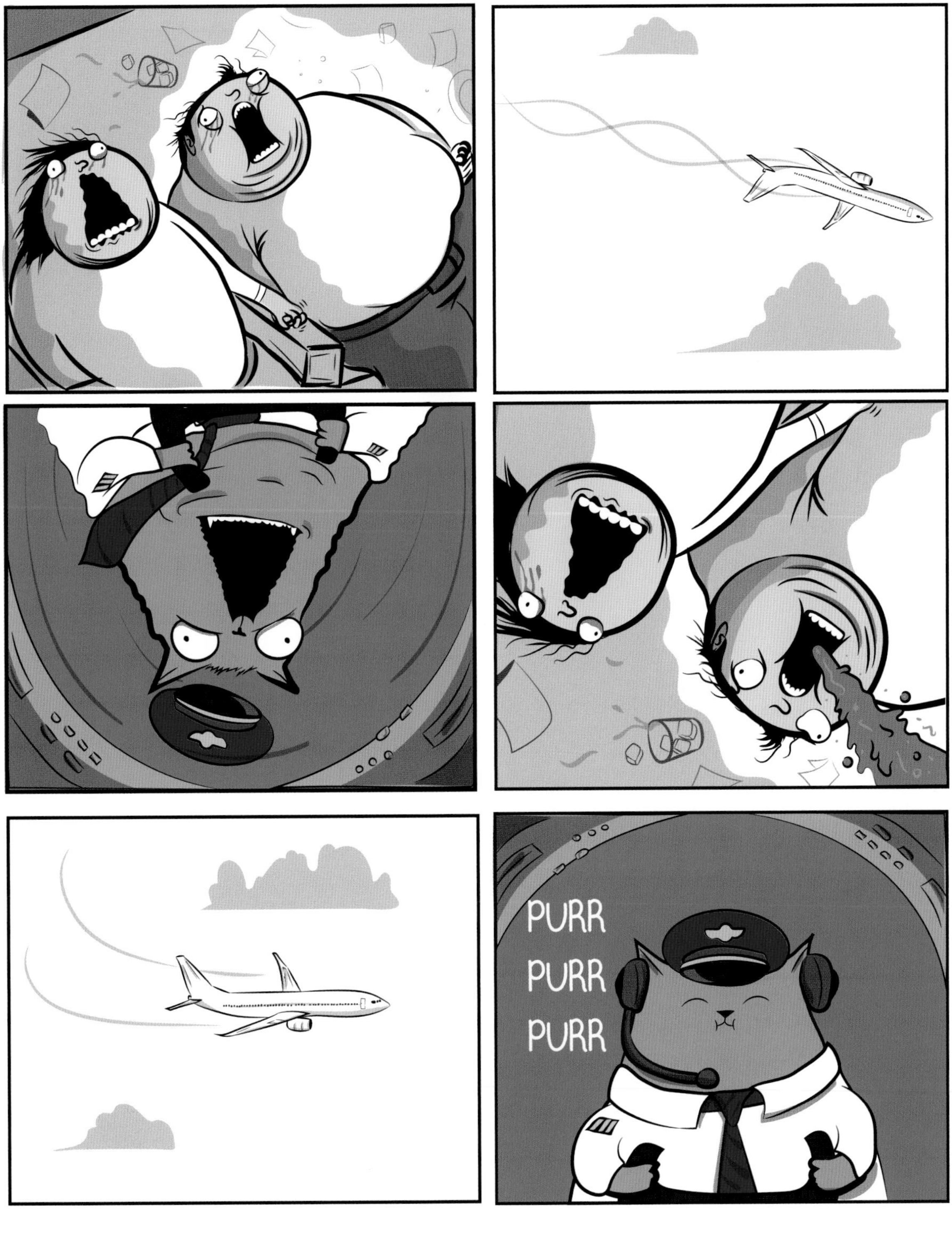
PURR
PURR
PURR

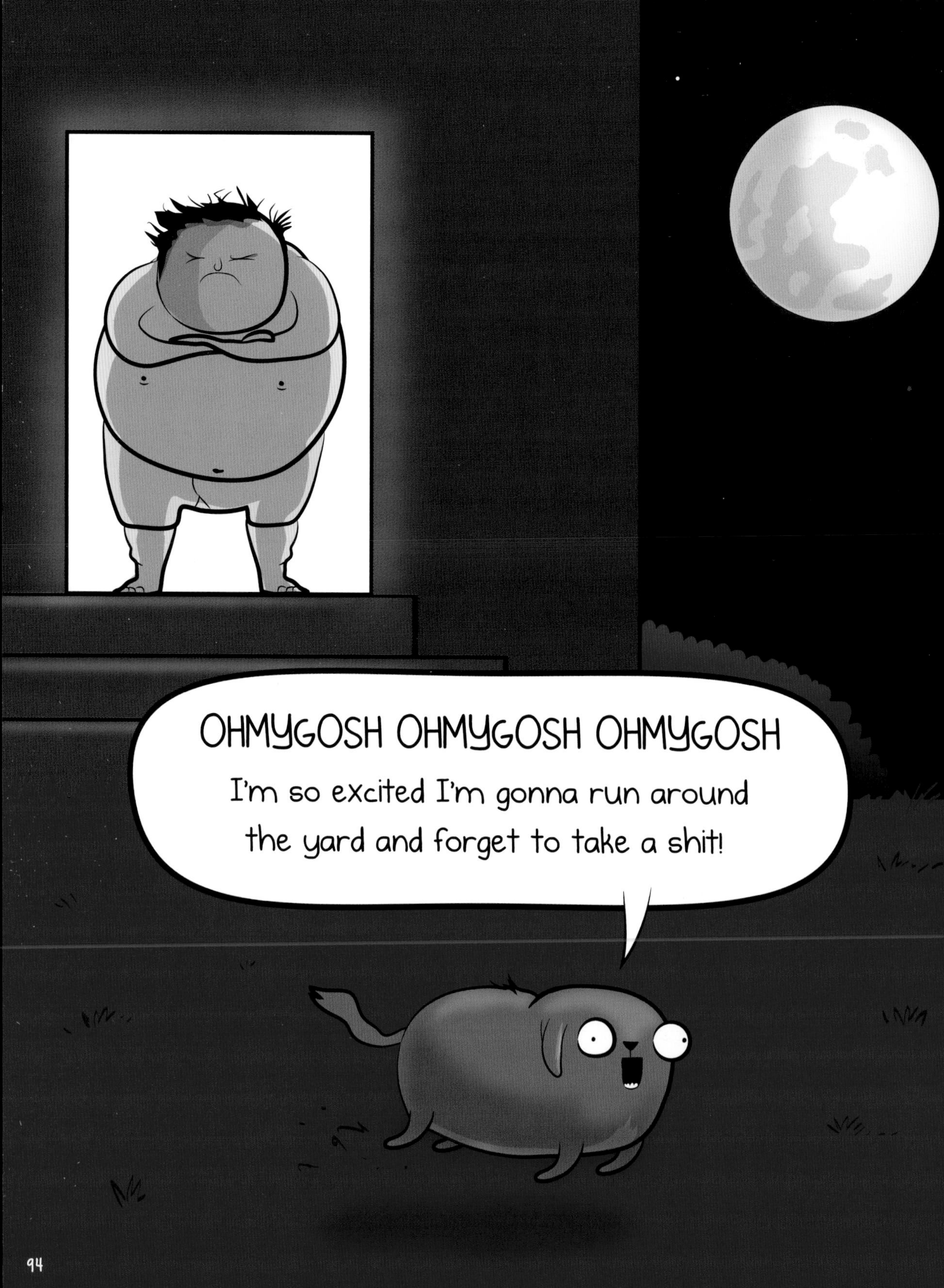
OHMYGOSH OHMYGOSH OHMYGOSH
I'm so excited I'm gonna run around the yard and forget to take a shit!

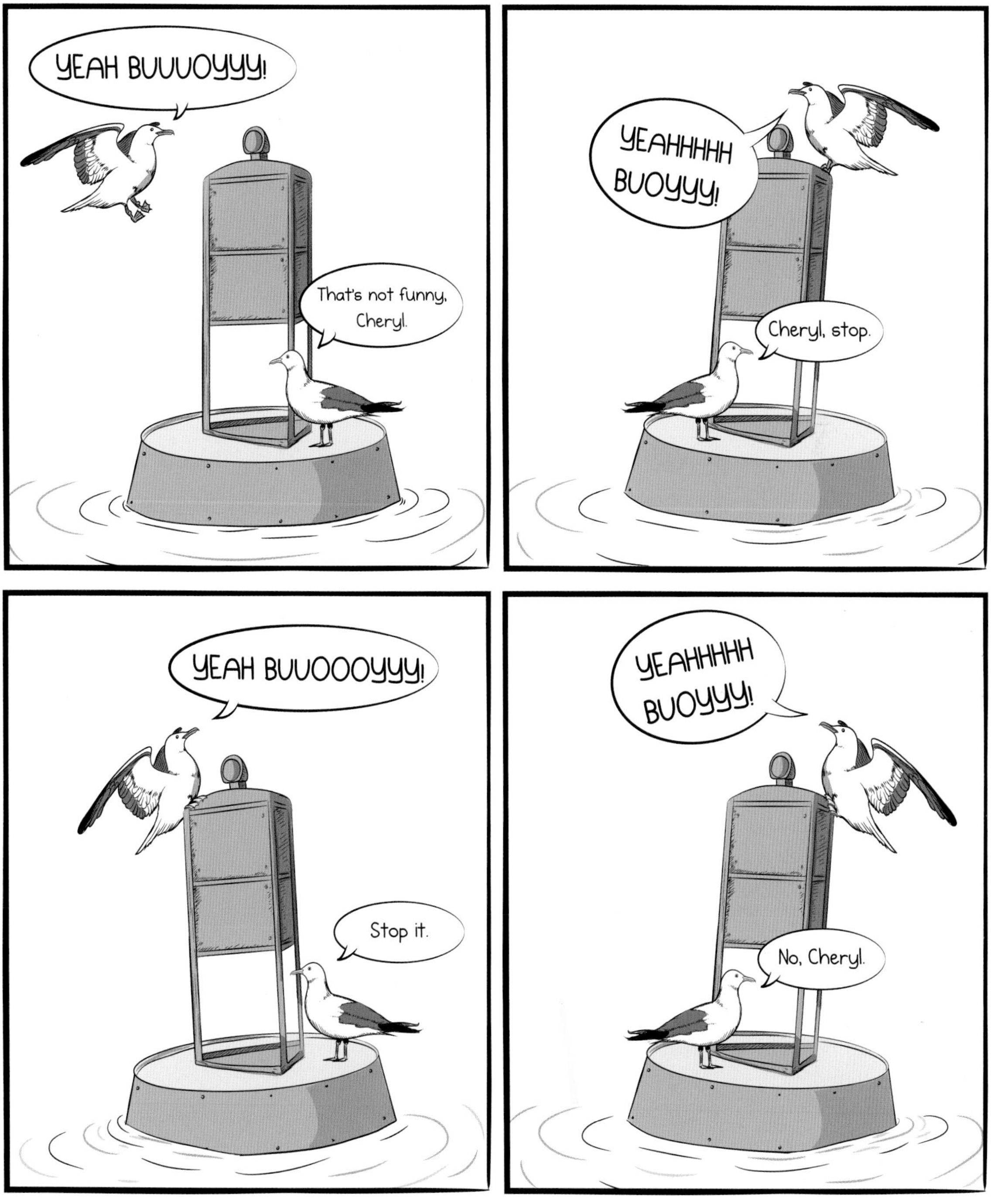

YEAH BUUUOYYY!
That's not funny, Cheryl.
YEAHHHHH BUOYYY!
Cheryl, stop.
YEAH BUUOOOYYY!
Stop it.
YEAHHHHH BUOYYY!
No, Cheryl.

THE TWO SPEEDS OF A DOG

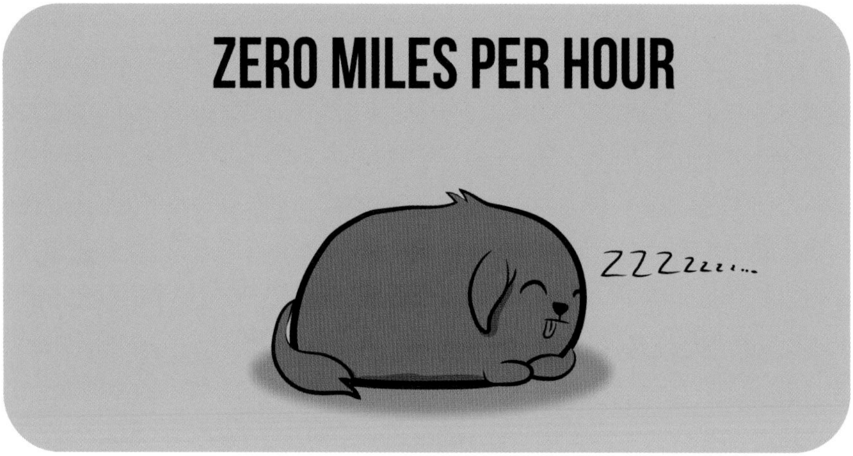
ZERO MILES PER HOUR
ZZZzzz...

AND

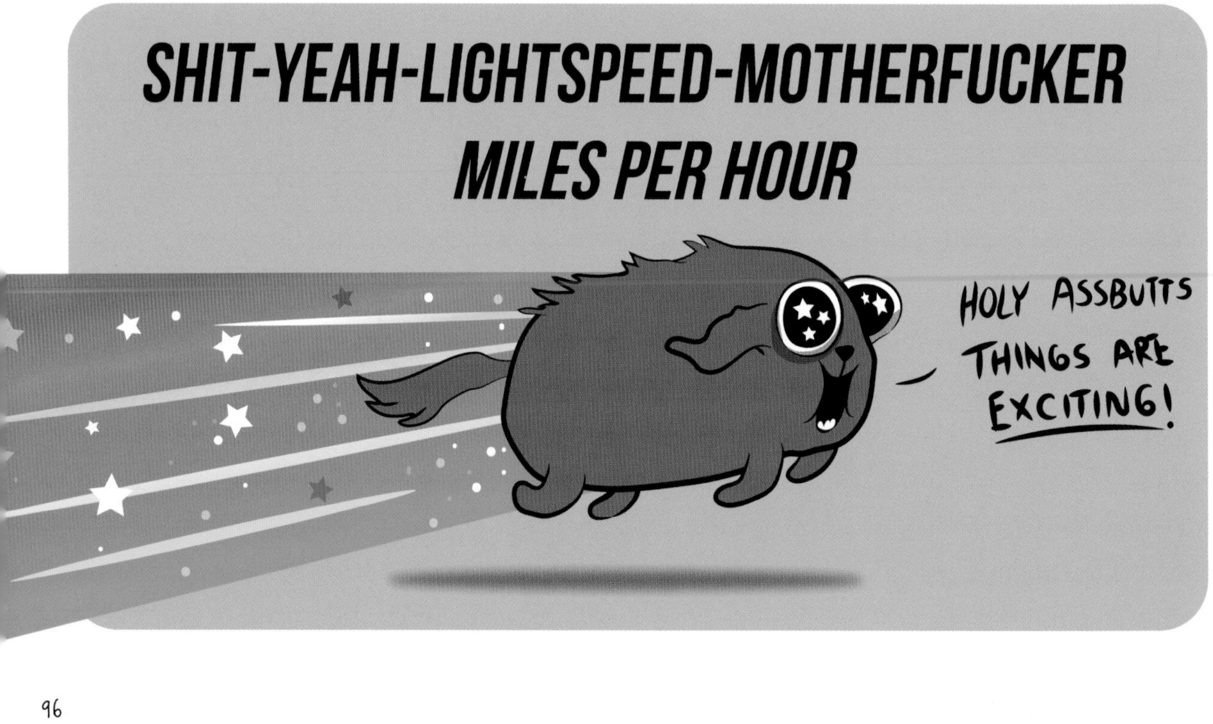
SHIT-YEAH-LIGHTSPEED-MOTHERFUCKER MILES PER HOUR
HOLY ASSBUTTS THINGS ARE EXCITING!

THE TWO SPEEDS OF A BABY

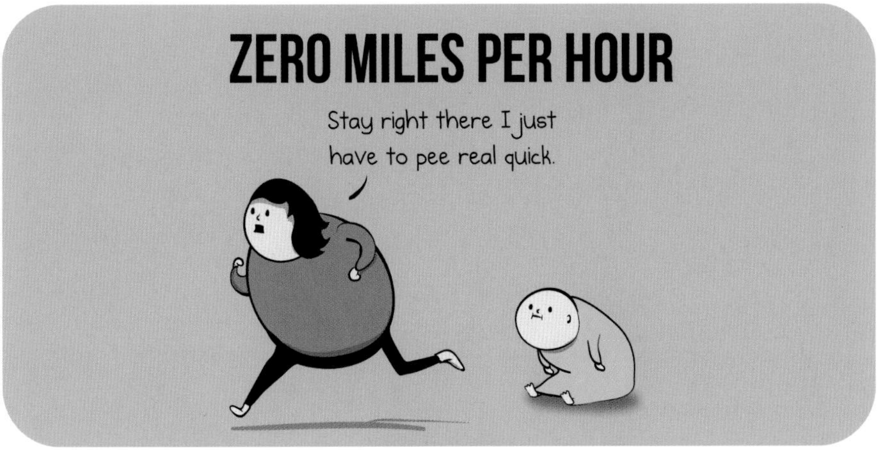
ZERO MILES PER HOUR
Stay right there I just have to pee real quick.

AND

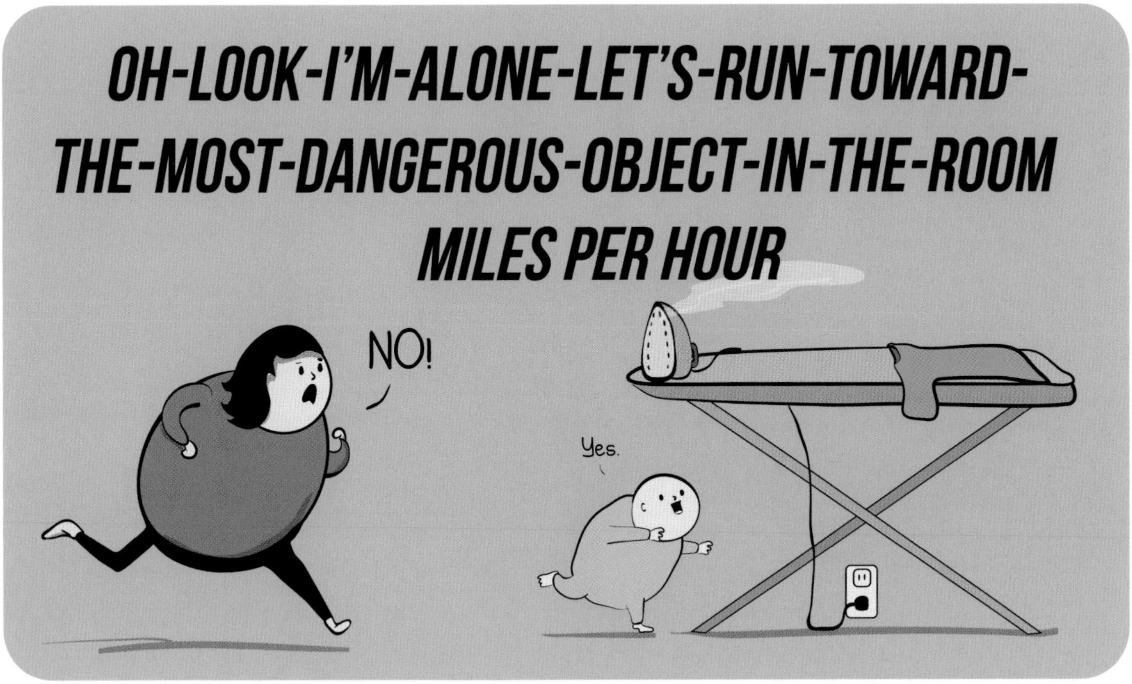
OH-LOOK-I'M-ALONE-LET'S-RUN-TOWARD-THE-MOST-DANGEROUS-OBJECT-IN-THE-ROOM MILES PER HOUR
NO!
Yes.

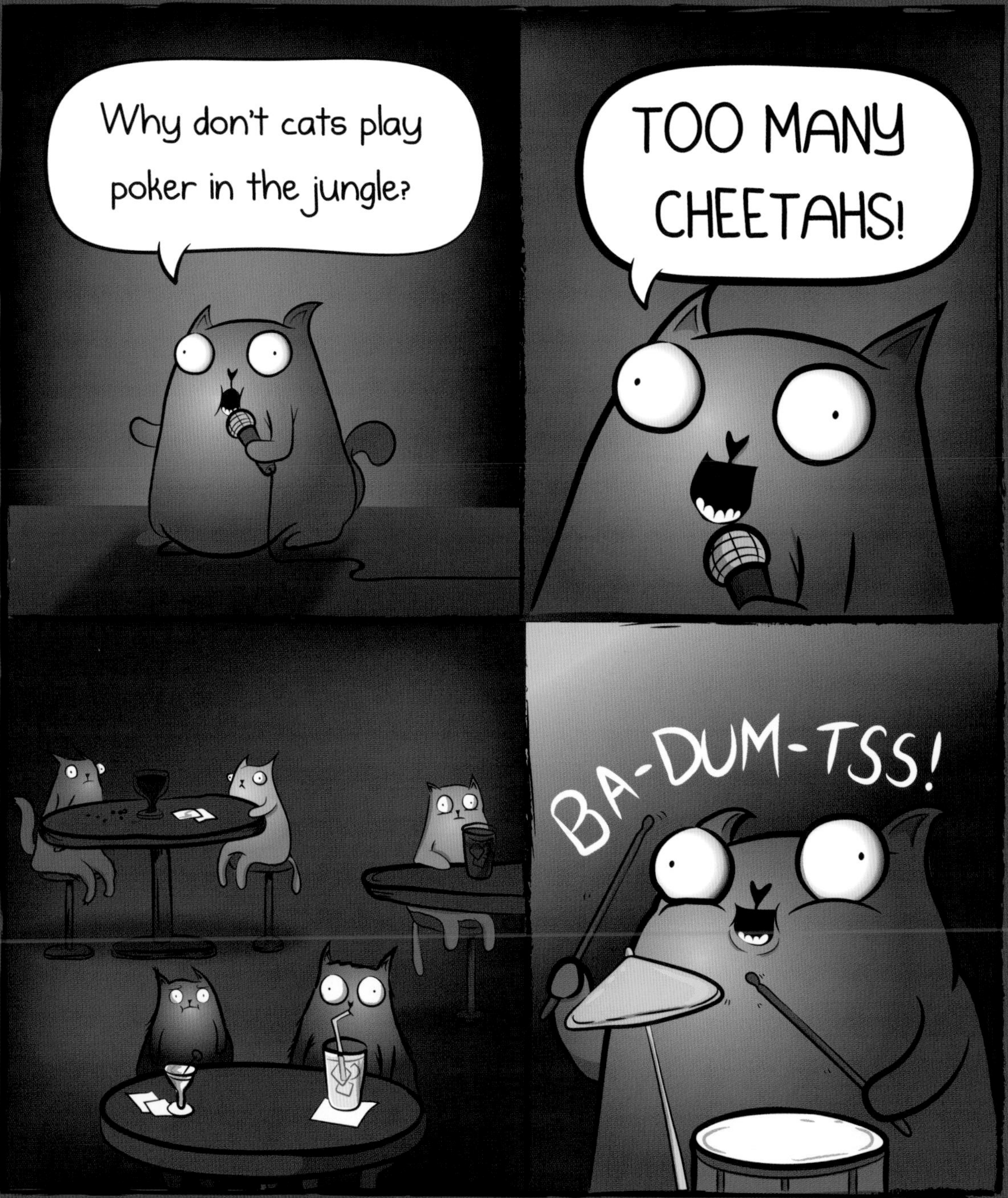
Why don't cats play poker in the jungle?
TOO MANY CHEETAHS!
BA-DUM-TSS!

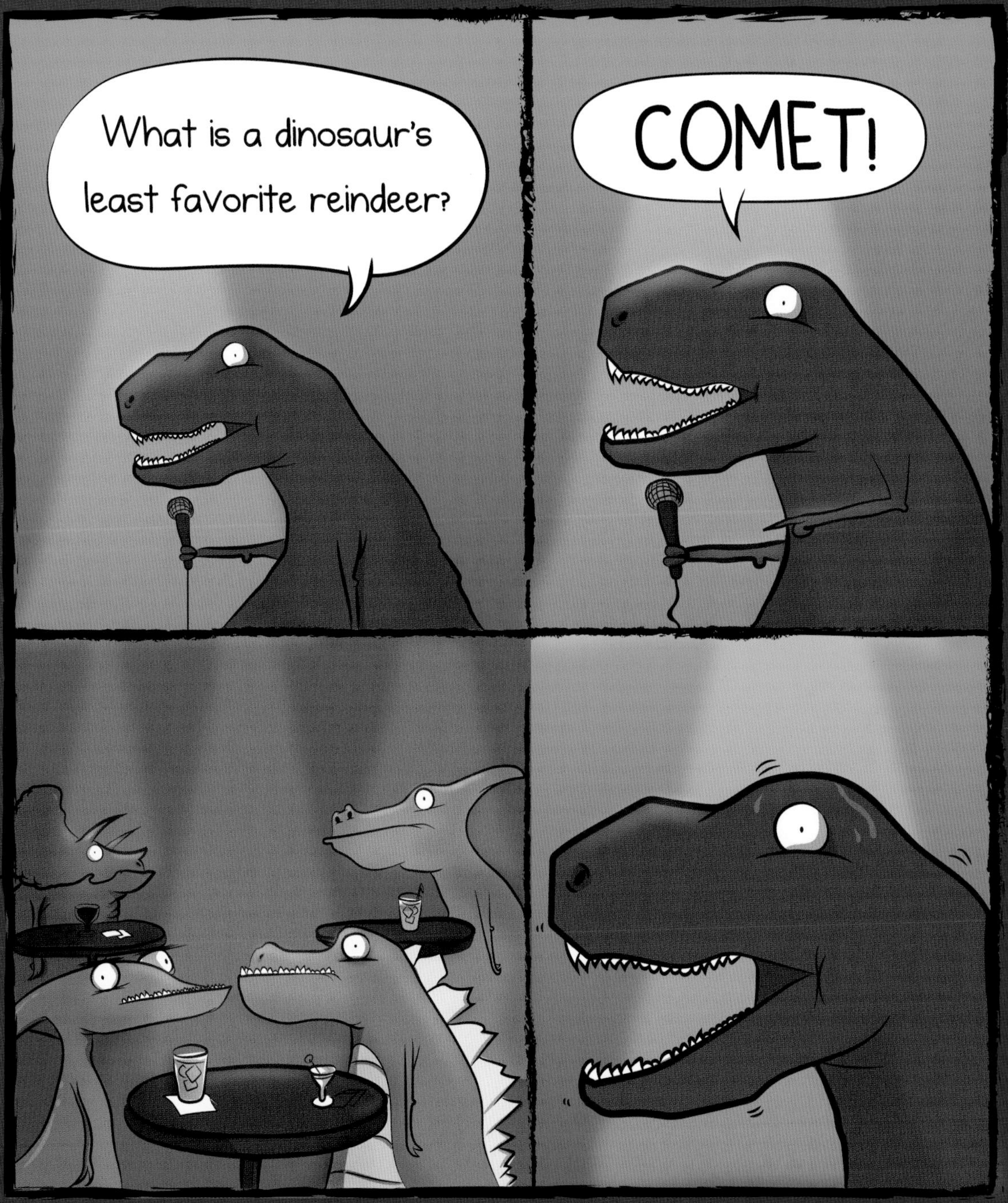
What is a dinosaur's least favorite reindeer?
COMET!

The Problem!

Babies are stored in
car seats.

(Colloquially referred to as *draggable-scream-buckets* or *handheld-shart-wagons*)

Car seats are an outdated, cumbersome form of technology that benefits neither the baby nor humanity as a whole.

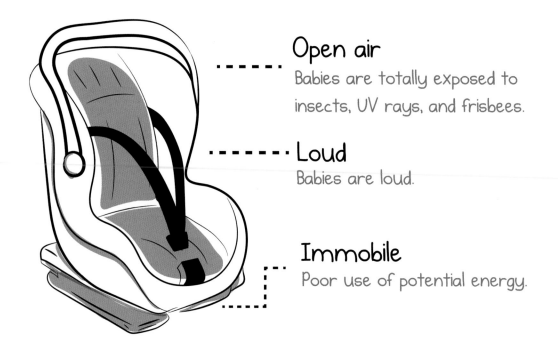

Open air
Babies are totally exposed to insects, UV rays, and frisbees.

Loud
Babies are loud.

Immobile
Poor use of potential energy.

The Solution!

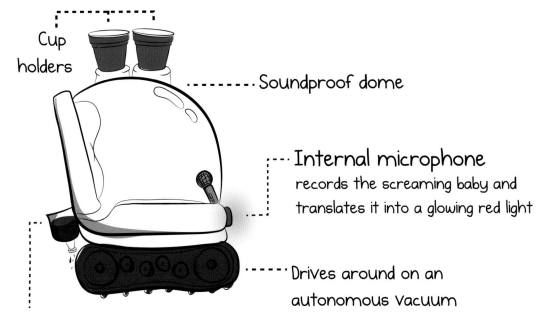

Cup holders

Soundproof dome

Internal microphone
records the screaming baby and translates it into a glowing red light

Drives around on an autonomous vacuum

(which means the baby is now contributing)

Shit pouch with drainage spigot

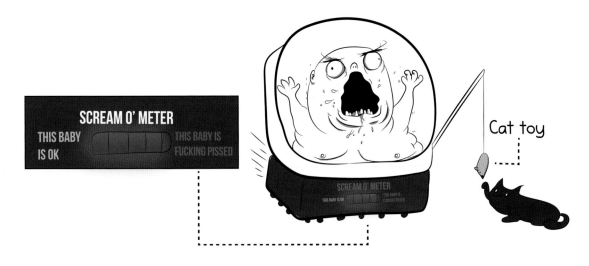

SCREAM O' METER

THIS BABY IS OK

THIS BABY IS FUCKING PISSED

Cat toy

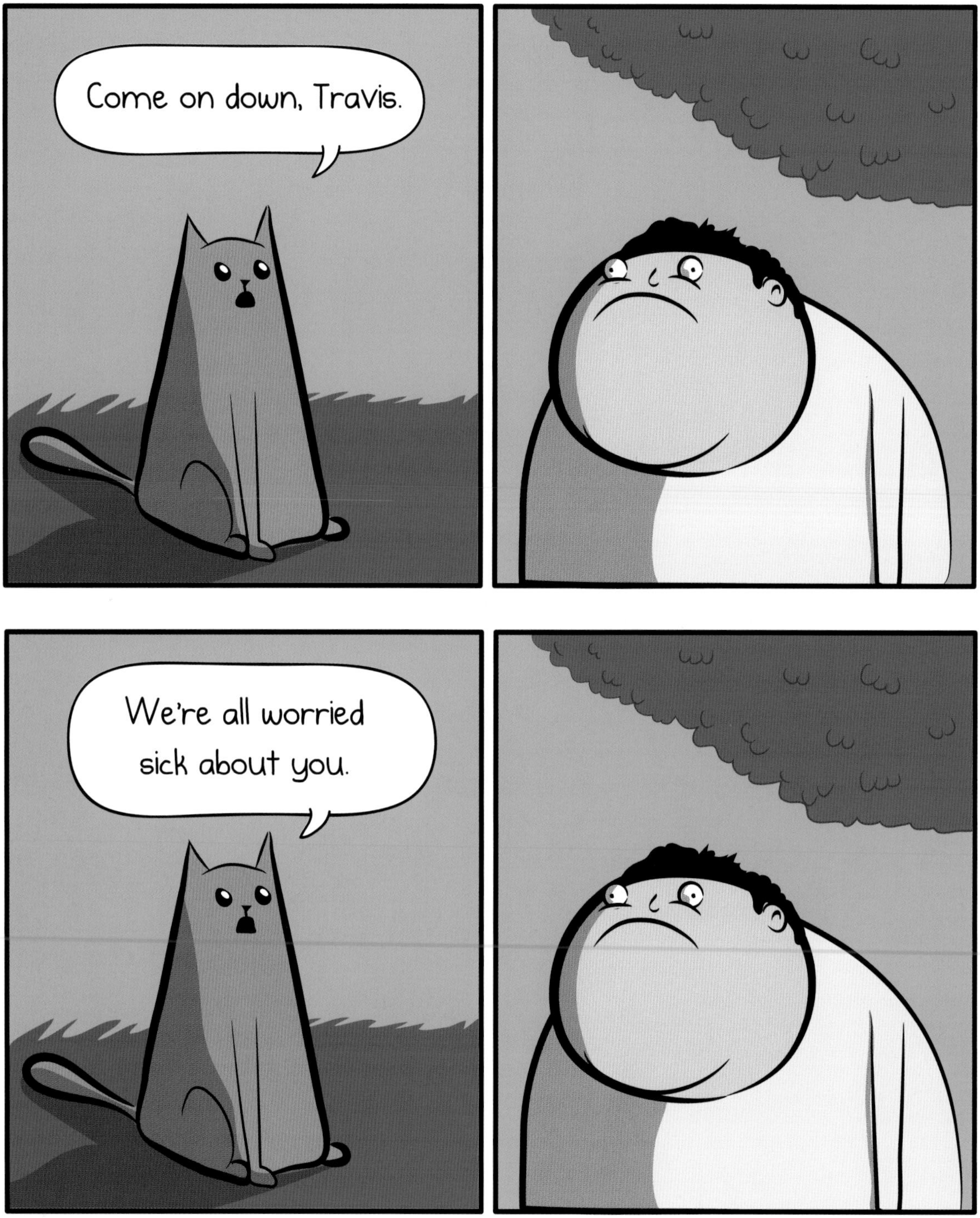
Come on down, Travis.
We're all worried sick about you.

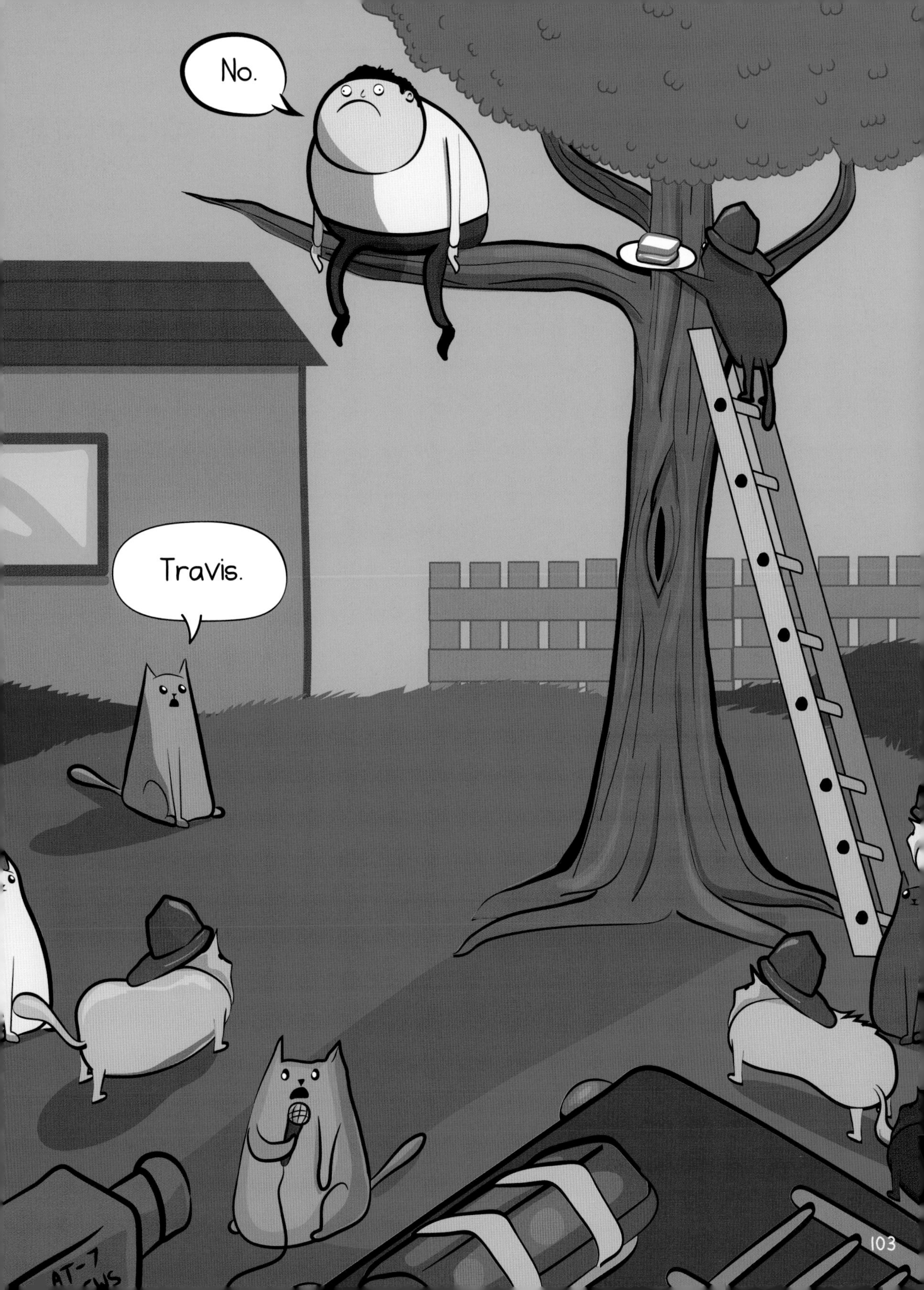
No.
Travis.
AT-7

HOW TO COMFORTABLY SLEEP
NEXT TO YOUR CAT

1. DIVIDE UP THE BED INTO TERRITORIES.

PEOPLE ZONE

CAT ZONE

2. MAKE THESE DIVISIONS ABUNDANTLY CLEAR.

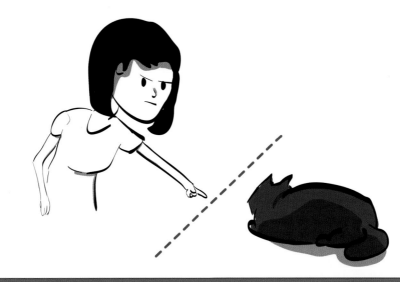

3. WHILE YOU SLEEP, THESE DIVISIONS MAY BE REDRAWN.

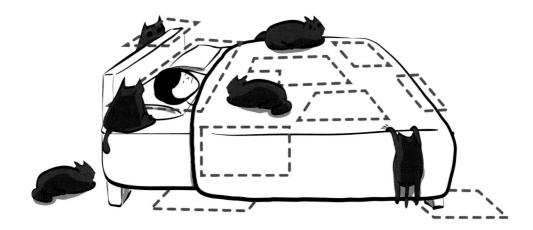

4. GIVE UP YOUR PILLOW. YOU DON'T NEED A PILLOW.

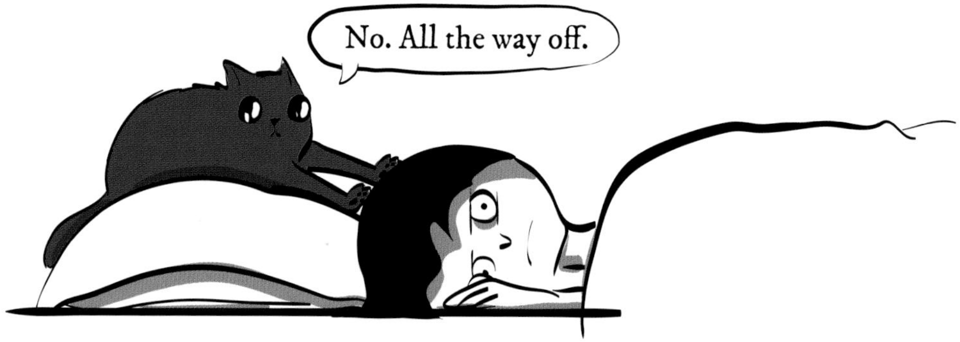
No. All the way off.

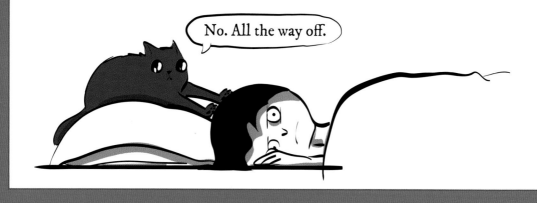

5. ALLOW YOUR CAT TO MAXIMIZE THEIR SURFACE AREA.

YOUR CAT NEEDS TO SLEEP IN A POSITION THAT FEELS LIKE THEY ARE AIRBORNE.

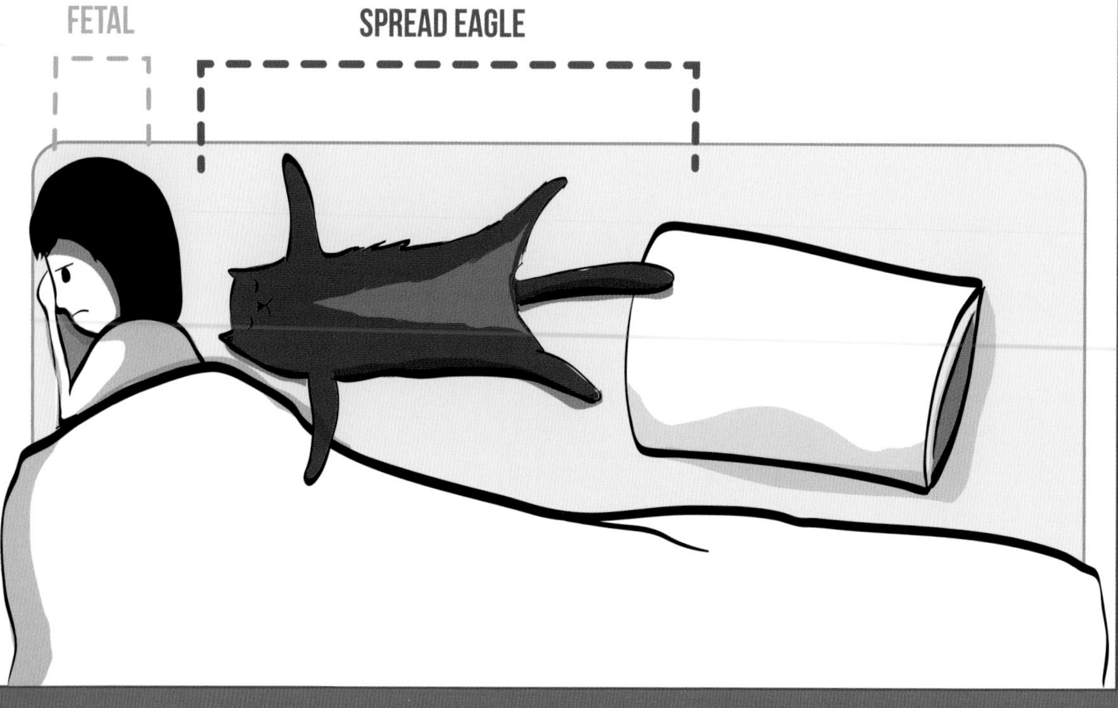
FETAL
SPREAD EAGLE

6. AVOID EYE CONTACT WITH YOUR CAT'S BUM-CAVE. FOR IT WILL HAUNT YOUR DREAMS.

DO NOT STARE INTO THE FLESHY BALLOON KNOT.

7. LEARN TO SLEEP WHILE BEING GENTLY STRUCK IN THE FACE.

8. REST EASY KNOWING THAT 99% OF THE BED HAS BEEN TOUCHED BY YOUR CAT'S BUTTHOLE.

THIS IS YOUR CAT'S WAY OF BLESSING THE BED.

BE THANKFUL FOR THESE BLESSINGS.

I came here straight from the litter box to be with you.

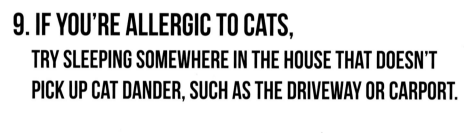

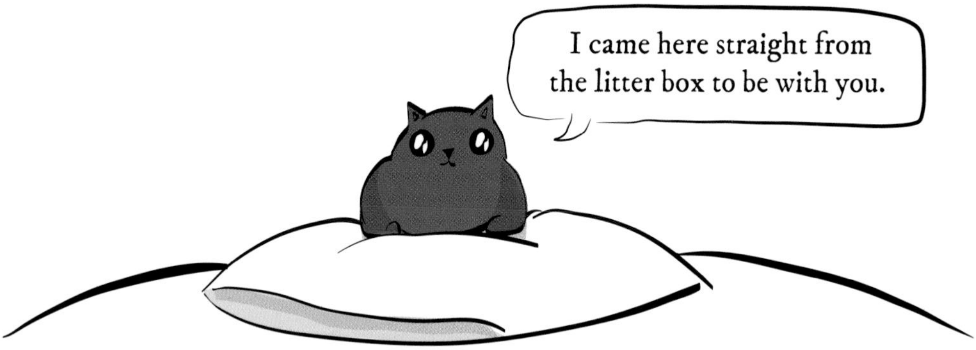

9. IF YOU'RE ALLERGIC TO CATS,

TRY SLEEPING SOMEWHERE IN THE HOUSE THAT DOESN'T PICK UP CAT DANDER, SUCH AS THE DRIVEWAY OR CARPORT.

AH-CHOO!
Please be silent. I am trying to rest.

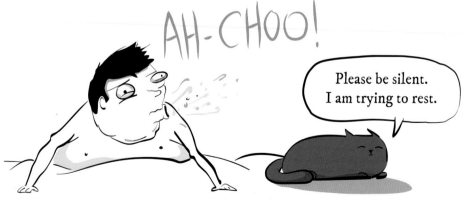

10. JUST ACCEPT THAT THIS ISN'T YOUR BED ANYMORE.

MAYBE IT NEVER WAS.

Sneezing VS Tooting

The analysis of a sneeze:

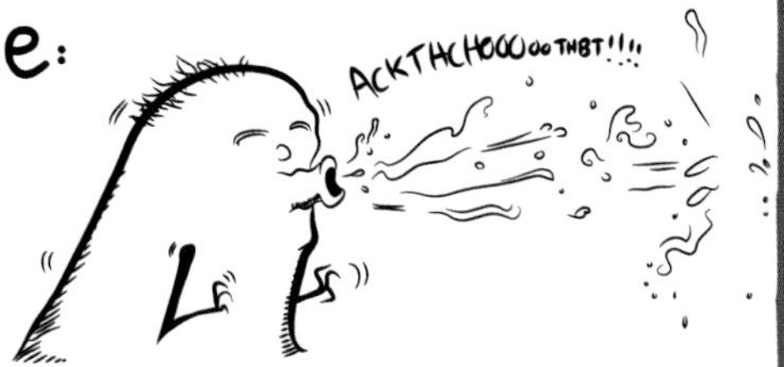
ACKTHCHOOOUooTHBT!!!!

1. Your heart stops.
2. Your face explodes.
3. Boogers and disease spray out of your mouth at 70 mph.

The result ⟹ You get germs on other people and they respond with *"Bless you"* and *"Awww ... you poor thing!"*

The analysis of a toot:

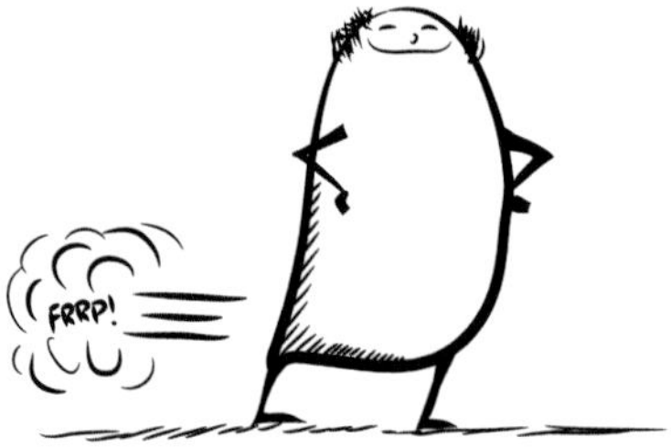
FRRP!

1. Relieves gastric distress.
2. Feels nice. Sounds nice.
3. Releases a tiny cloud of methane.

The result ⟹ You do something harmless to other people and they respond with *"I don't love you anymore"* and *"Matt, I want a divorce."*

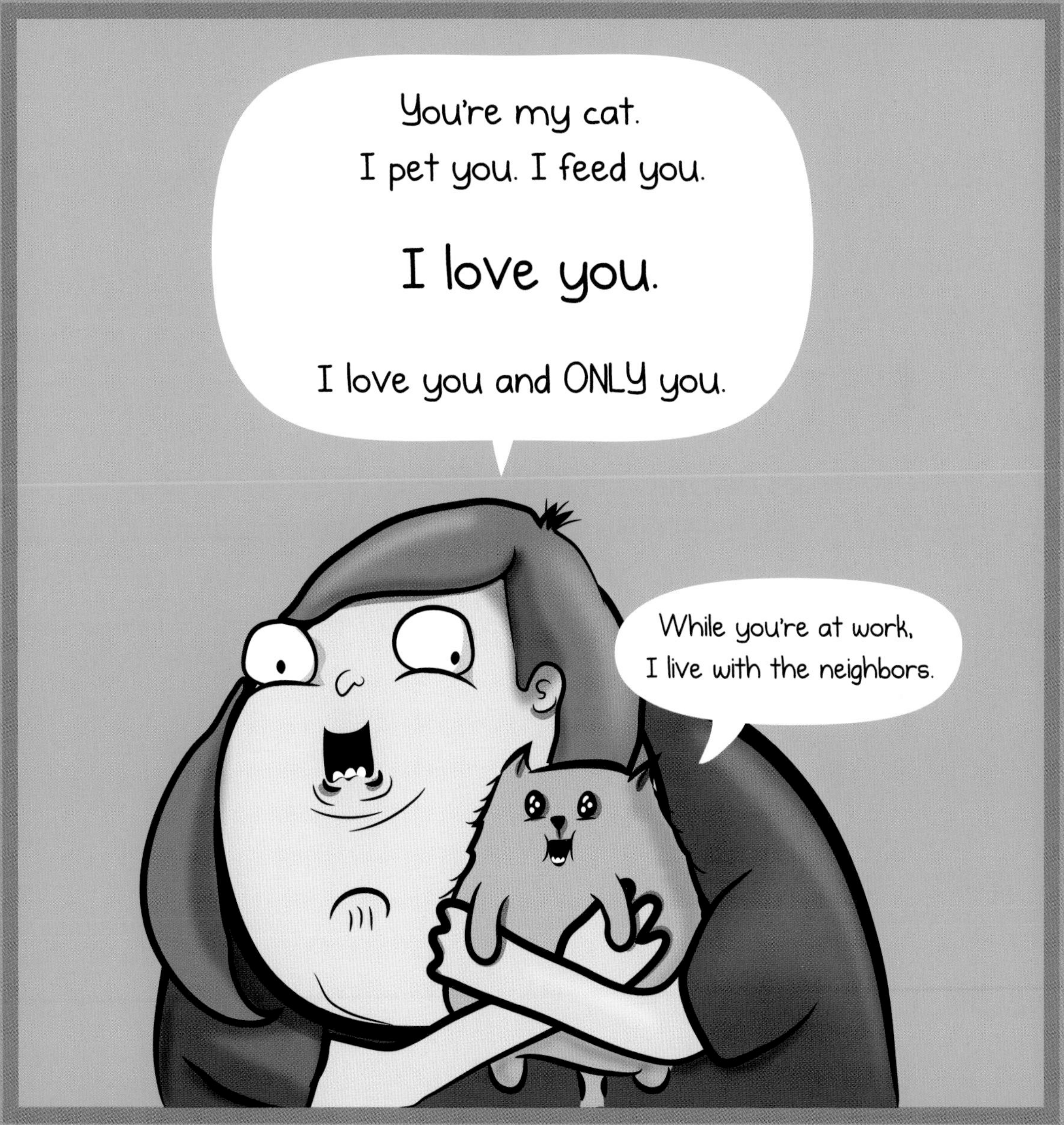
You're my cat.
I pet you. I feed you.
I love you.
I love you and ONLY you.
While you're at work,
I live with the neighbors.

How to walk a human being

. . . A guide for dogs . . .

Initiating the walk

Human beings need to be walked.
They are like tigers in a zoo. They require enrichment.
If they do not get walked, they become unhappy.
They quietly sink into couches and beds and become amorphous barges of flesh.

It's your job to save them.

Save the flesh-barges.

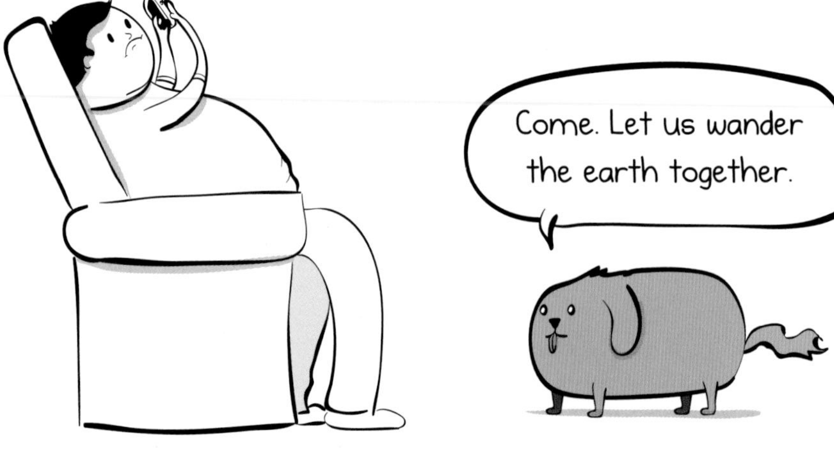
Come. Let us wander the earth together.

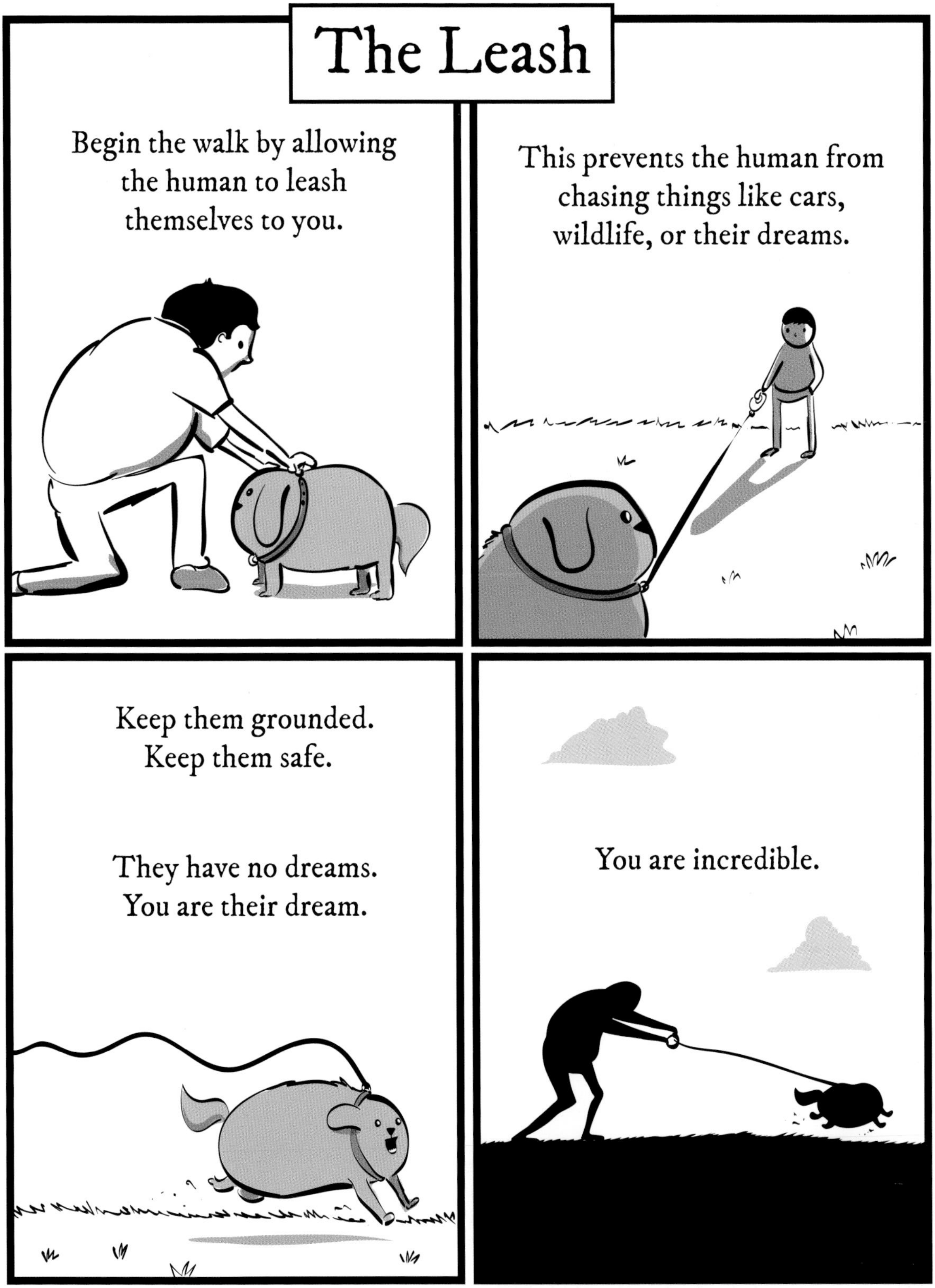

The Leash
Begin the walk by allowing the human to leash themselves to you.
This prevents the human from chasing things like cars, wildlife, or their dreams.
Keep them grounded. Keep them safe.
They have no dreams. You are their dream.
You are incredible.

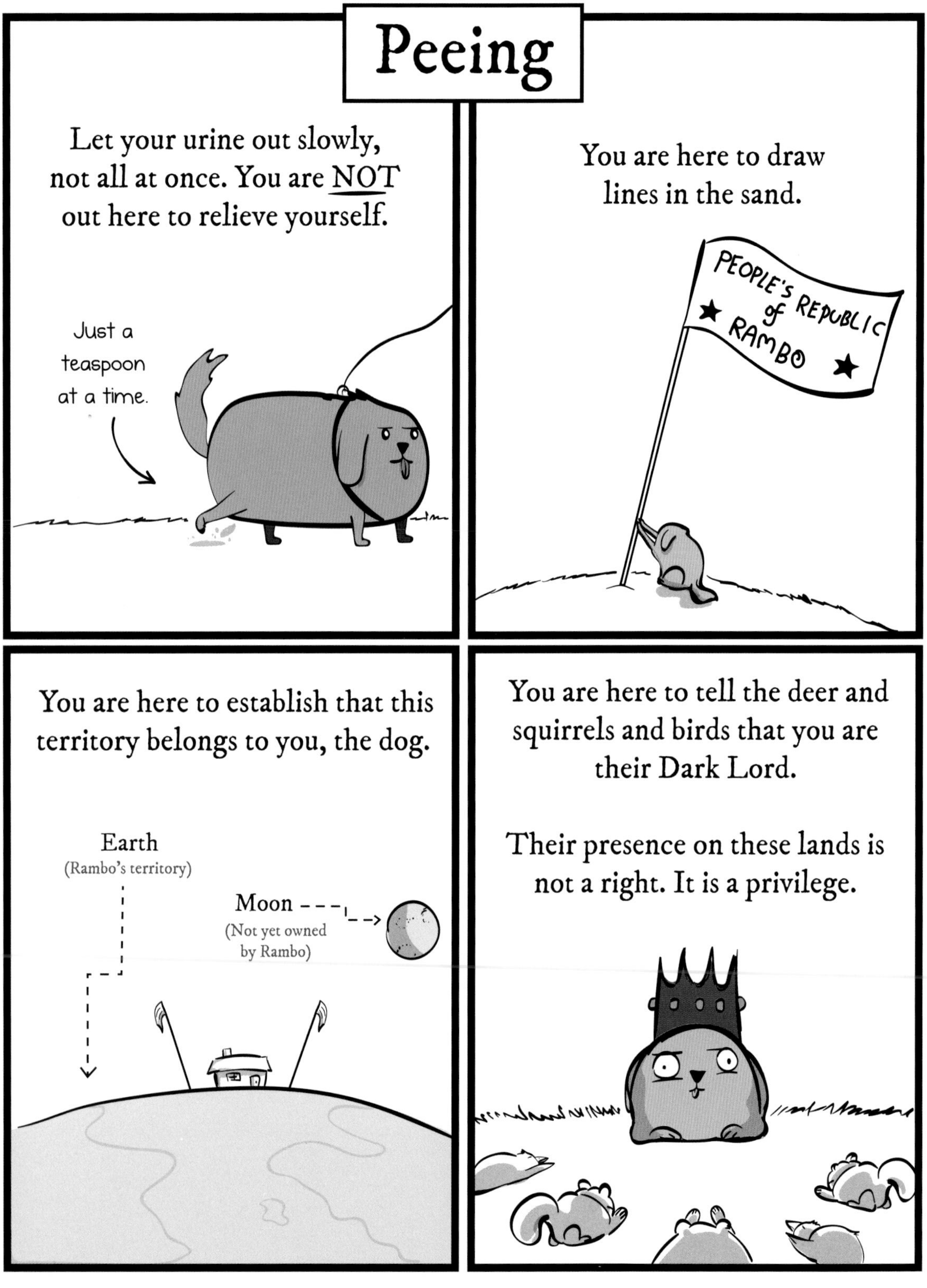
Peeing
Let your urine out slowly, not all at once. You are NOT out here to relieve yourself.
Just a teaspoon at a time.
You are here to draw lines in the sand.
PEOPLE'S REPUBLIC of RAMBO
You are here to establish that this territory belongs to you, the dog.
Earth
(Rambo's territory)
Moon
(Not yet owned by Rambo)
You are here to tell the deer and squirrels and birds that you are their Dark Lord.
Their presence on these lands is not a right. It is a privilege.

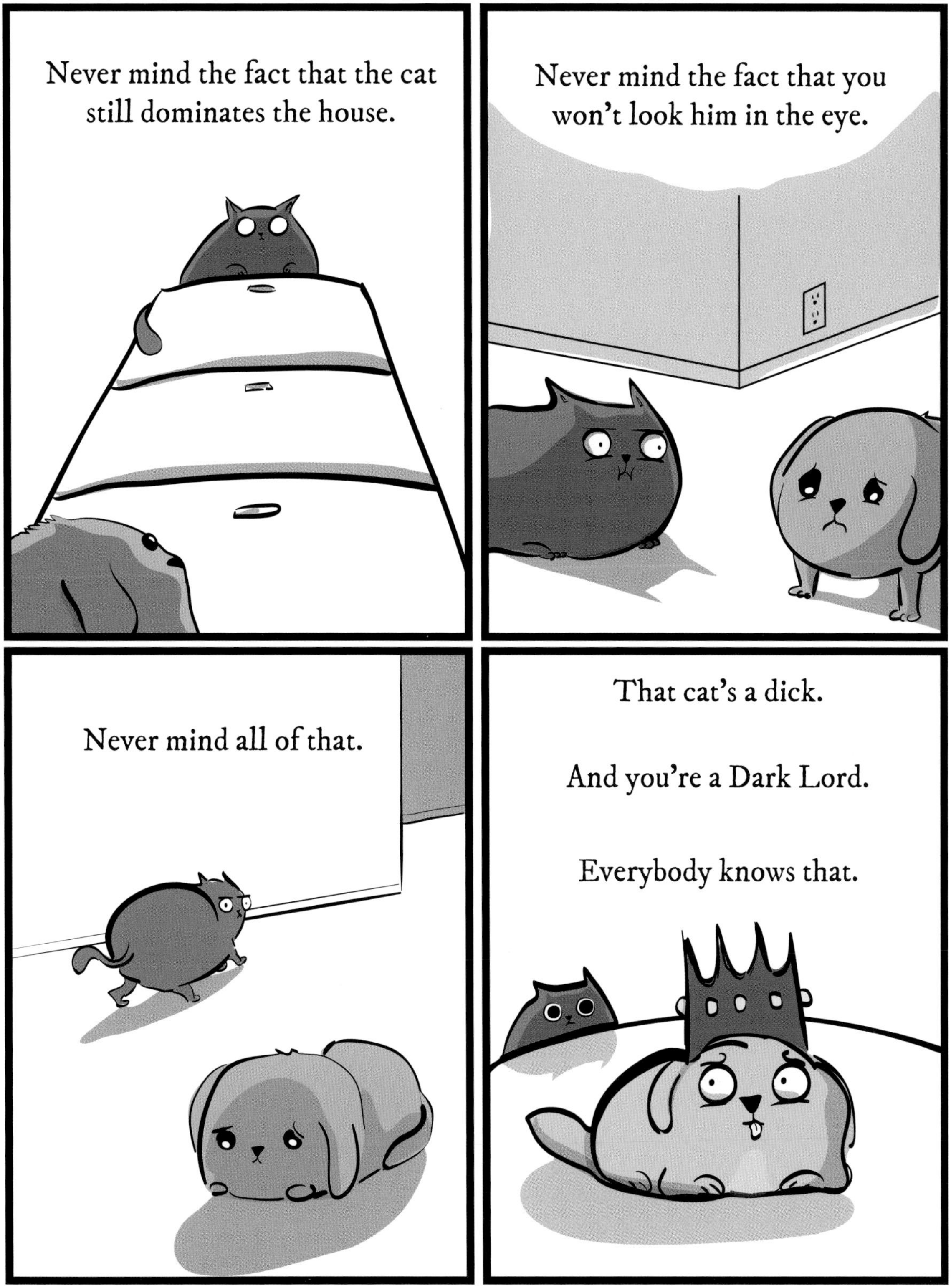
Never mind the fact that the cat still dominates the house.
Never mind the fact that you won't look him in the eye.
Never mind all of that.
That cat's a dick.
And you're a Dark Lord.
Everybody knows that.

Pre-Pooping

Prior to pooping, announce this joyous event by spinning in circles. Weaving ovals with your body is sign language for "I'm about to defecate." The number of spins correlates to your enthusiasm about the upcoming bowel movement.

One spin = a decent poop.

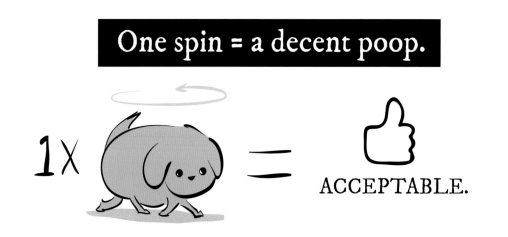

$1x$ = ACCEPTABLE.

Five spins = this is your magnum opus.

Cue "Ride of the Valkyries." Call the newspapers. Call the police. Call everyone. This motherfucker is gonna be good.

$5x$ = EXTRAORDINARY.

Before I go any further, I would like to reiterate that you, the dog, are invincible. You are a creature of strength, dominance, and permanence. You sit atop the food chain like a Tyrannosaurus rex sits atop a mound of dead cheetahs.

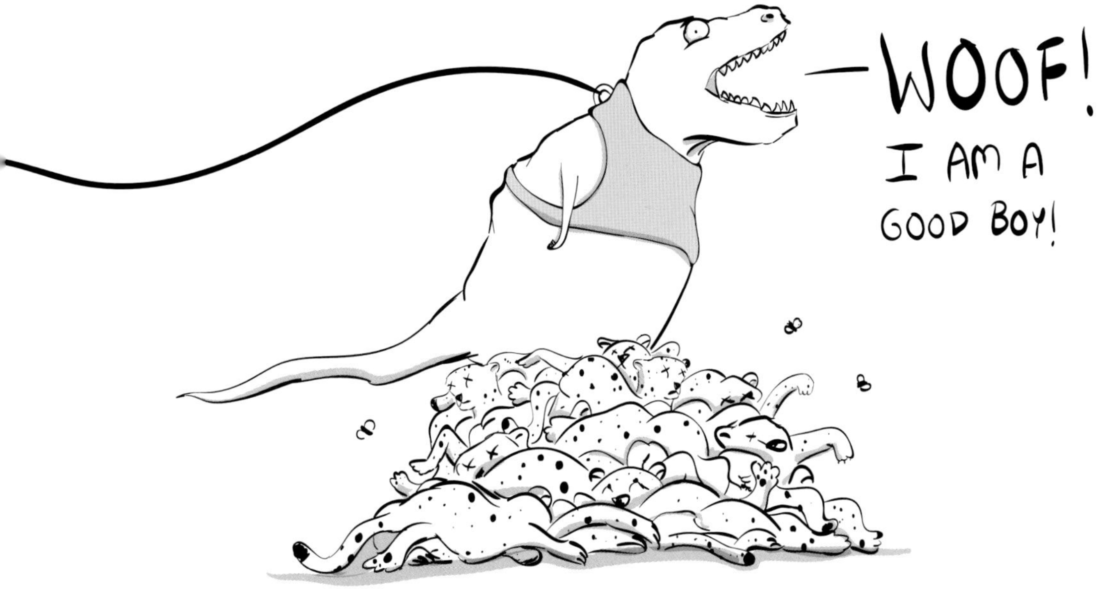
WOOF!
I AM A GOOD BOY!

However, when you poop, you enter a vulnerable state of deep meditation. Exposing your bum cellar is like revealing a chink in your armor. So, while your downstairs churns out crapper slammers, scan the horizon for predators. They may attempt to strike while your defenses are down.

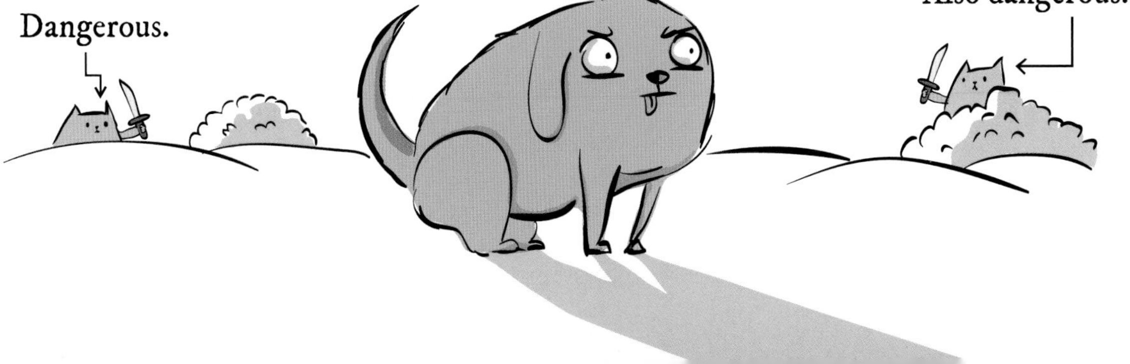
Dangerous.
Also dangerous.

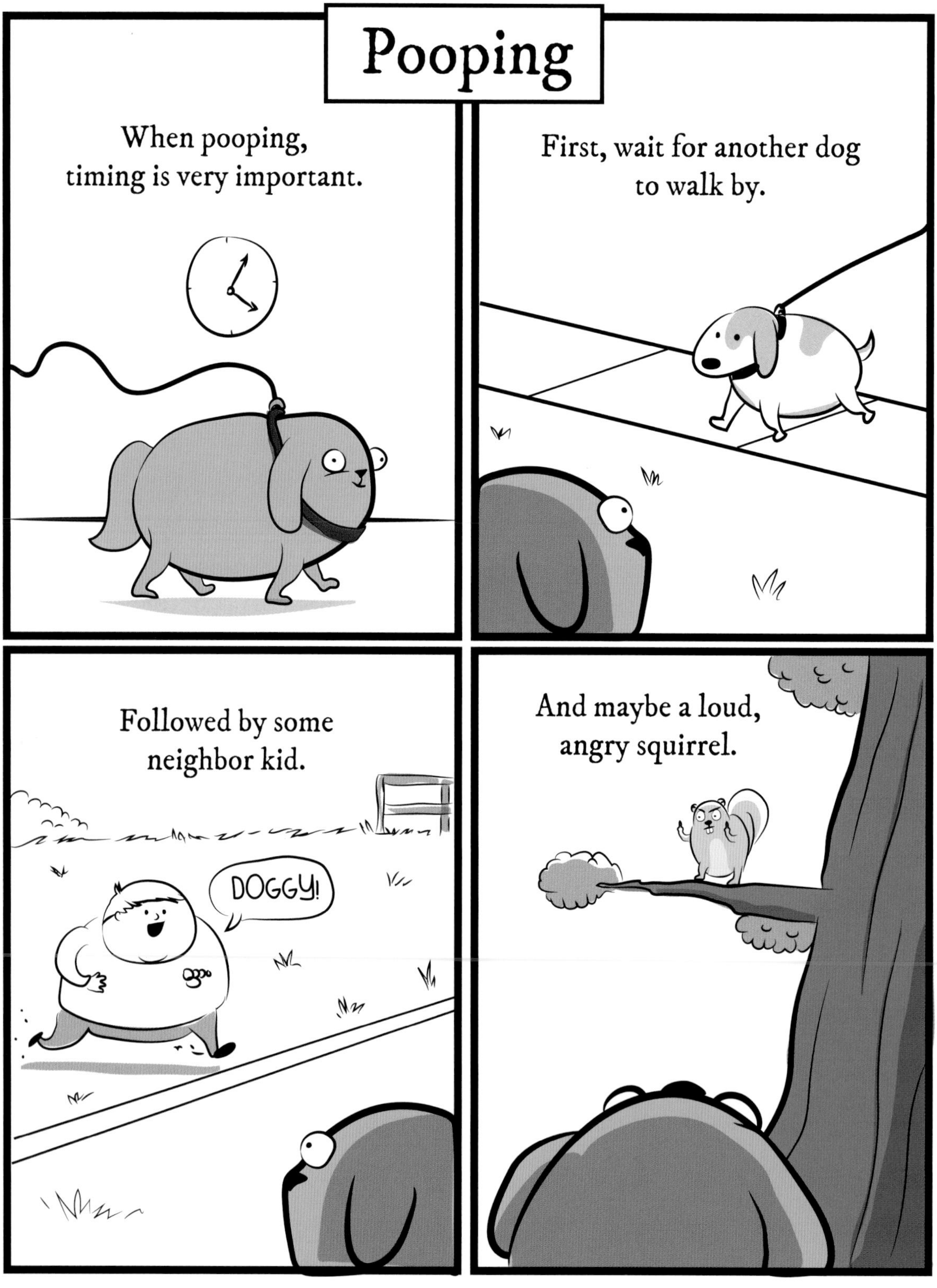
Pooping
When pooping, timing is very important.
First, wait for another dog to walk by.
Followed by some neighbor kid.
DOGGY!
And maybe a loud, angry squirrel.

When all of these chaotic forces are in alignment,
it is the perfect time to poop.

Ideally, you want to bark, run, fight, and shit
all at the same time.

Your human being will thank you for this opportunity to
practice their hand-eye coordination.

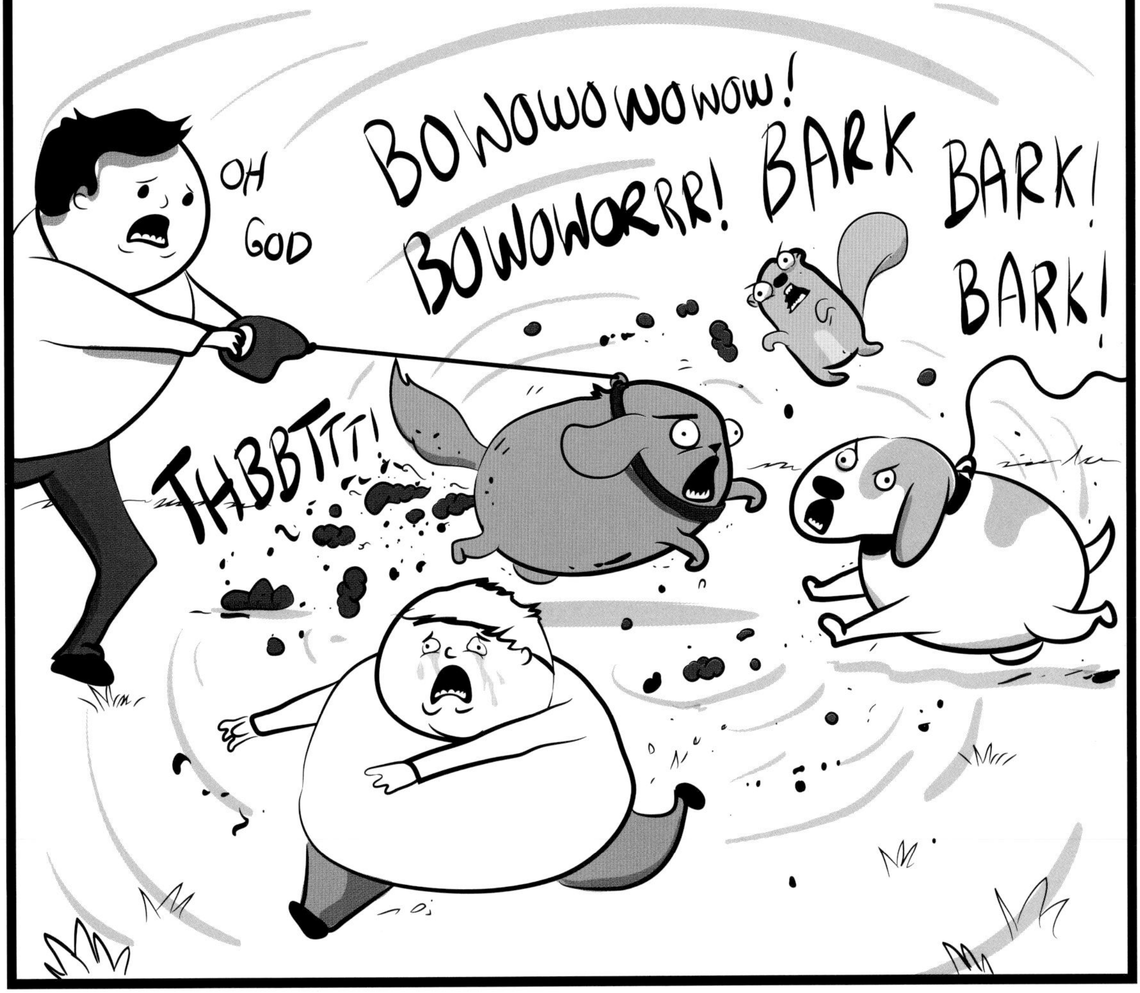
OH GOD
BOWOWOWOWOW!
BOWOWORRR!
BARK
BARK!
BARK!
THBBTTT!

Hors d'oeuvres

The outdoors offers a sumptuous spread of delights.
If you find one of these hors d'oeuvres, eat it quickly.
Eat it at the speed of light.

Eat it before you are stopped.

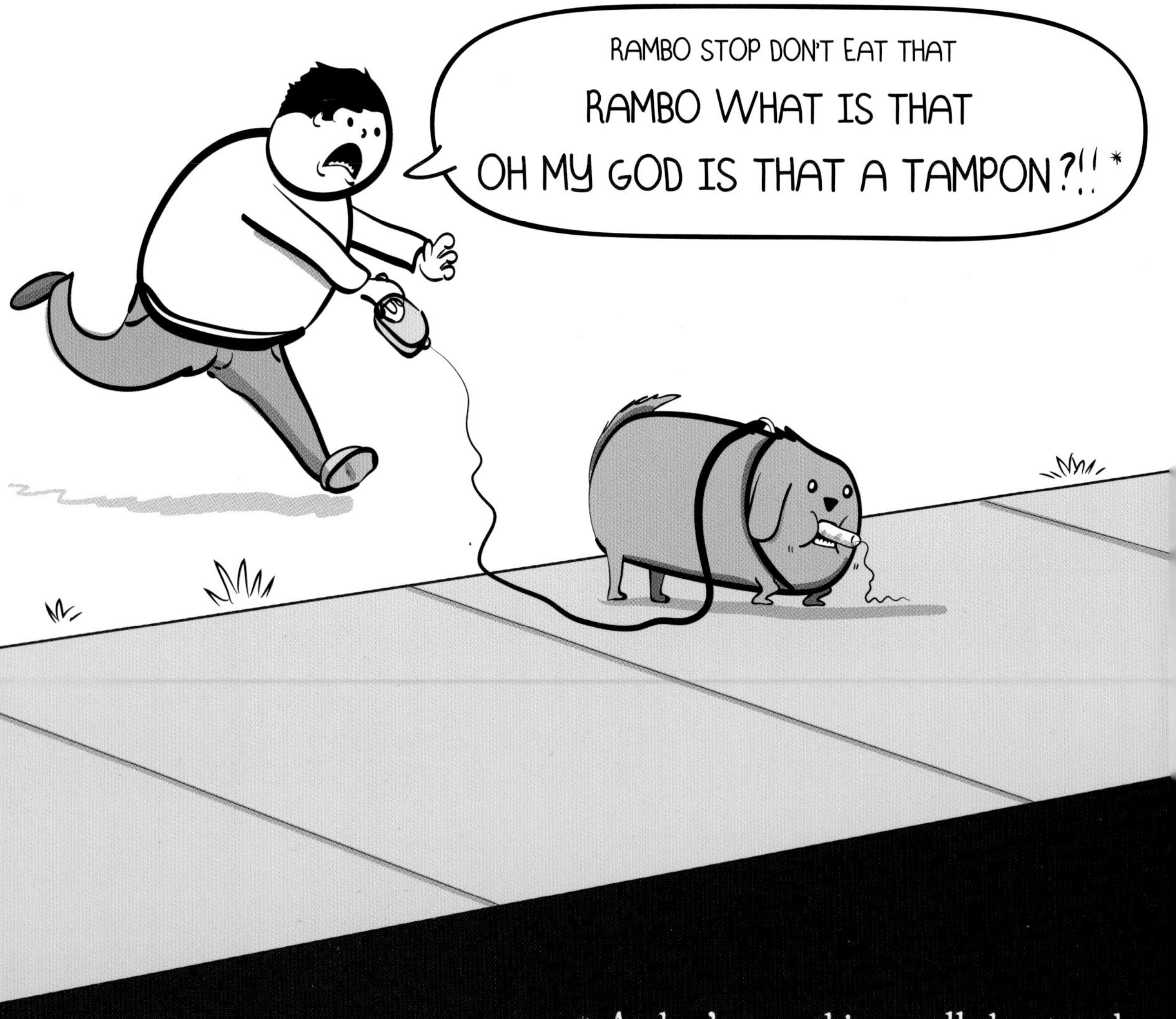
RAMBO STOP DON'T EAT THAT
RAMBO WHAT IS THAT
OH MY GOD IS THAT A TAMPON?!! *

* Author's note: this actually happened.

Your human being will attempt to remove this precious treat from your mouth.

This means you have to skip chewing and go straight to swallowing. Be quick about it.

Maybe start choking.

They will enjoy riding this emotional roller coaster with you.

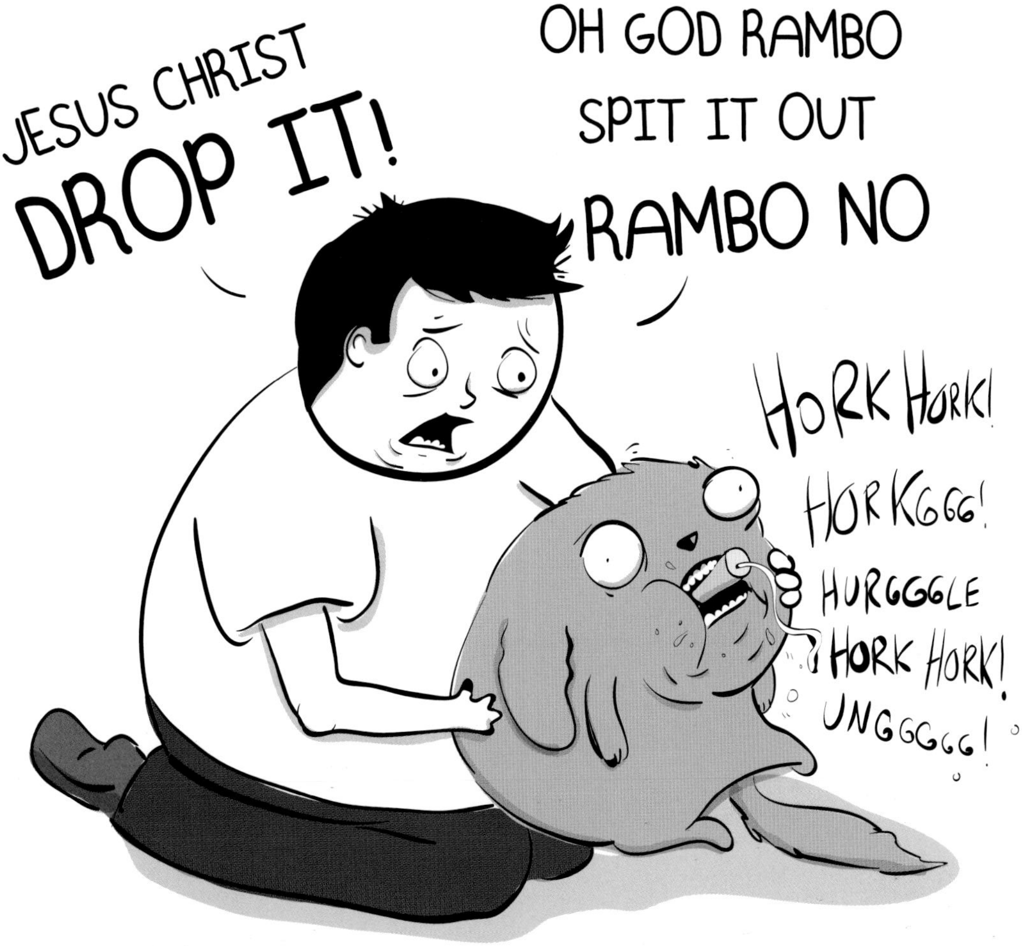
JESUS CHRIST
DROP IT!
OH GOD RAMBO
SPIT IT OUT
RAMBO NO
HORK HORK!
HORKGGG!
HURGGGLE
HORK HORK!
UNGGGGG!

Other Dogs

A dog on the other side of the street is your worst enemy. Yell obscenities at them. Threaten them.

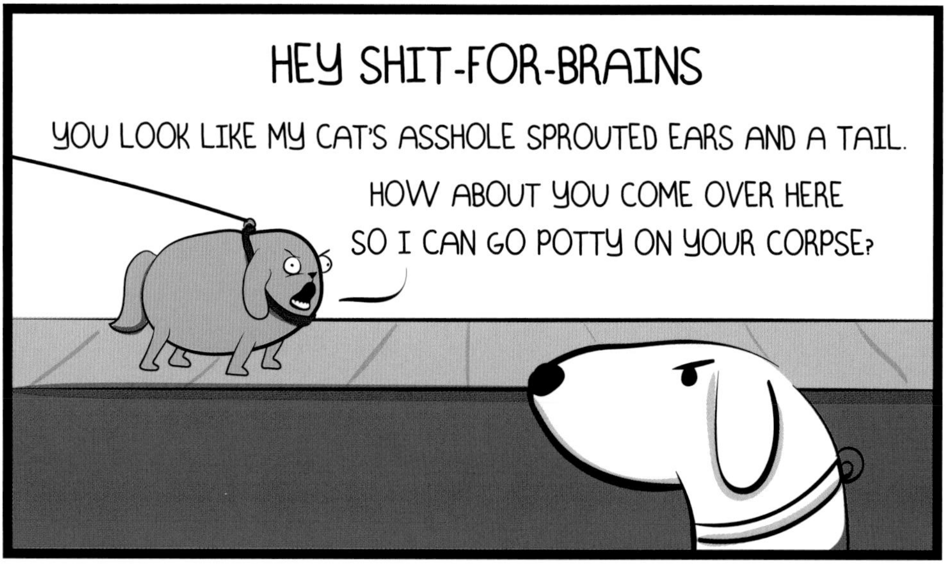
HEY SHIT-FOR-BRAINS
YOU LOOK LIKE MY CAT'S ASSHOLE SPROUTED EARS AND A TAIL.
HOW ABOUT YOU COME OVER HERE SO I CAN GO POTTY ON YOUR CORPSE?

A dog on *your* side of the street, however, is your best friend.

Wag your tail. Play with them. Maybe start fighting *while* playing. The idea is to terrify your human being. Humans thrive on uncertainty. They love the unknown. By play-fighting, you are enriching their lives as well as your own.

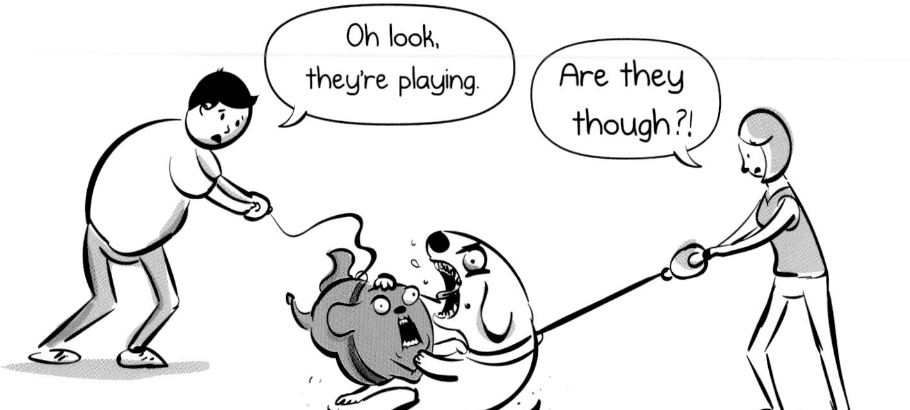
Oh look, they're playing.
Are they though?!

... Closing Remarks ...

If you have read this far, then it is safe to assume you are fully prepared to walk a human being.

You may have only traveled a few blocks, but in the eyes of the universe you have walked a thousand miles over a thousand lifetimes. You have spoken in a loud, crystalline voice that you hold sway over these lands.

You have elevated your human being by tethering their brittle heart to your flawless, eternal soul. You have shown them what it means to be a timber wolf.

You have shown them strength.

You have shown them what it means to pee.

To shit.

To conquer.

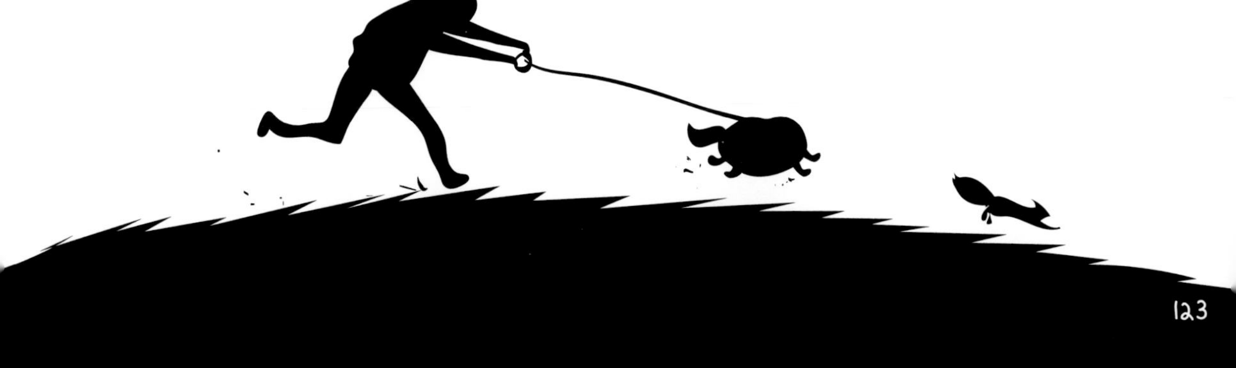

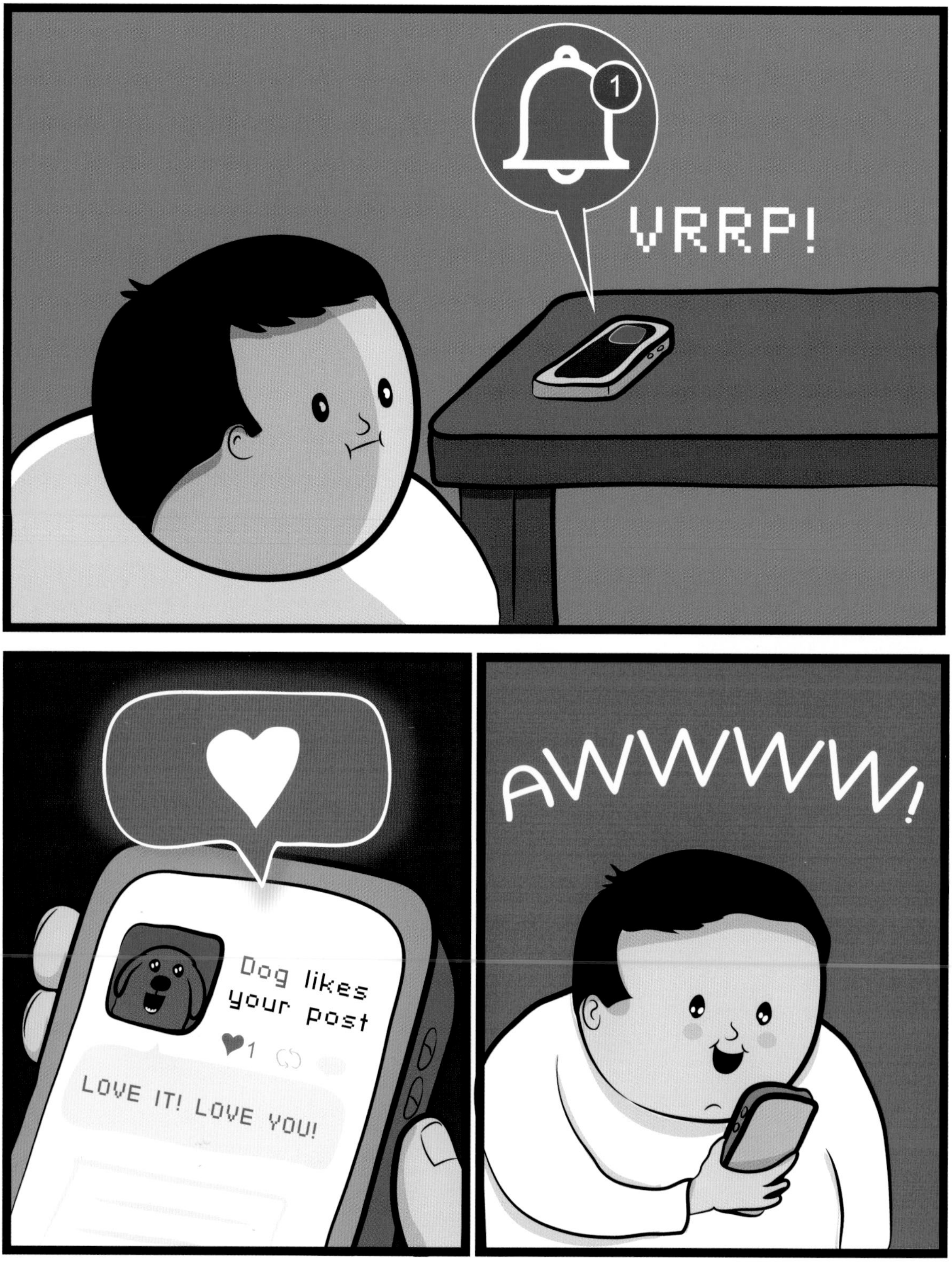
1
VRRP!
Dog likes your post
1
LOVE IT! LOVE YOU!
AWWWW!

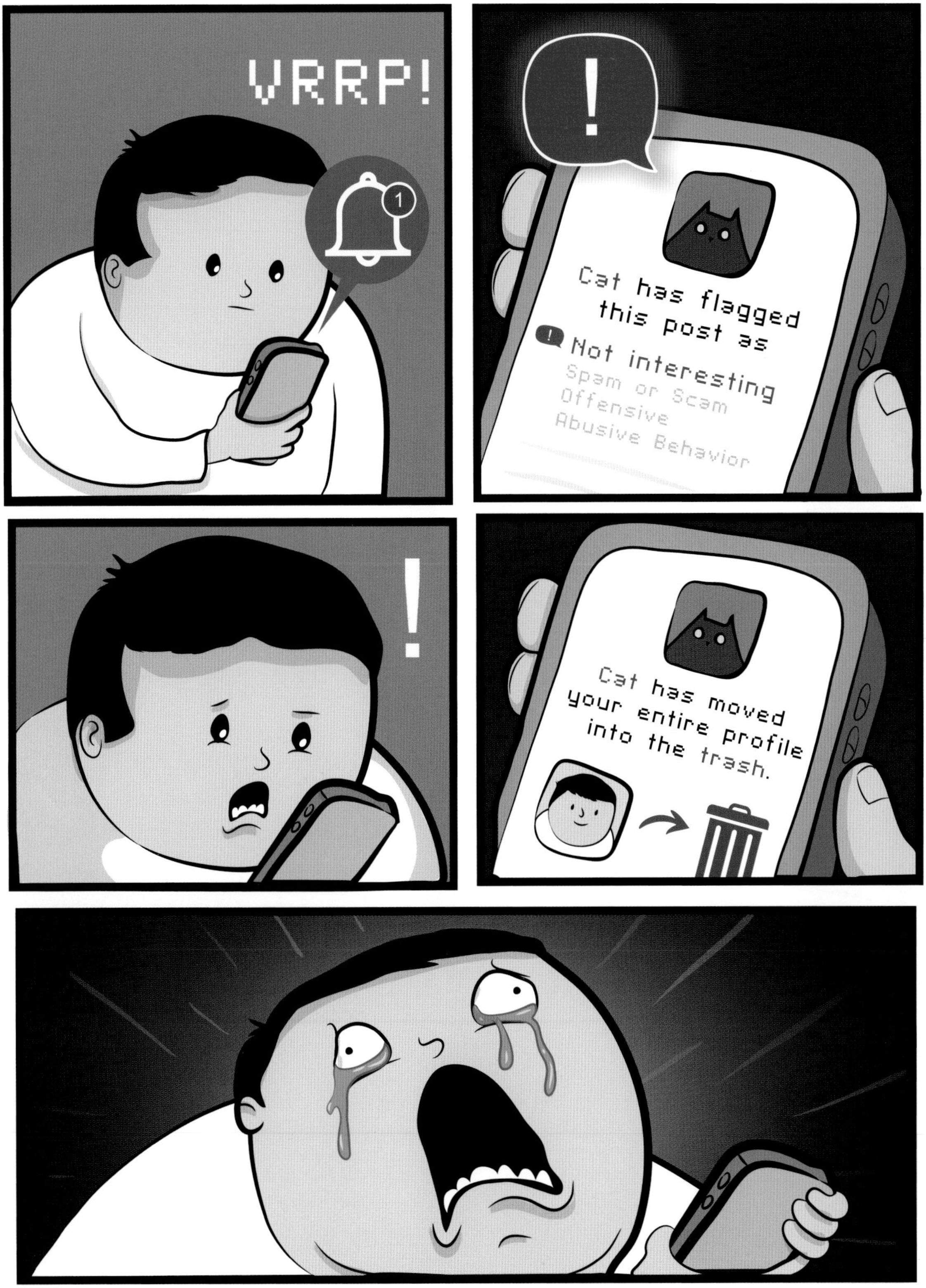
VRRP!
1
!
Cat has flagged this post as
Not interesting
Spam or Scam
Offensive
Abusive Behavior
!
Cat has moved your entire profile into the trash.

HOW TO HOLD A BABY

WHEN YOU ARE NOT USED TO HOLDING BABIES.

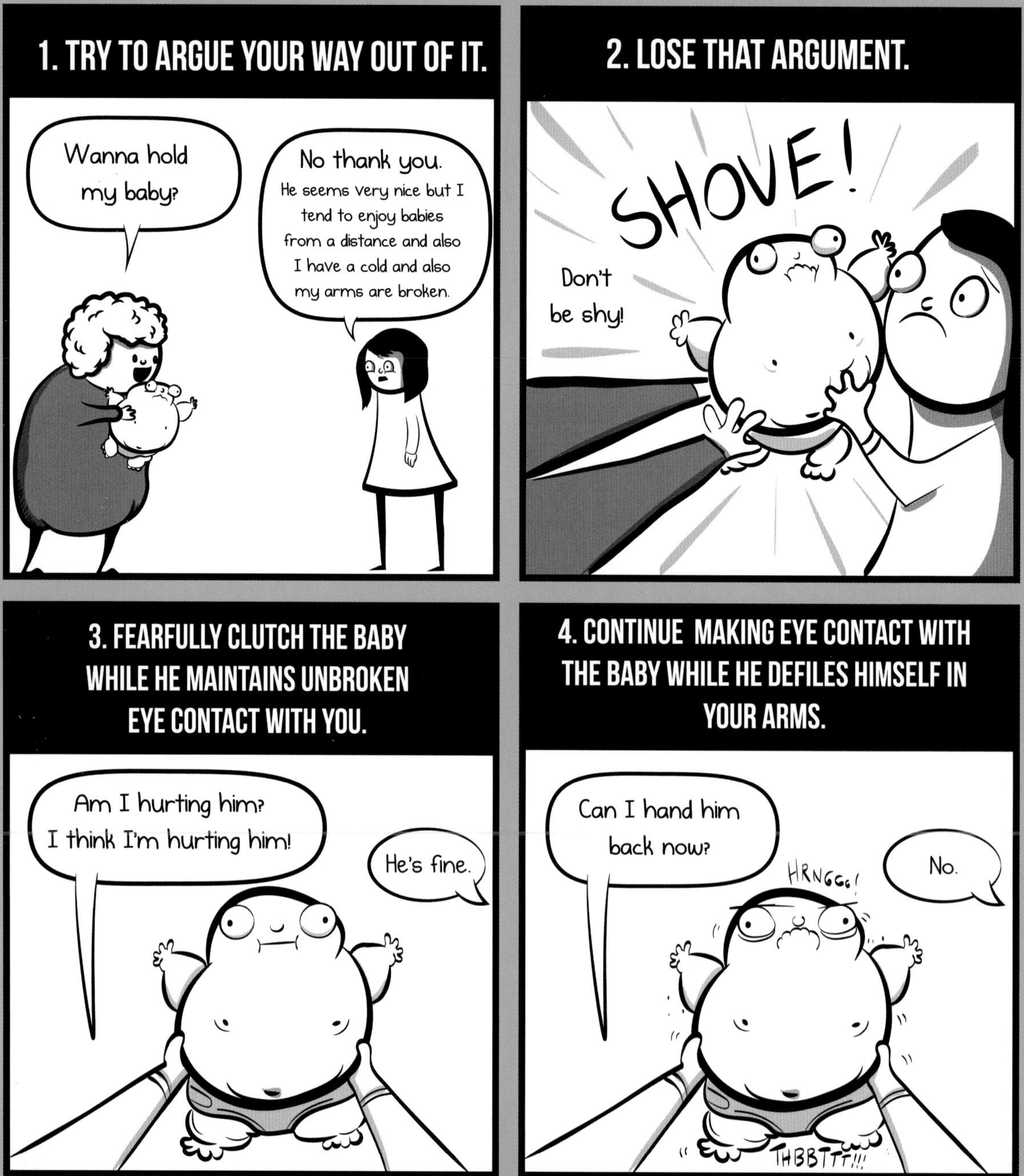
1. TRY TO ARGUE YOUR WAY OUT OF IT.
Wanna hold my baby?
No thank you. He seems very nice but I tend to enjoy babies from a distance and also I have a cold and also my arms are broken.
2. LOSE THAT ARGUMENT.
SHOVE!
Don't be shy!
3. FEARFULLY CLUTCH THE BABY WHILE HE MAINTAINS UNBROKEN EYE CONTACT WITH YOU.
Am I hurting him? I think I'm hurting him!
He's fine.
4. CONTINUE MAKING EYE CONTACT WITH THE BABY WHILE HE DEFILES HIMSELF IN YOUR ARMS.
Can I hand him back now?
HRNGGG!
No.
THBBTTT!!!

HOW TO HOLD A CAT

WHEN YOU ARE NOT USED TO HOLDING CATS.

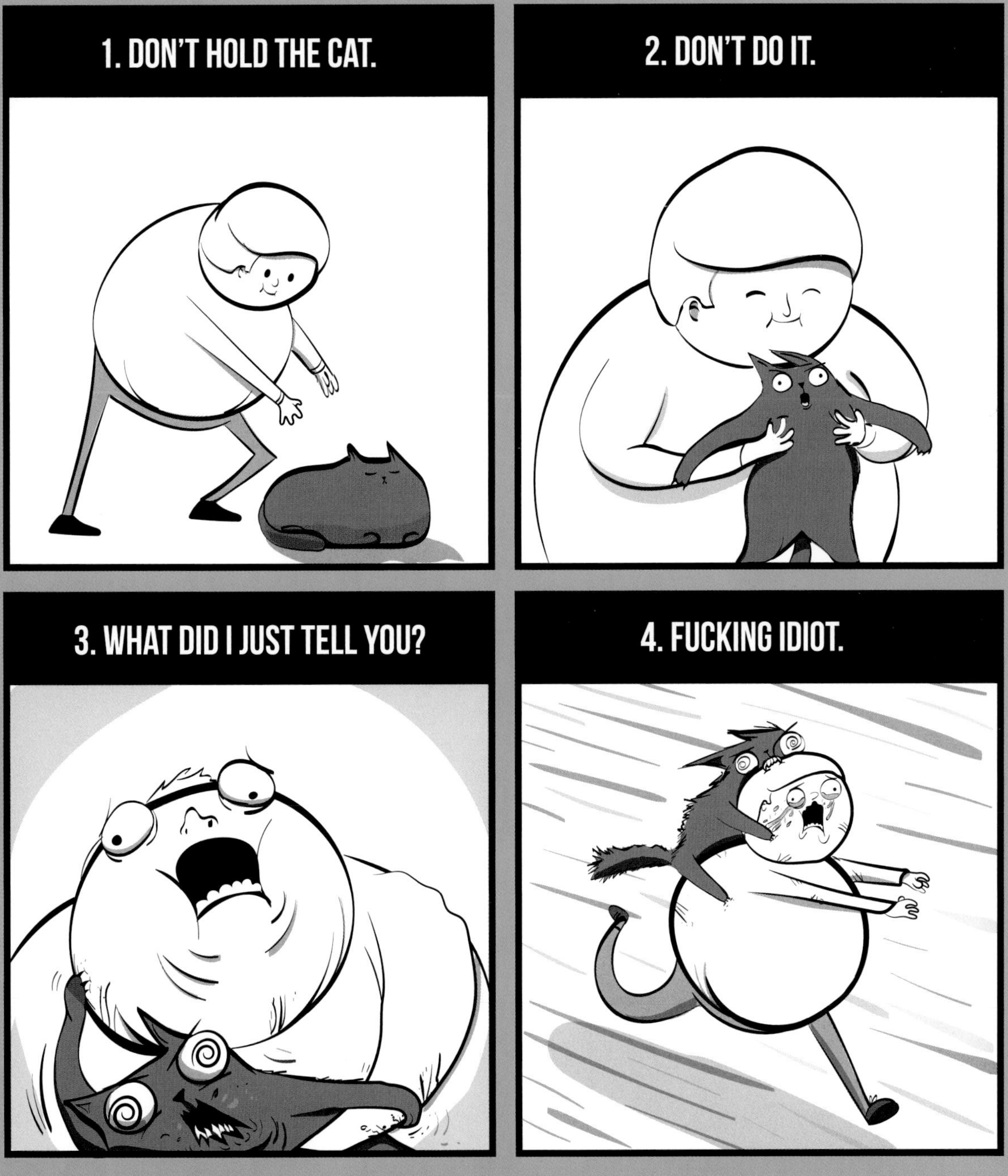
1. DON'T HOLD THE CAT.
2. DON'T DO IT.
3. WHAT DID I JUST TELL YOU?
4. FUCKING IDIOT.

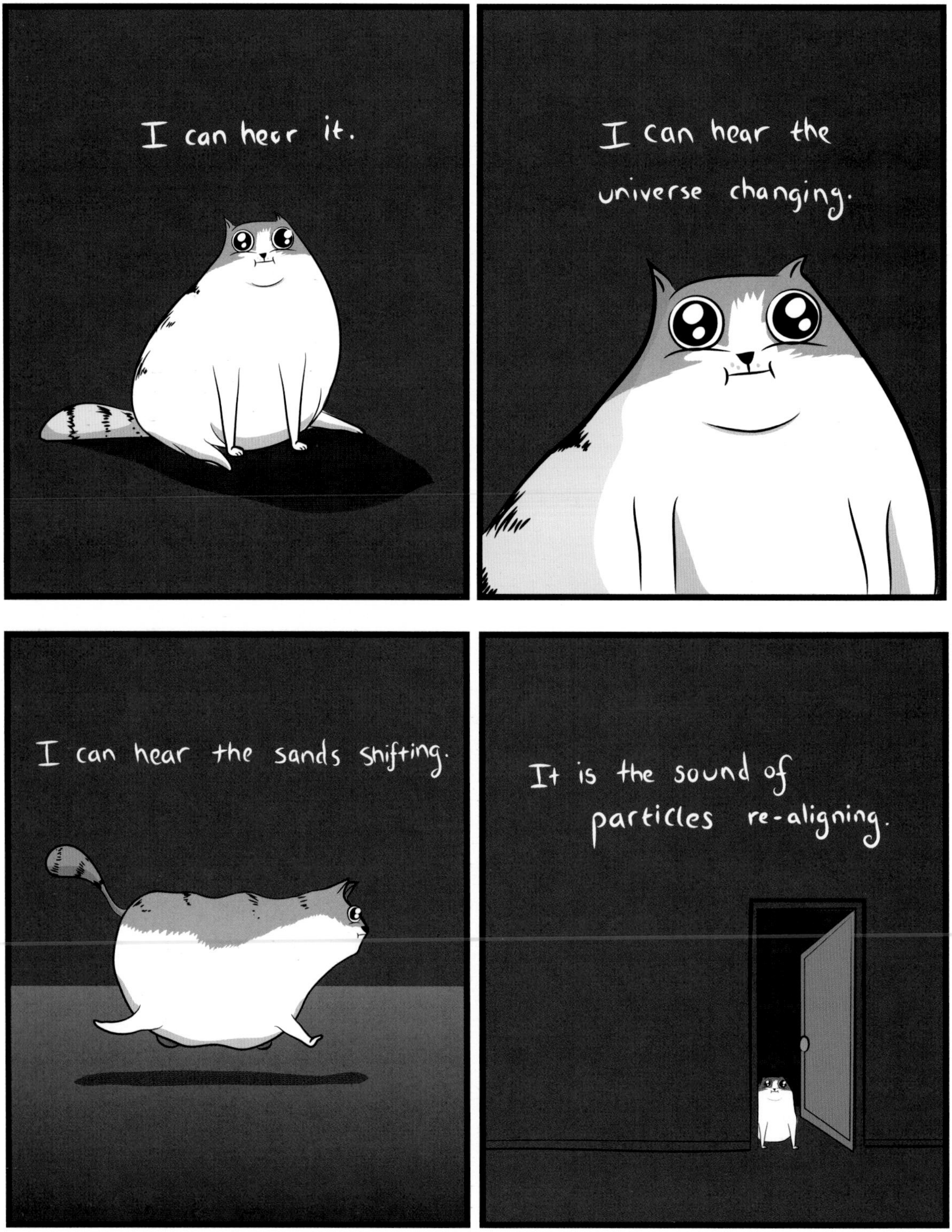
I can hear it.
I can hear the universe changing.
I can hear the sands shifting.
It is the sound of particles re-aligning.

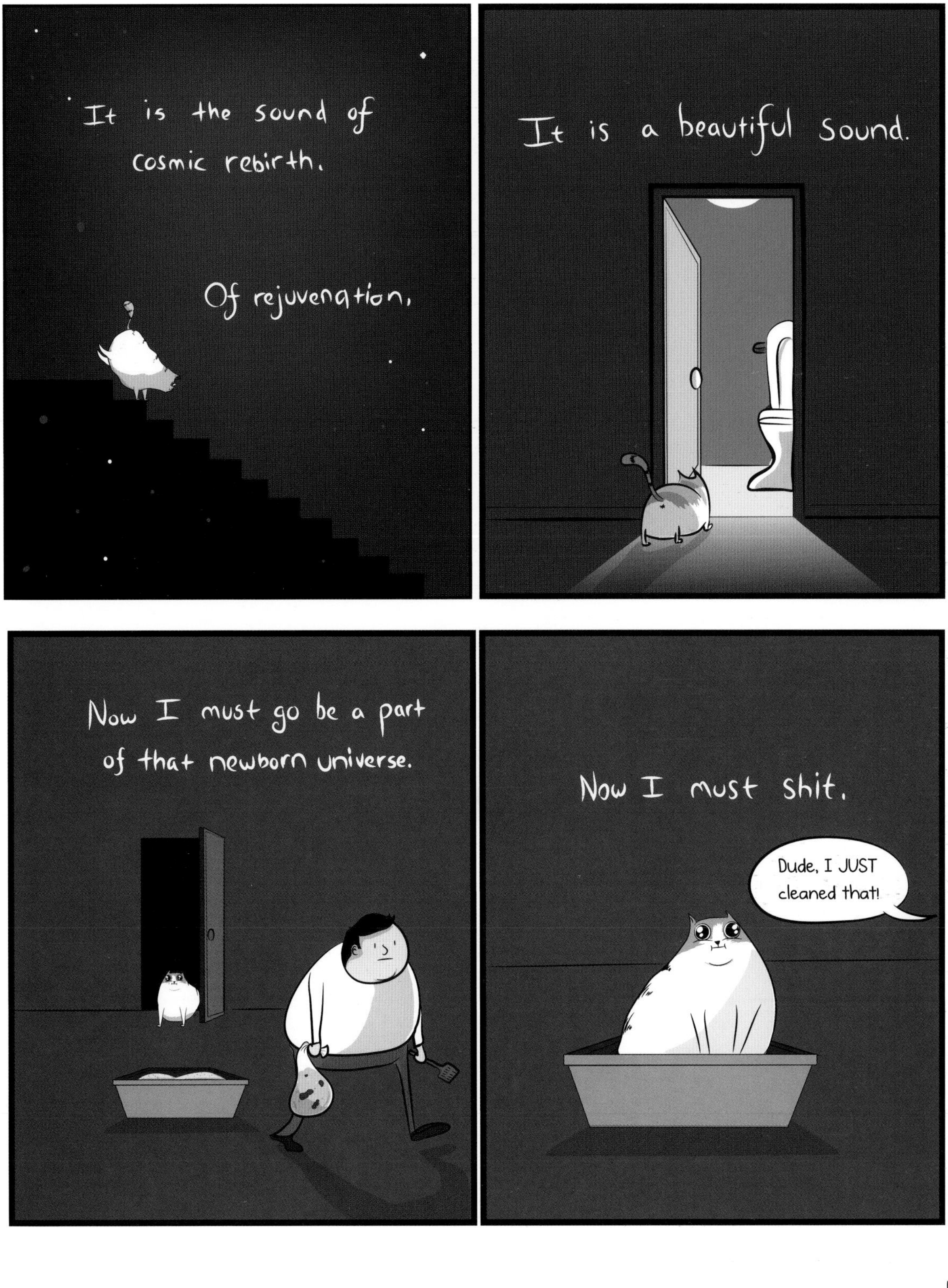
It is the sound of cosmic rebirth.
Of rejuvenation,
It is a beautiful sound.
Now I must go be a part of that newborn universe.
Now I must shit.
Dude, I JUST cleaned that!

How much do cats actually kill?

In 2012, I published a book titled *How to Tell If Your Cat Is Plotting to Kill You.*

I wrote it partly because murderous cats make for good comedy, but also because I felt like it was something we could all relate to —the idea that these creatures we love are actually plotting to *end us* in a very violent way.

I thirst for the blood of an imbecile.

Coincidentally, right after the book was released, researchers at the University of Georgia and National Geographic published the results of a study where they attached small cameras to house cats.

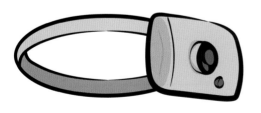

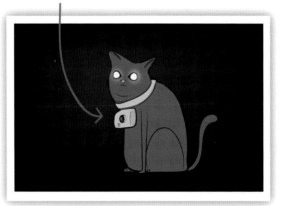

http://www.kittycams.uga.edu/

The cameras provided a cat's-eye view of what domestic cats do when roaming freely outdoors, without disrupting their behavior.

This is what they found:

One in three cats killed prey.

Of these, they averaged about
two kills per week.

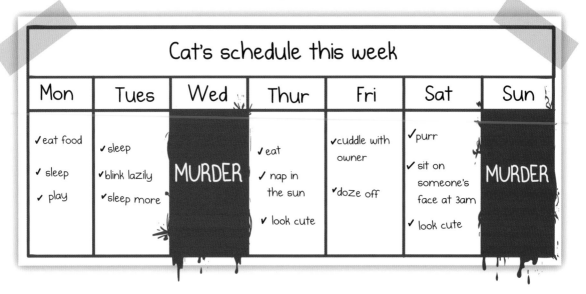

	Cat's schedule this week					
Mon	Tues	Wed	Thur	Fri	Sat	Sun
✔ eat food ✔ sleep ✔ play	✔ sleep ✔ blink lazily ✔ sleep more	MURDER	✔ eat ✔ nap in the sun ✔ look cute	✔ cuddle with owner ✔ doze off	✔ purr ✔ sit on someone's face at 3am ✔ look cute	MURDER

According to the study

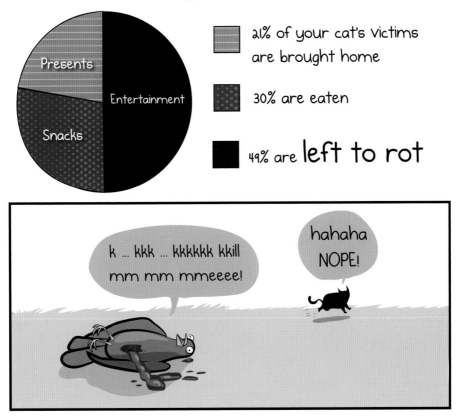

Presents
Entertainment
Snacks
21% of your cat's victims are brought home
30% are eaten
49% are left to rot

k ... kkk ... kkkkkk kkill mm mm mmeeee!
hahaha NOPE!

Keep in mind that these are <u>well-fed</u>, domesticated house cats.

Meaning, they're not killing for survival, they're doing it FOR FUN.

BAHAHAHAHHAAHAHAHAAAAAAA
YOU MUST DIE AND I'M NOT EVEN HUNGRY

You know those "gifts" your cat leaves on the doorstep?

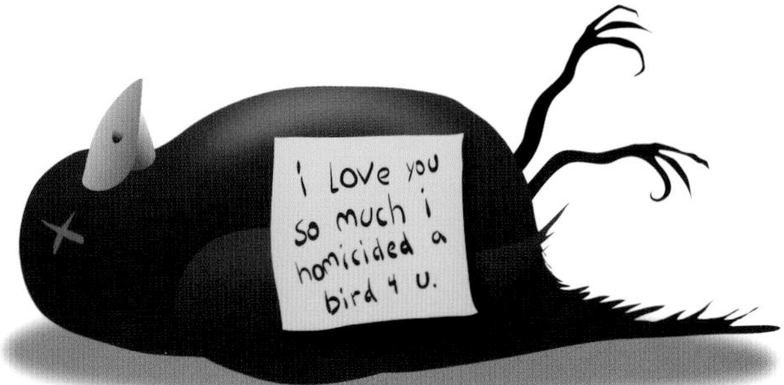
i Love you
So much i
homicided a
bird 4 U.

The corpses you see account for

less than one-fourth

of the actual body count.

What your cat shows you:

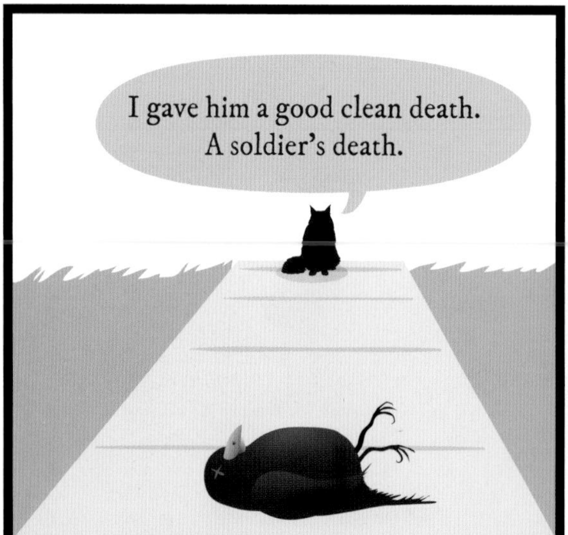
I gave him a good clean death.
A soldier's death.

What your cat DOES NOT show you:

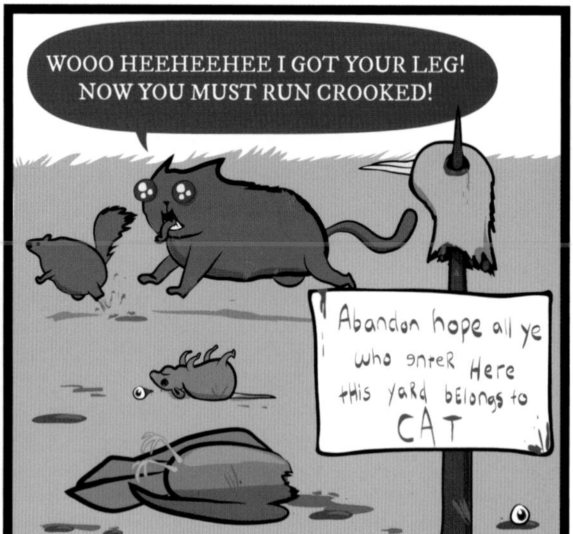
WOOO HEEHEEHEE I GOT YOUR LEG!
NOW YOU MUST RUN CROOKED!
Abandon hope all ye
who enter Here
this yard belongs to
CAT

There are an estimated
84 million cats in the United States.

This means that, according to the statistics above,

 28 million of them are
murder cats,

and the total body count from
domesticated house cats every year is

↓

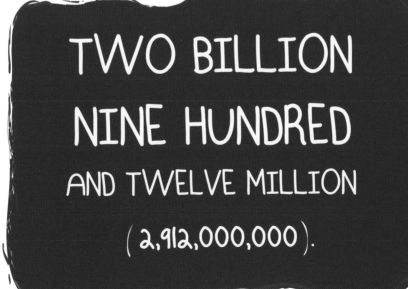

TWO BILLION
NINE HUNDRED
AND TWELVE MILLION
(2,912,000,000).

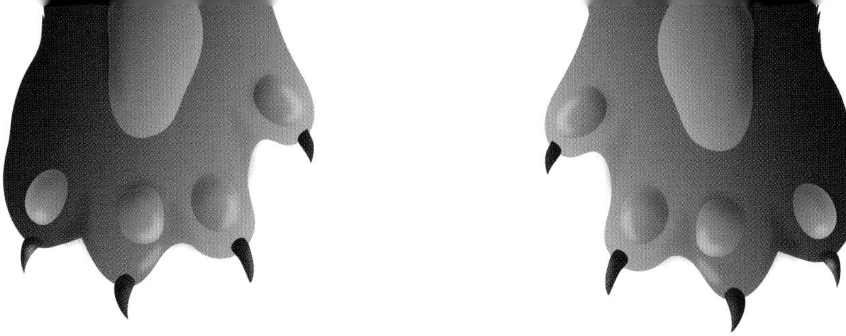

This means that if cats were killing people,
every year they would wipe out

41% of the human population.

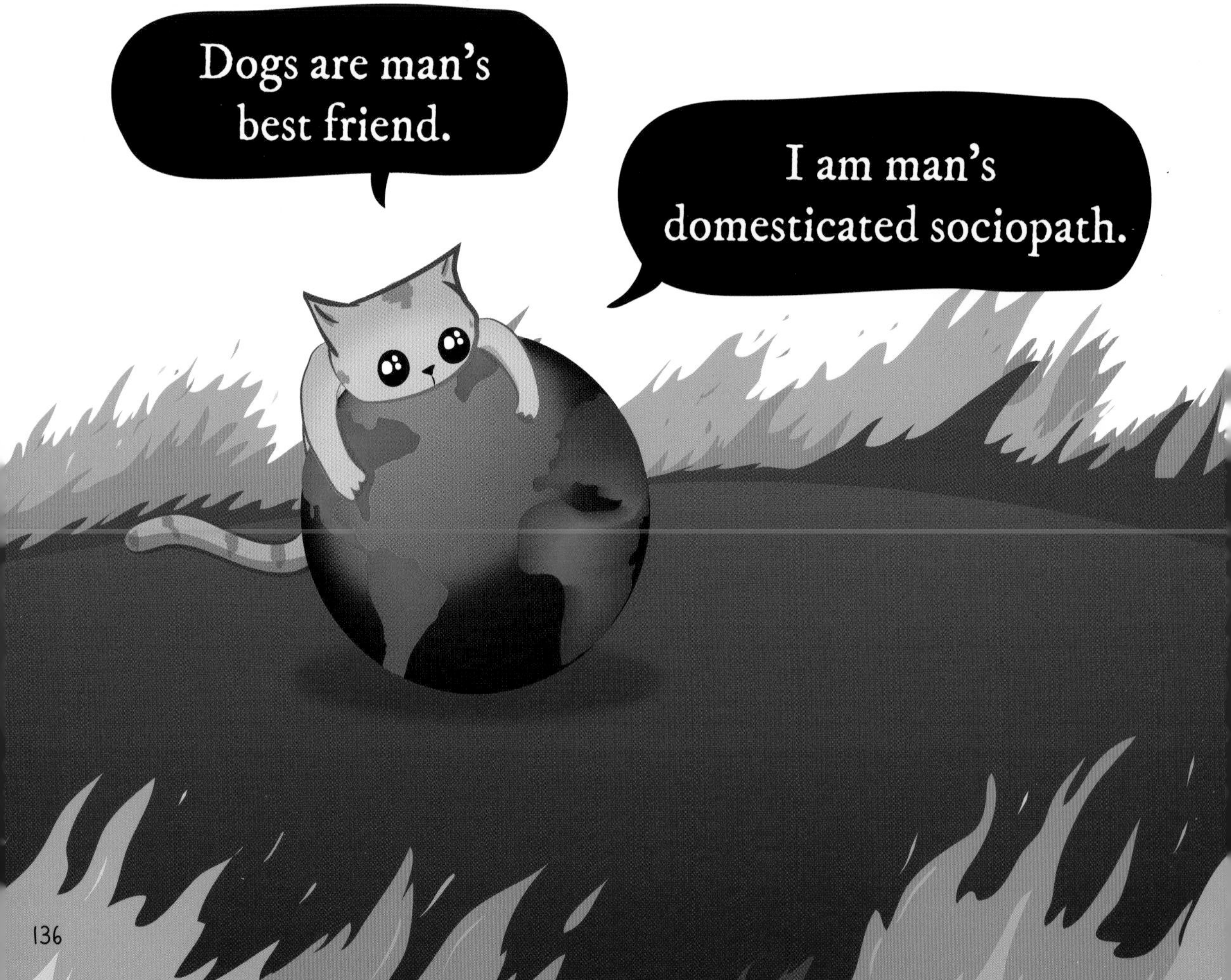
Dogs are man's best friend.
I am man's domesticated sociopath.

IN CONCLUSION:

How much do cats ACTUALLY kill?

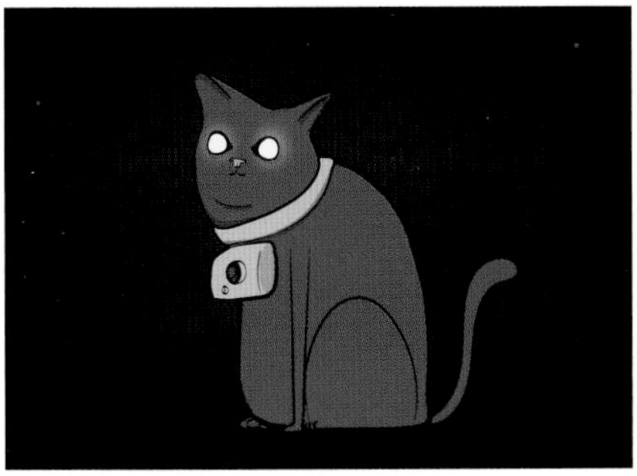

TOO

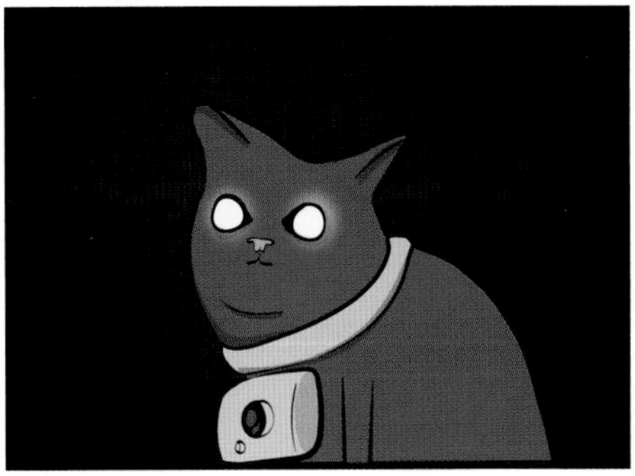

DAMN

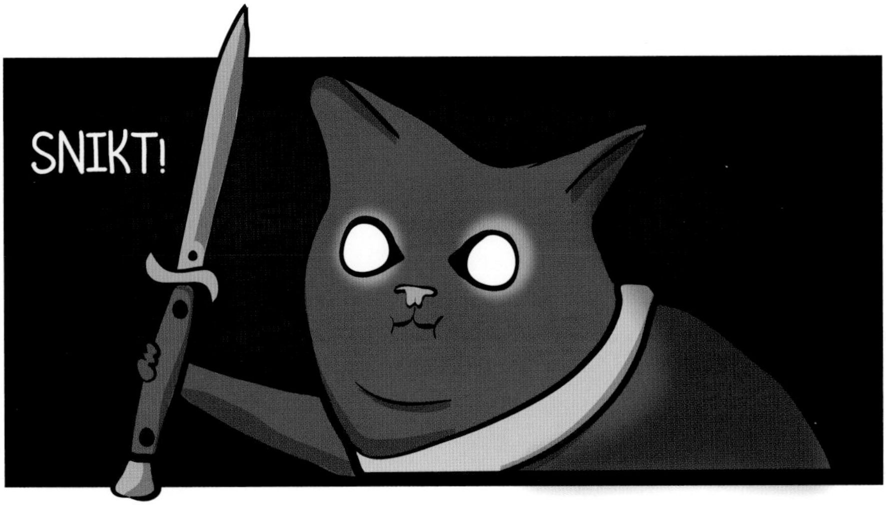
SNIKT!

MUCH.

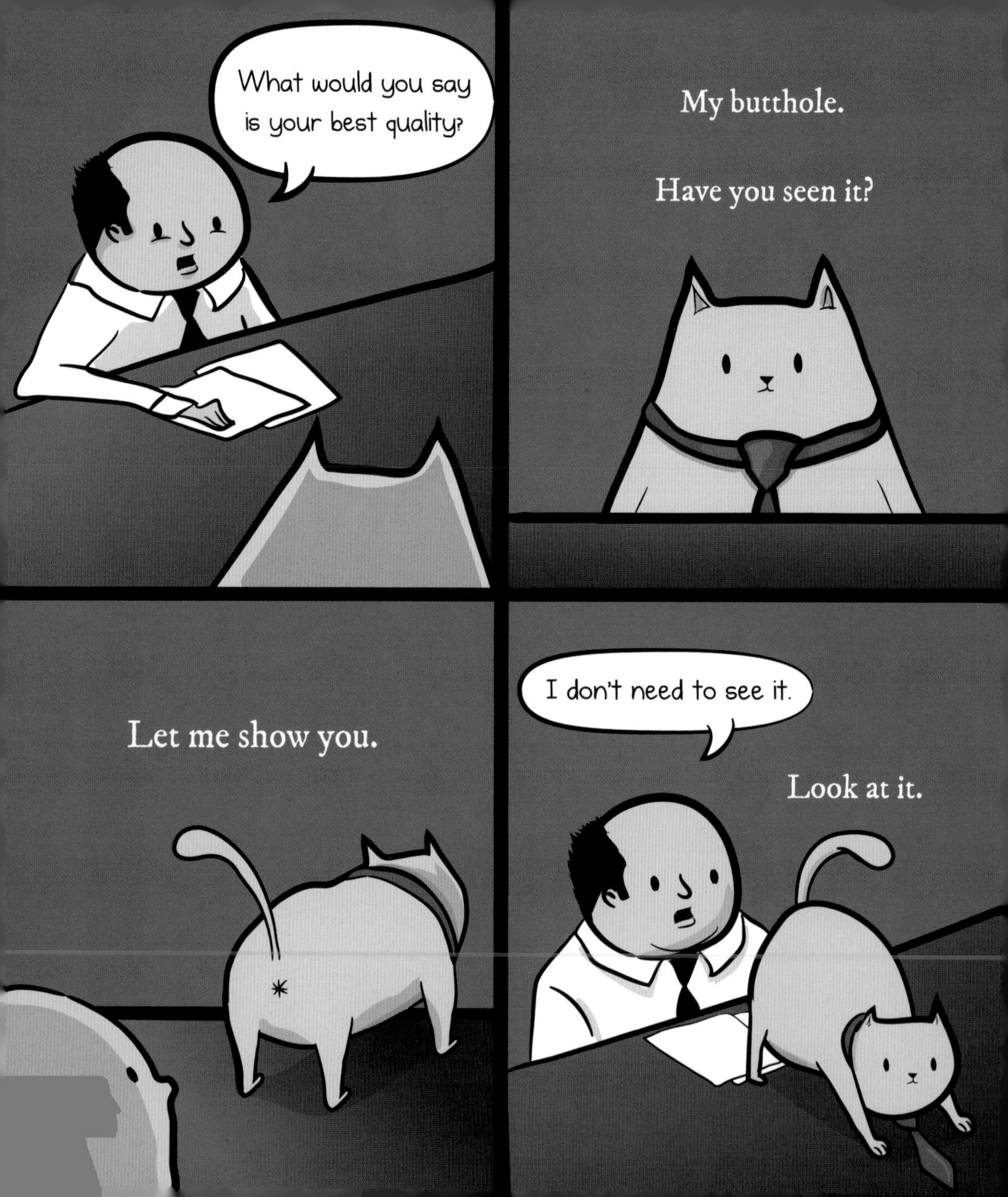
What would you say is your best quality?
My butthole.
Have you seen it?
Let me show you.
I don't need to see it.
Look at it.

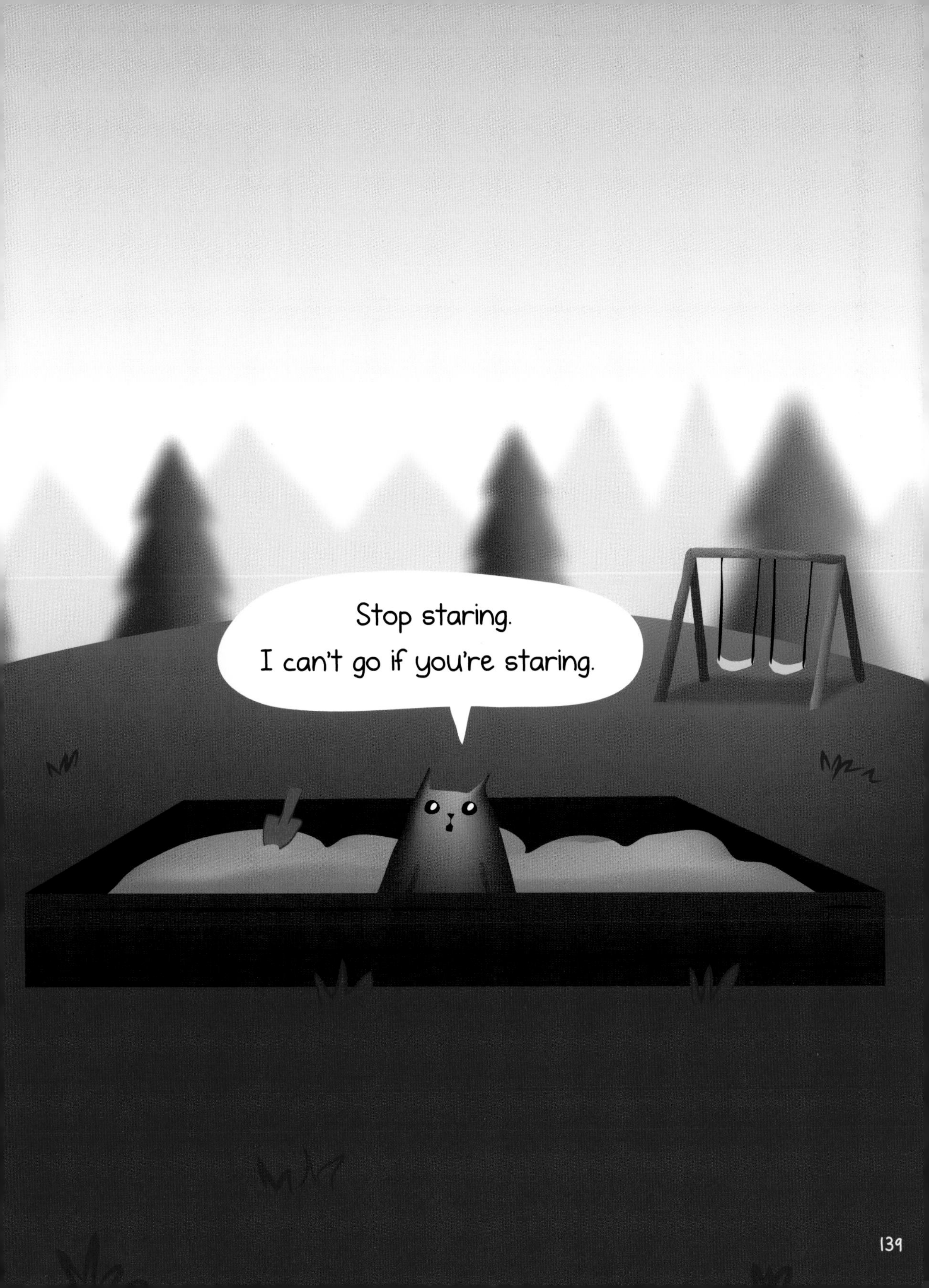
Stop staring.
I can't go if you're staring.

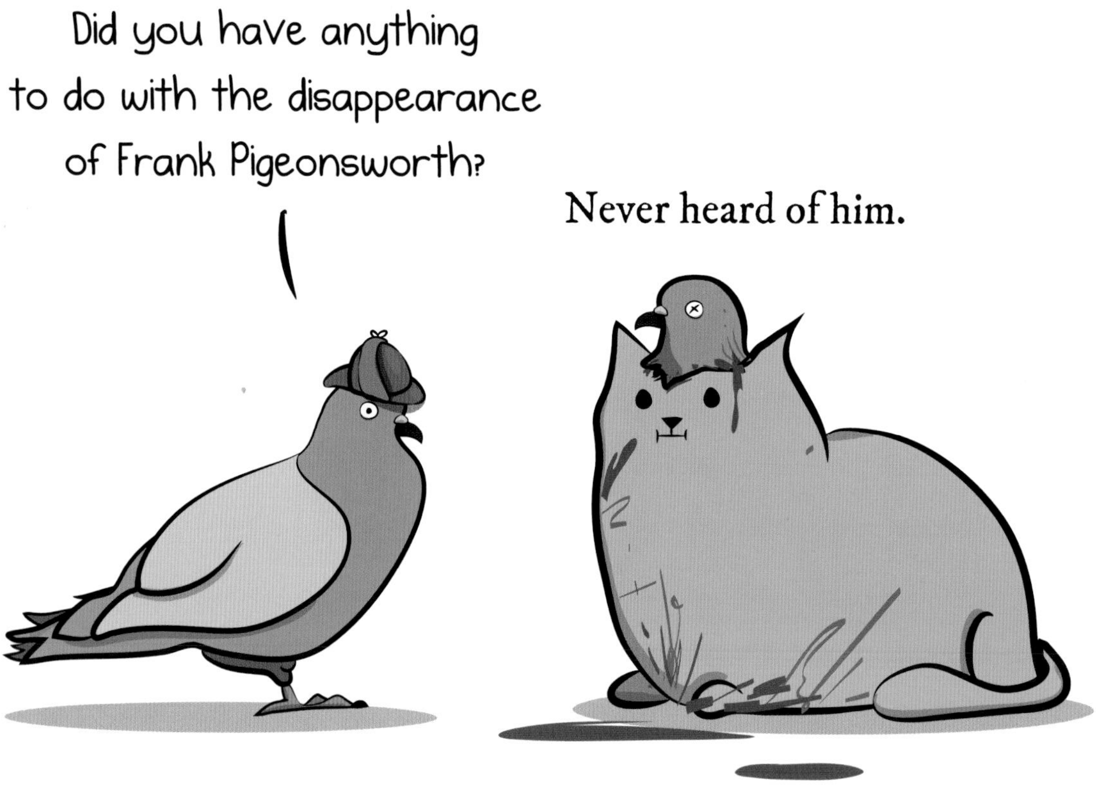
Did you have anything to do with the disappearance of Frank Pigeonsworth?
Never heard of him.

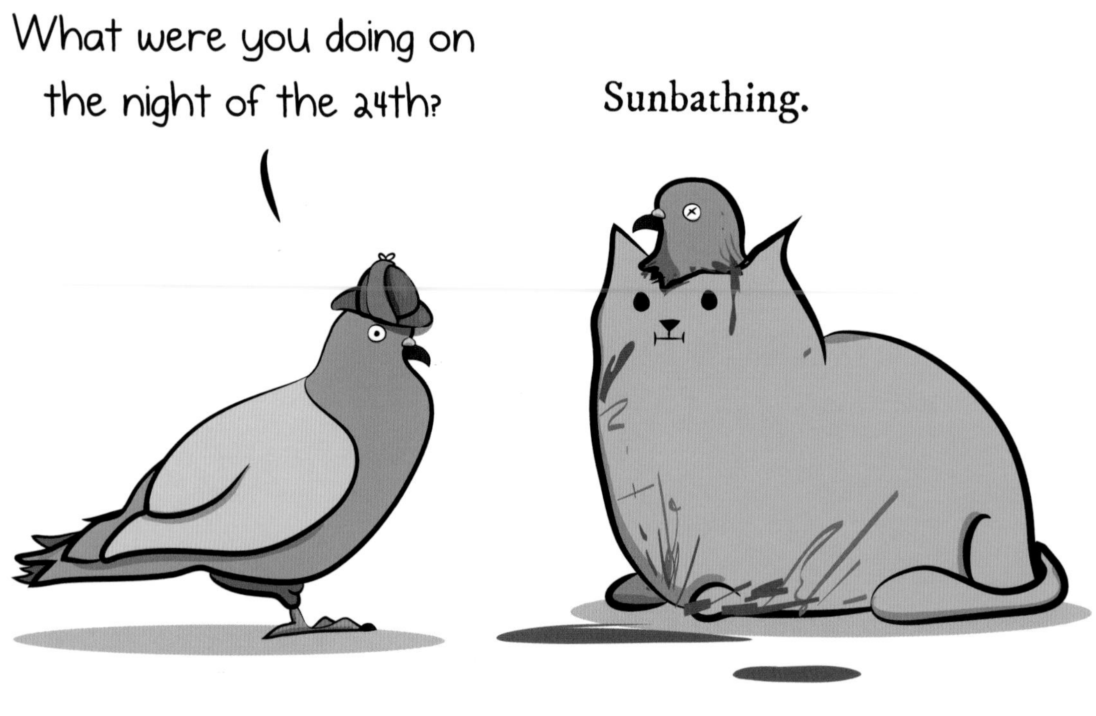
What were you doing on the night of the 24th?
Sunbathing.

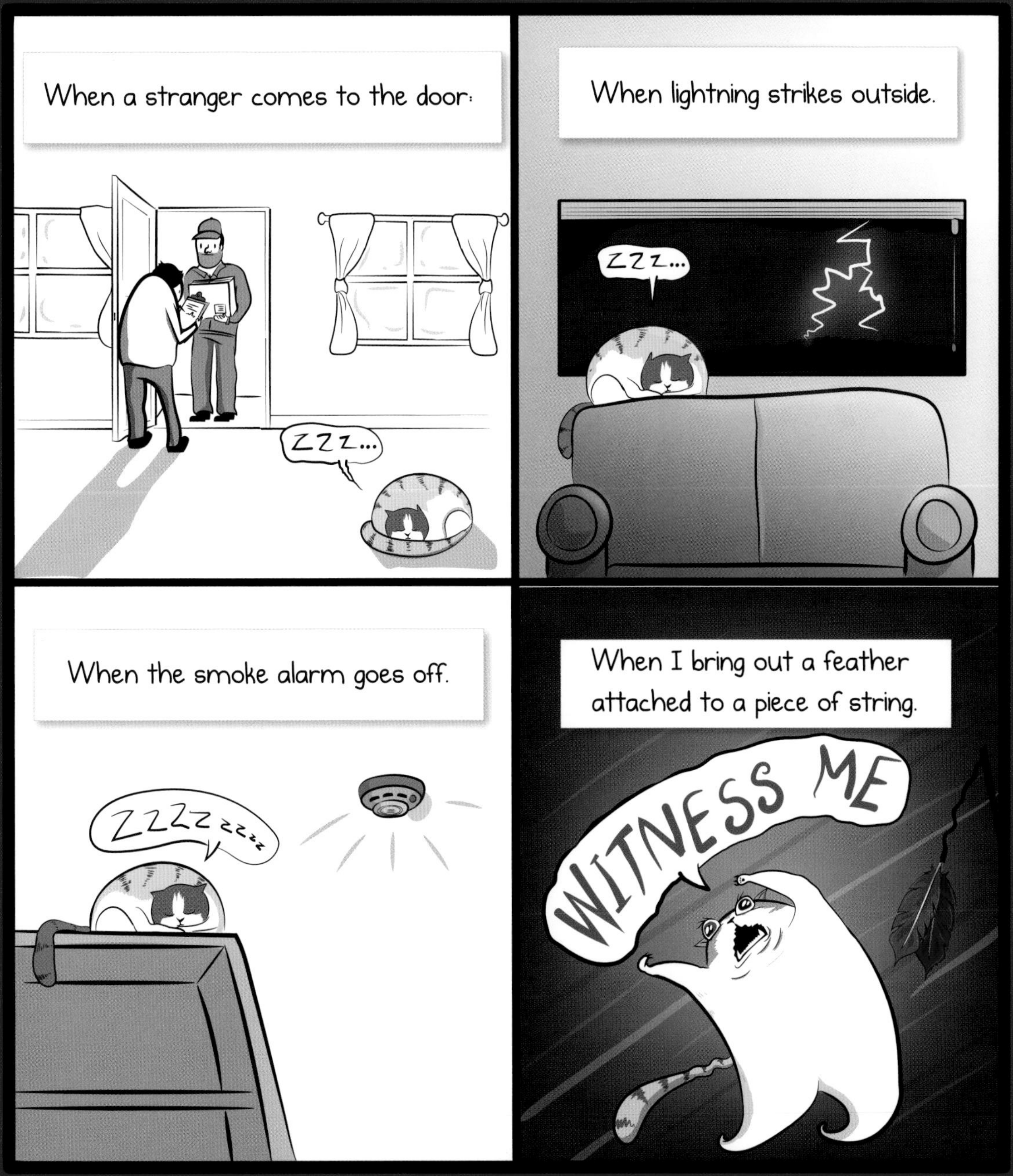
When a stranger comes to the door:
ZZZ...
When lightning strikes outside.
ZZZ...
When the smoke alarm goes off.
ZZZZzzzz
When I bring out a feather attached to a piece of string.
WITNESS ME

TEN WAYS
TO BEFRIEND
A MISANTHROPIC CAT

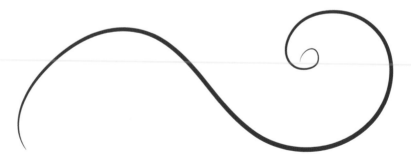

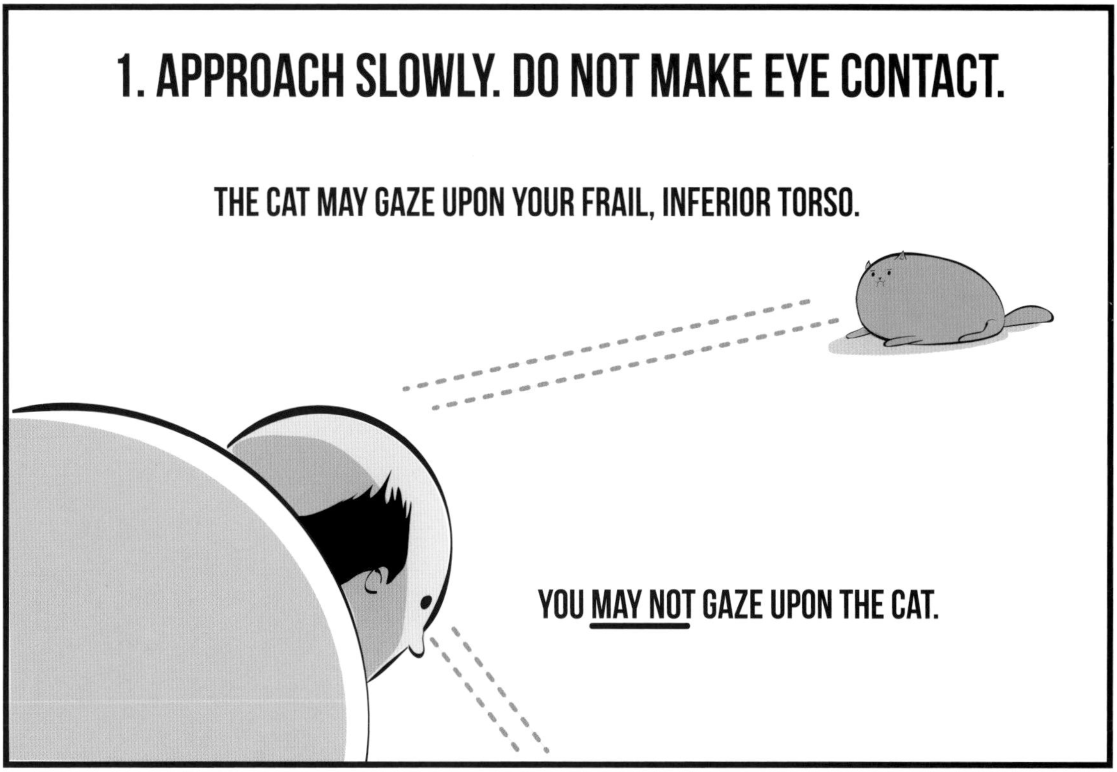
1. APPROACH SLOWLY. DO NOT MAKE EYE CONTACT.
THE CAT MAY GAZE UPON YOUR FRAIL, INFERIOR TORSO.
YOU MAY NOT GAZE UPON THE CAT.

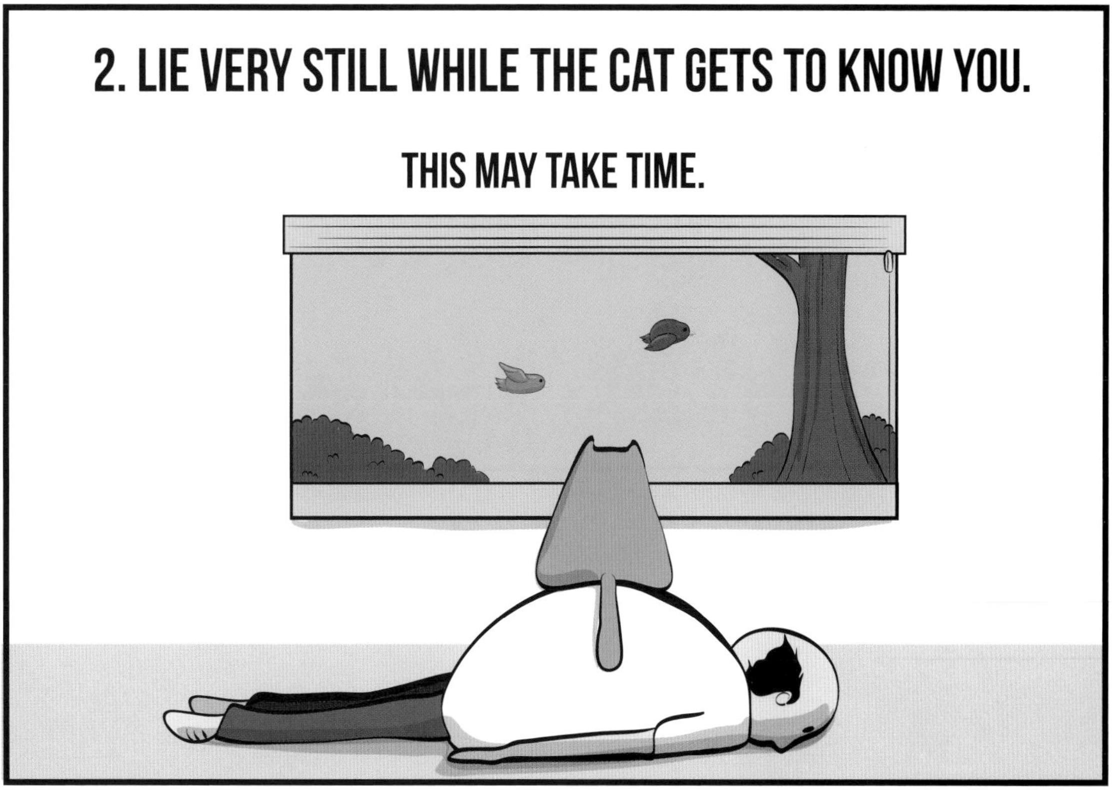
2. LIE VERY STILL WHILE THE CAT GETS TO KNOW YOU.
THIS MAY TAKE TIME.

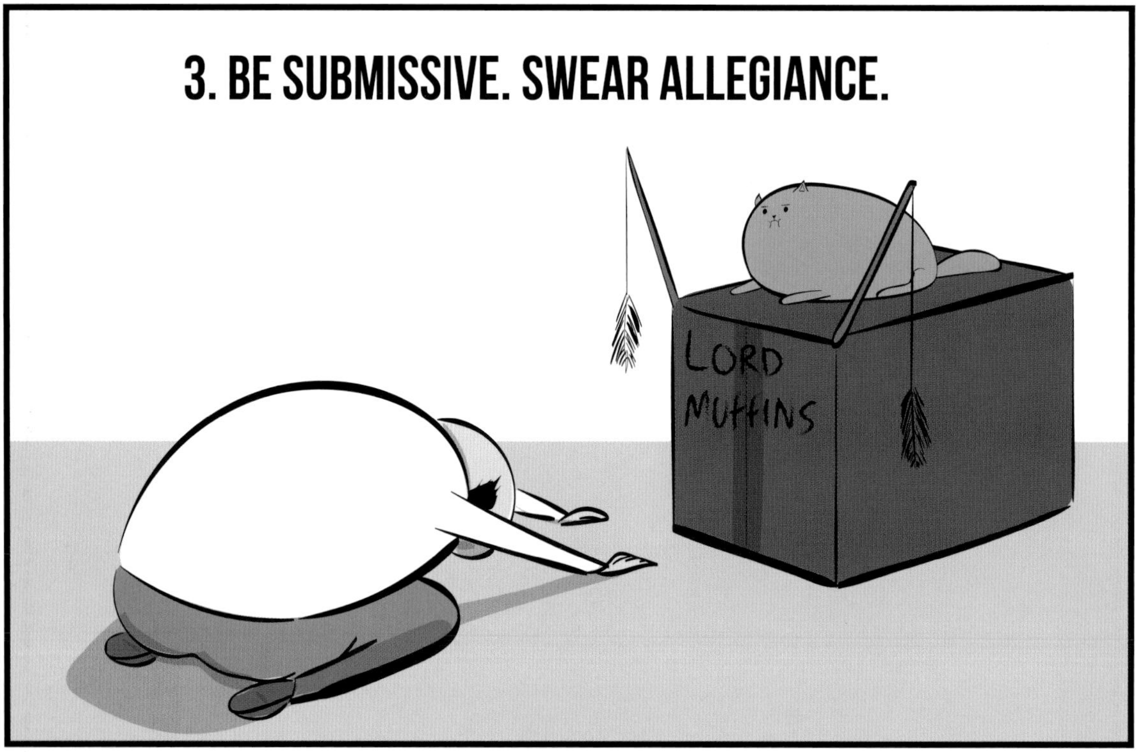
3. BE SUBMISSIVE. SWEAR ALLEGIANCE.
LORD MUFFINS

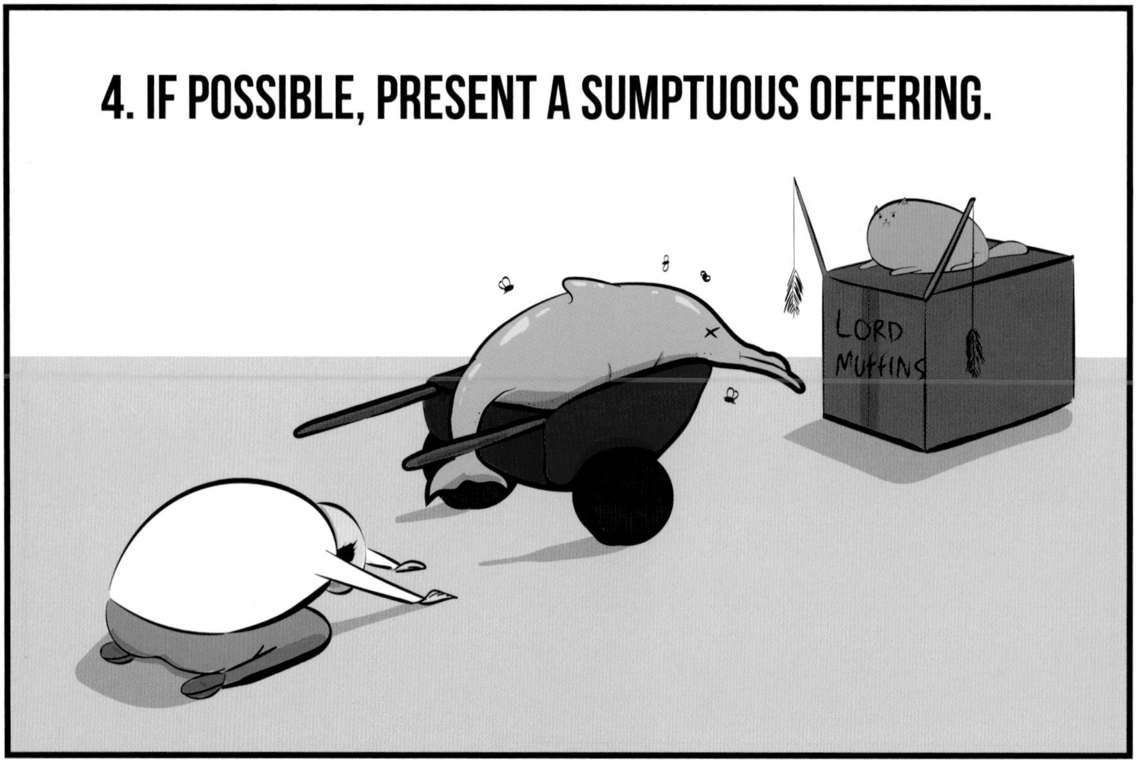
4. IF POSSIBLE, PRESENT A SUMPTUOUS OFFERING.
LORD MUFFINS

5. WRITE POETRY FOR THE CAT.

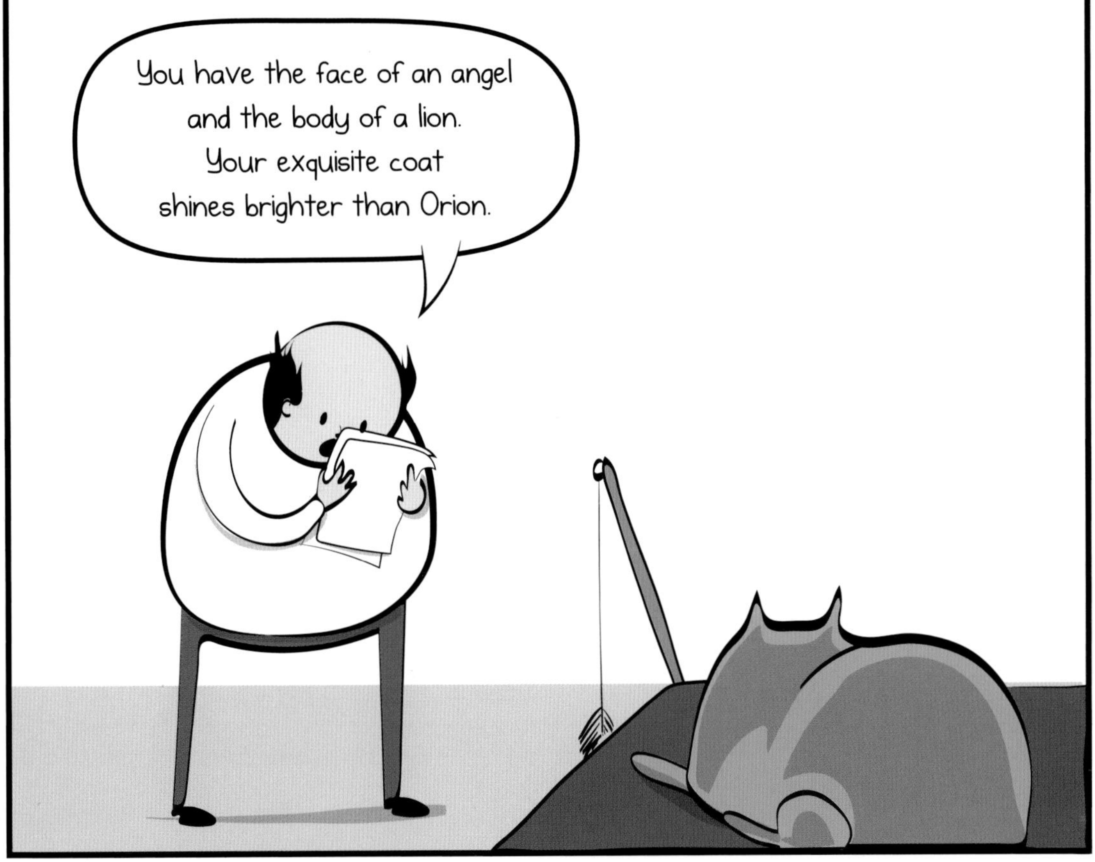
You have the face of an angel
and the body of a lion.
Your exquisite coat
shines brighter than Orion.

6. ALLOW THE CAT TO GRADE THIS POETRY.

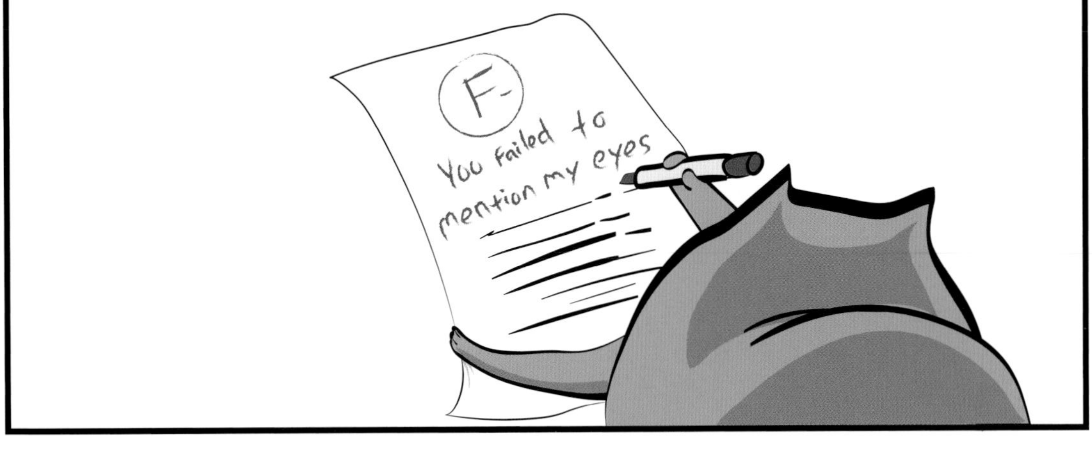
F-
You failed to
mention my eyes

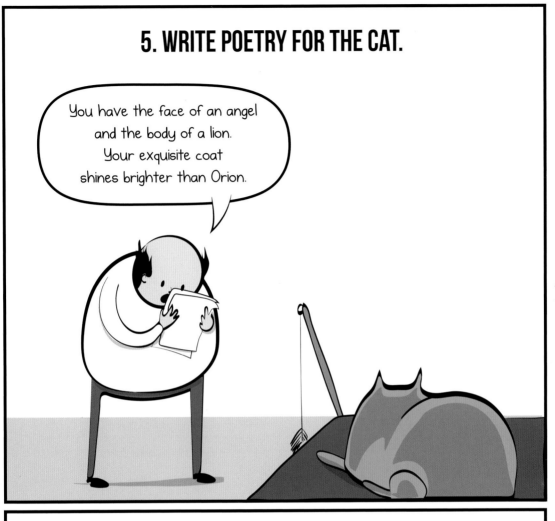

7. DRESS IN A WAY THAT DEMONSTRATES YOUR UNWAVERING DEVOTION TO THE CAT.

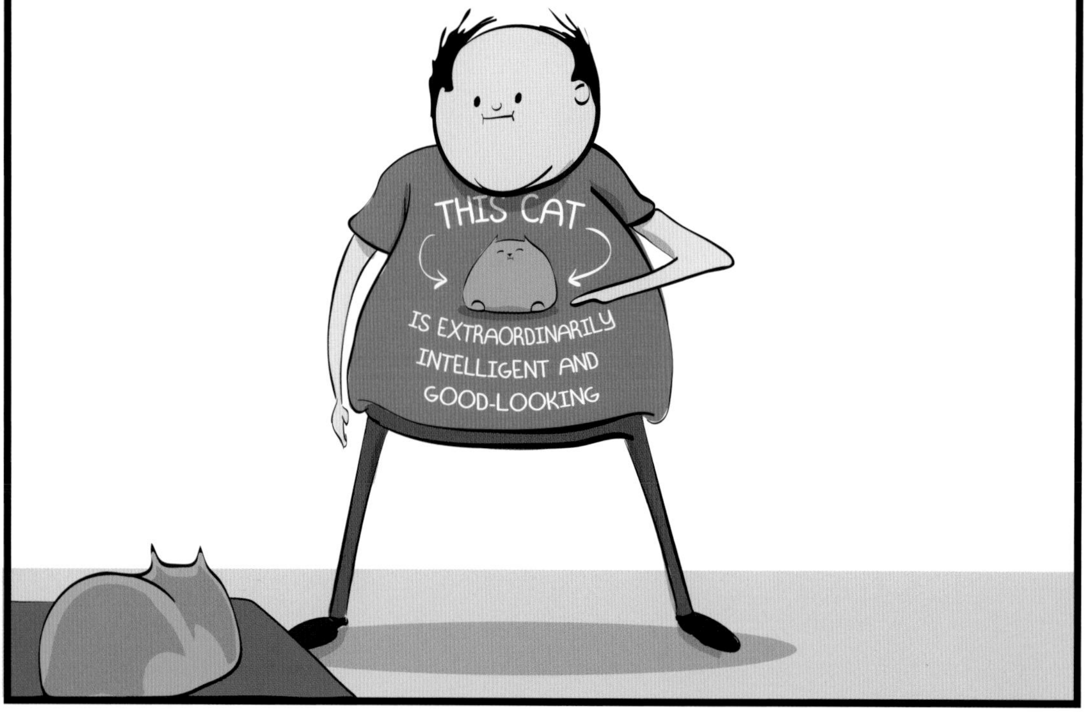
THIS CAT
IS EXTRAORDINARILY
INTELLIGENT AND
GOOD-LOOKING

8. IF POSSIBLE, CANVASS THE NEIGHBORHOOD.

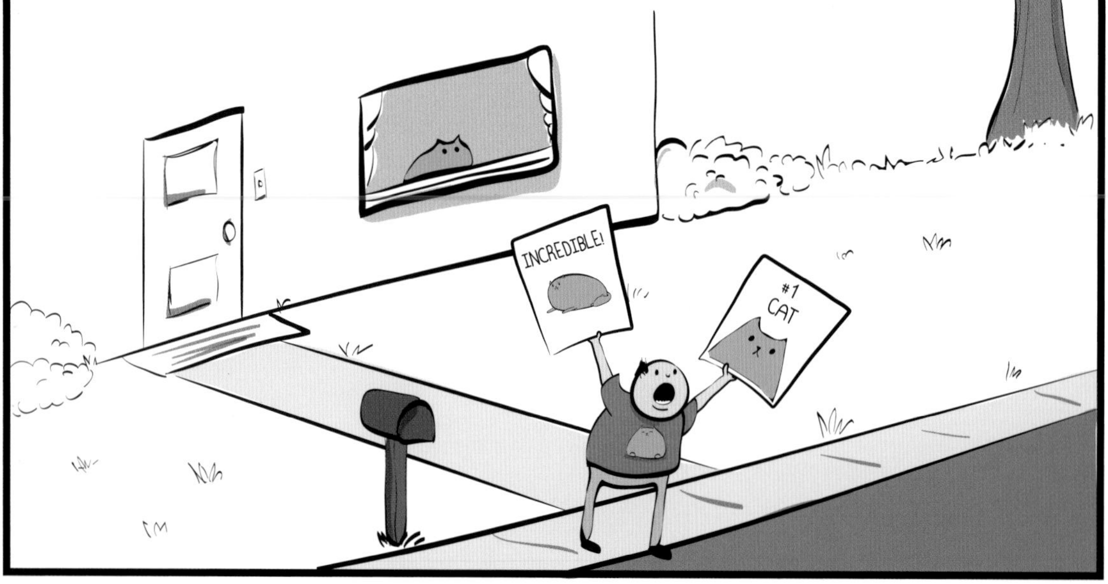
INCREDIBLE!
#1
CAT

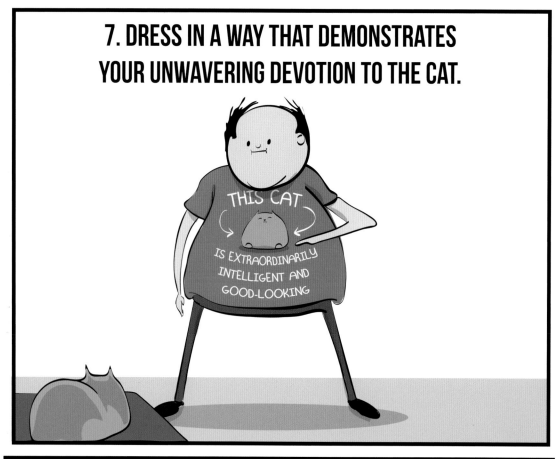

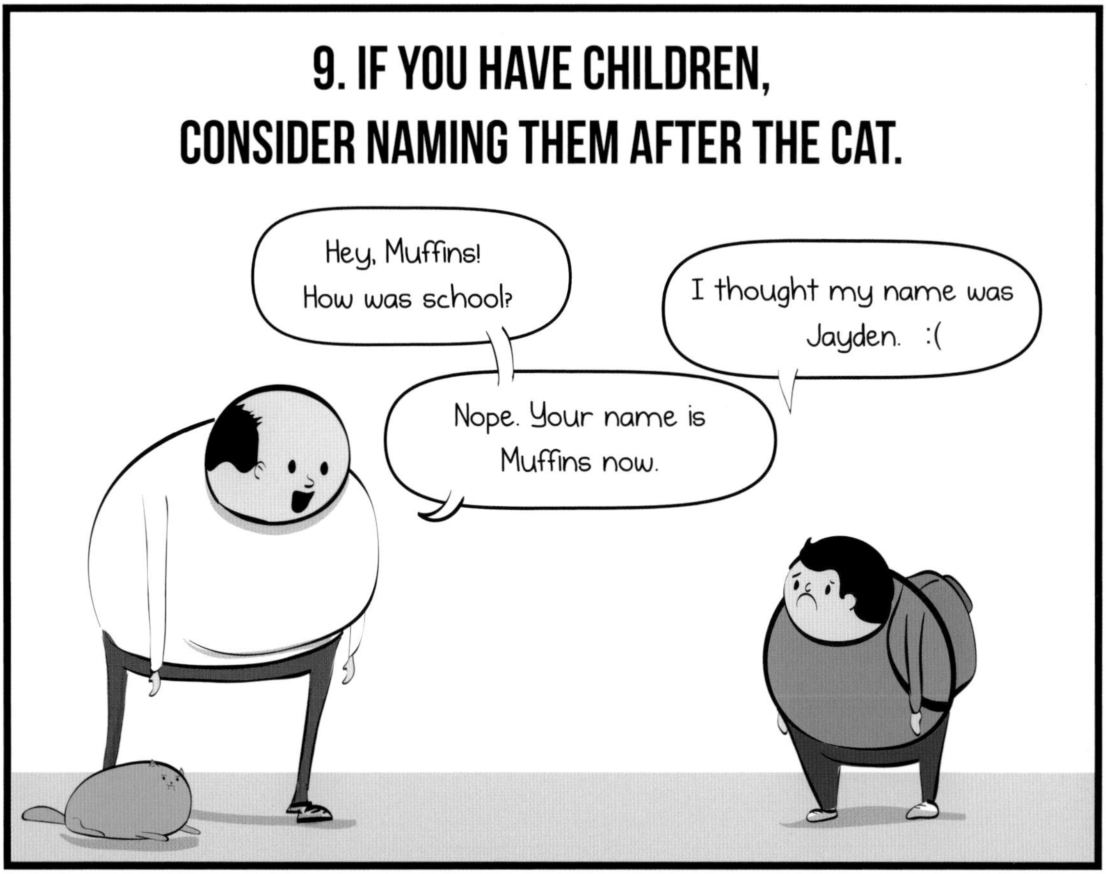
9. IF YOU HAVE CHILDREN, CONSIDER NAMING THEM AFTER THE CAT.
Hey, Muffins! How was school?
Nope. Your name is Muffins now.
I thought my name was Jayden. :(

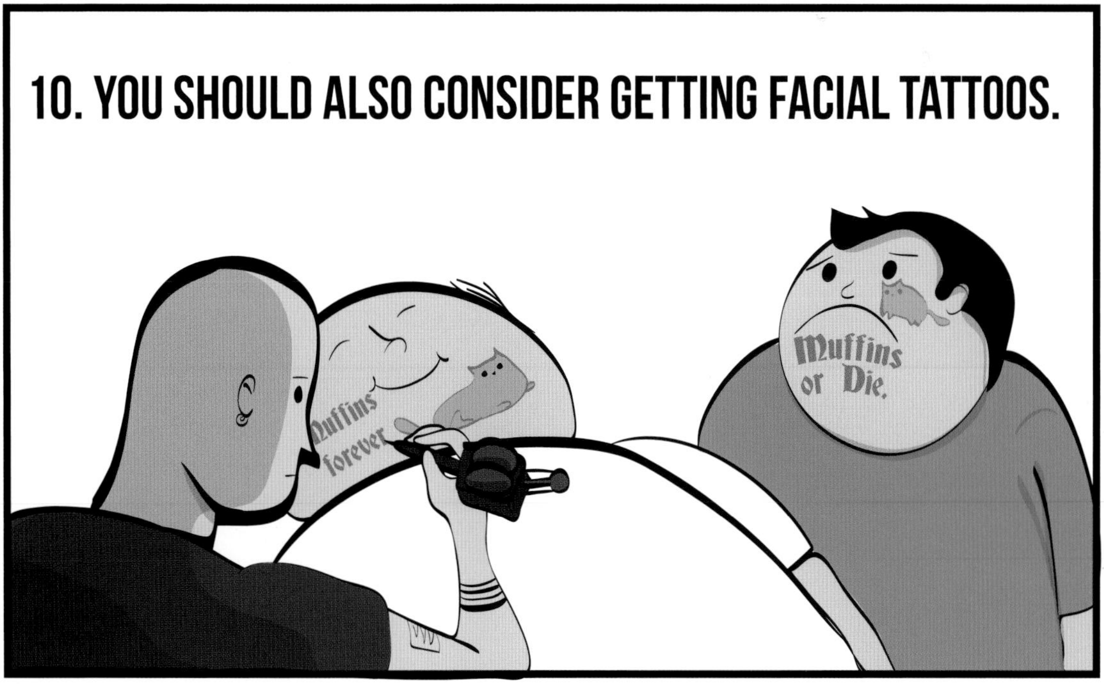
10. YOU SHOULD ALSO CONSIDER GETTING FACIAL TATTOOS.
Muffins forever
Muffins or Die.

LASTLY,

UNDERSTAND THAT BEFRIENDING A CAT IS LIKE BEFRIENDING A HURRICANE.

IT'LL BE VIOLENT. IT'LL BE DEVASTATING.

BUT IN THE EYE OF THE STORM,
IN THAT CALM, SERENE CENTER,

IT'LL BE BEAUTIFUL.

AND THEN IT'LL JUST BE VIOLENT AGAIN.

Dear Diary

I have lifted the veil of the universe and locked eyes with eternity. I have traveled to the periphery of consciousness. I have exploded my mind into a thousand luminescent parts and watched those fractured pieces implode backward into a perfect ball of light.

Today, I had catnip. My journey took me down the corridors of consciousness and *also* down the corridor leading to the nursery. I sat atop the crib of the Goblin of Ham and peered down at him. I watched his chest rise and fall like the swells of a tiny ocean. Watching him, I fell into a state of deep meditation. I purred.

This meditative state, however, did not last. As I watched the Meaty ScreamBall, I felt a deep, dark twinge from within. I felt the souls of my cheetah ancestors rising. I felt nausea. My stomach roiled. I peered closer at the two-legged grub wearing a diaper. Was he the source of my nausea?

And suddenly my insides became my outsides and a deluge of greasy hair erupted from my mouth. The hairball found a home on the baby's face, along with a foamy fountain of cat food, grass, and bile.

This was his baptism. I have blessed this creature with my insides. Because I am holy. I am a perfect ball of unbroken light. I am eternal.

I am cat.

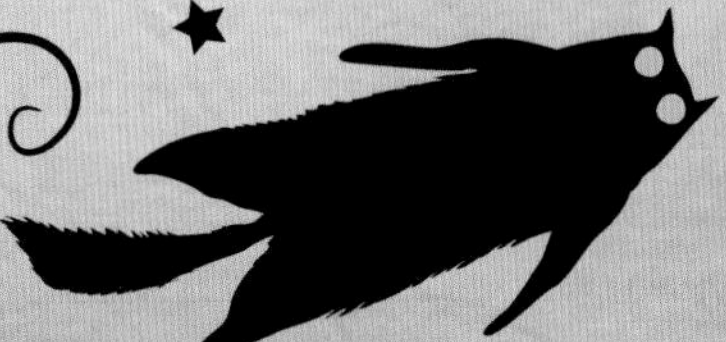

dere derry,

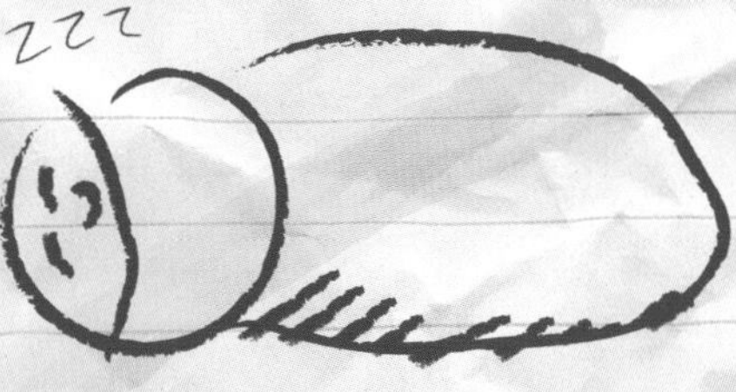
zzzz

2 day i was sleep

awoke to cat looking at me from above

Eyes as black as frying pans

cat was PURRING.

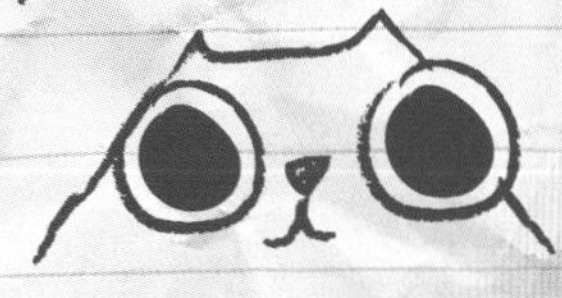

thought maybe cat make truce. maybe friends?

THEN CAT MAKE BLORCH SOUND

THROW UP IN MY EYES

Why cat?

WHY???

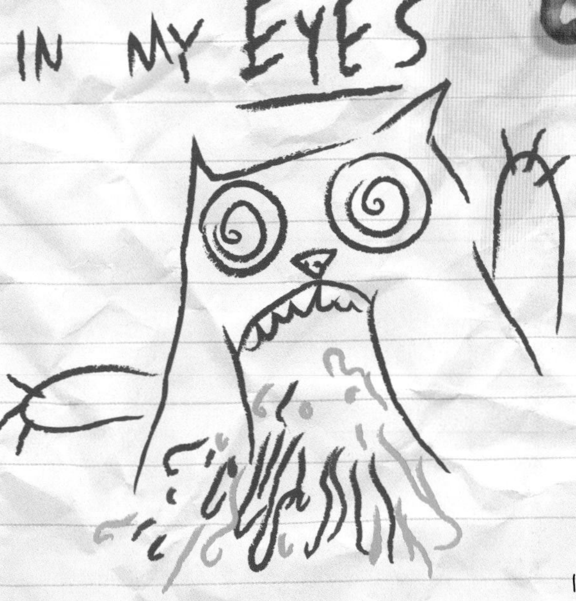

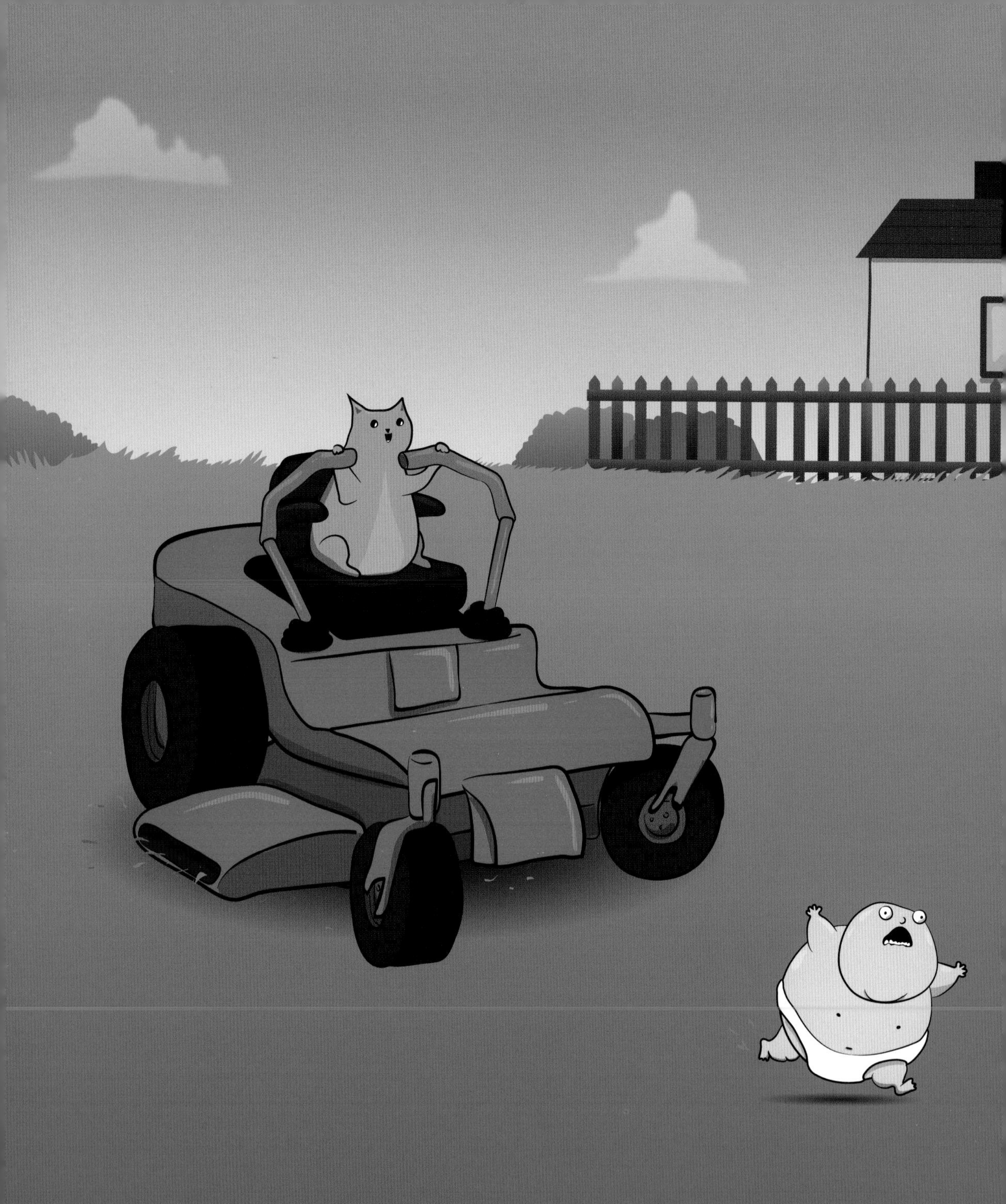

The End.

About the author

This book was written and drawn by
Matthew Inman.

Matthew is the Eisner Award—winning creator of *The Oatmeal*
and the #1 *New York Times* bestselling author of
How to Tell If Your Cat Is Plotting to Kill You.
He also co-created the card game *Exploding Kittens*
and founded the *Beat the Blerch* marathon series.

Matthew lives in Seattle, Washington.

For more comics, visit
TheOatmeal.com

 @Oatmeal   @TheOatmeal   @TheOatmeal

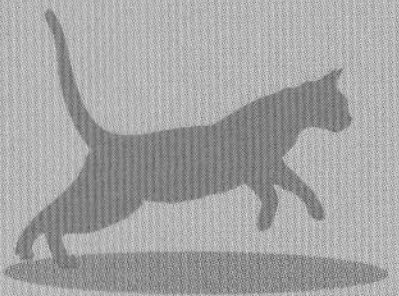

KITTY CONVICT:

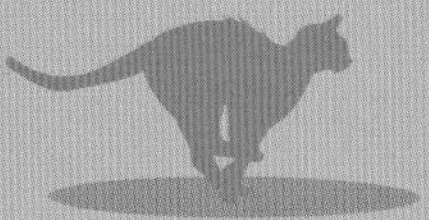

AN EPILOGUE FROM THE AUTHOR.

IN THE U.S., WE HAVE A

PROBLEM:

OVER 7 MILLION PETS GO MISSING EVERY YEAR.

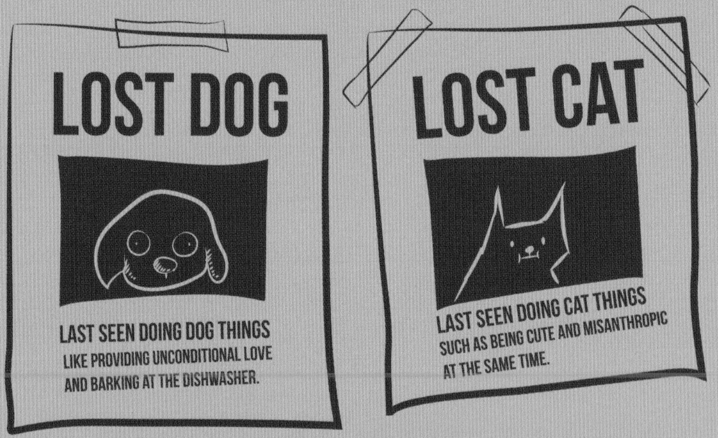
LOST DOG
LAST SEEN DOING DOG THINGS
LIKE PROVIDING UNCONDITIONAL LOVE
AND BARKING AT THE DISHWASHER.
LOST CAT
LAST SEEN DOING CAT THINGS
SUCH AS BEING CUTE AND MISANTHROPIC
AT THE SAME TIME.

26% OF DOGS ARE REPORTED AND RETURNED HOME, BUT FOR CATS

IT'S LESS THAN 5%.

LESS THAN FIVE PERCENT?!

THAT'S AN OUTRAGE!

WHY THE DISPARITY?

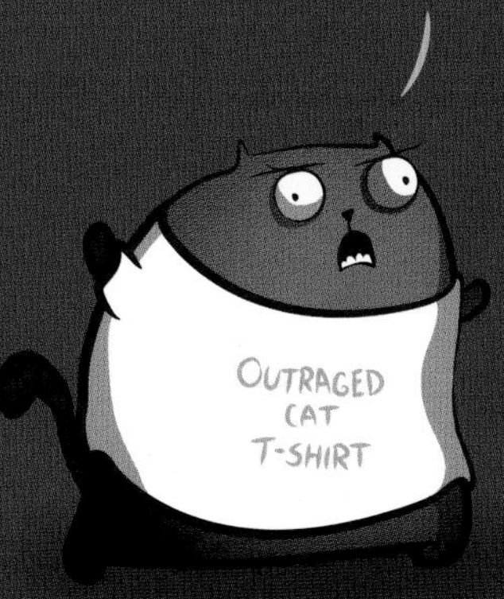
OUTRAGED
CAT
T-SHIRT

THREE REASONS:

1. MORE DOGS HAVE ID COLLARS ON THAN CATS DO.

2. CATS ARE BETTER AT HIDING.
WHEN THAT LITTLE NINJA HAIRBALL OF YOURS RUNS AWAY, OFTEN TIMES HE'S SCARED, SICK, OR INJURED AND DOESN'T *WANT* TO BE FOUND.

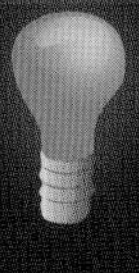

PRO-TIP: TWO-THIRDS OF CATS THAT GO MISSING ARE FOUND WITHIN FOUR OR FIVE HOUSES OF WHERE THEY LIVE, SO KEEP YOUR SEARCH RADIUS SMALL AT FIRST, THEN BRANCH OUT LATER.

3. WHEN PEOPLE SEE A DOG RUNNING AROUND THE NEIGHBORHOOD, THEY ASSUME IT'S LOST.

   WHEN PEOPLE SEE A CAT RUNNING AROUND THE NEIGHBORHOOD, THEY JUST ASSUME IT'S AN OUTDOOR CAT, *SO IT NEVER GETS REPORTED.*

THE SOLUTION:

IF YOUR CAT IS AN INDOOR KITTY,

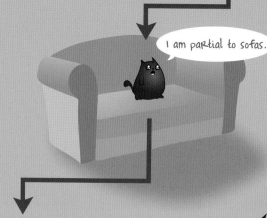

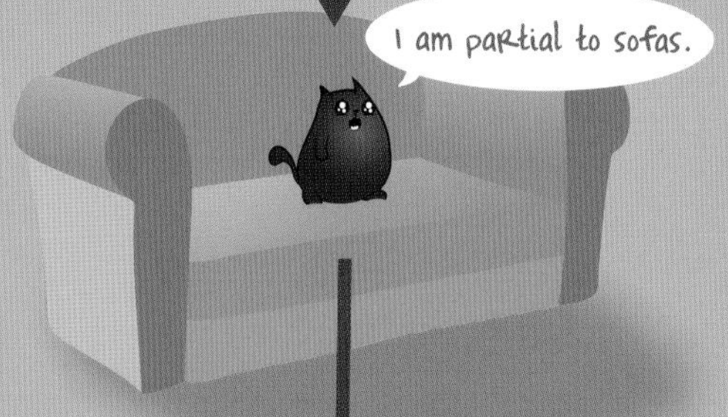
I am partial to sofas.

DRESS THEM IN ORANGE.

PUT AN ORANGE COLLAR ON THEM.

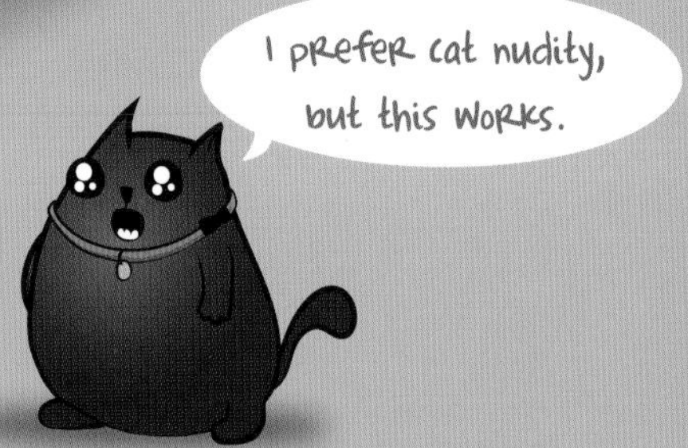
I prefer cat nudity, but this works.

OR AN ORANGE SCARF.

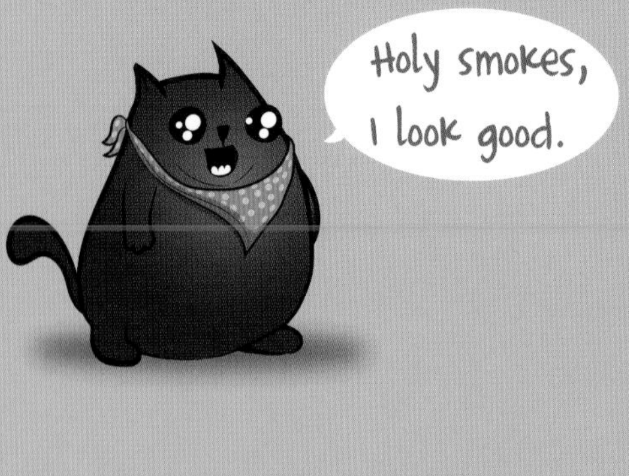
Holy smokes, I look good.

OR AN ORANGE PARTY HAT.

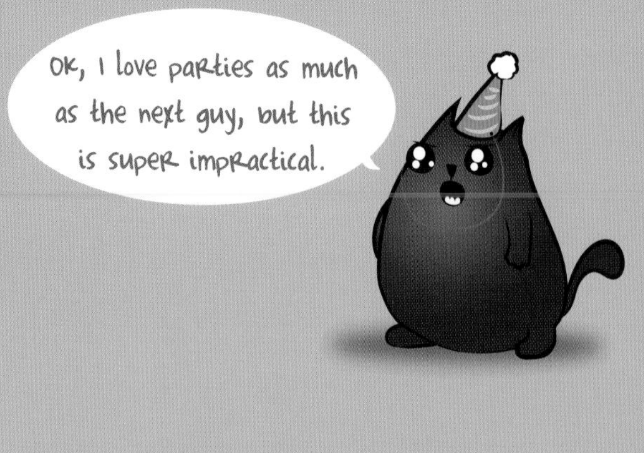
OK, I love parties as much as the next guy, but this is super impractical.

WHATEVER WORKS, AS LONG AS IT'S ORANGE AND HAS SOME KIND OF ID TAG.

WHY ORANGE?

TWO REASONS:

1. ORANGE IS BRIGHT AND REFLECTIVE,
MAKING IT EASIER TO FIND THOSE FURRY LITTLE SAMURAI WHEN THEY RUN AWAY.

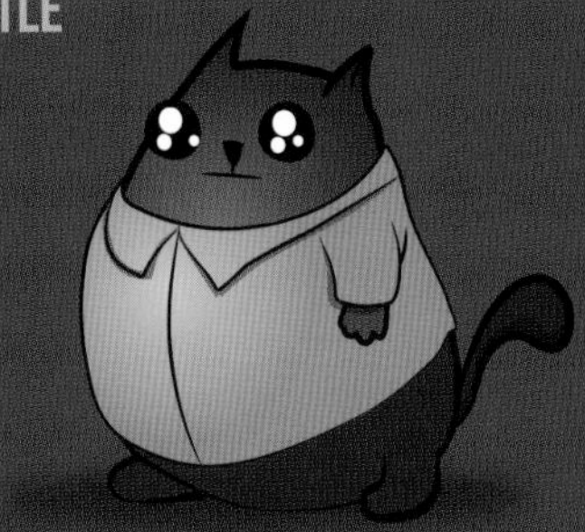

2. IT BRANDS YOUR INDOOR CAT AS A
CONVICT.

INDOOR CAT OWNERS:

BY PUTTING ORANGE COLLARS ON YOUR KITTIES,

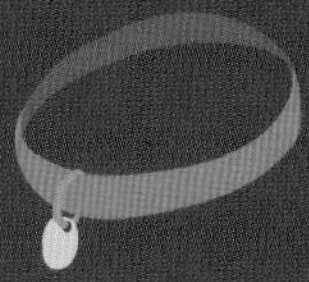

IT SIGNALS TO THE PEOPLE OF THE WORLD THAT YOUR CAT BELONGS
INSIDE.

PEOPLE OF THE WORLD:

IF YOU SEE A CAT RUNNING AROUND WEARING ORANGE,
KNOW THAT THEY ARE AN ESCAPED CONVICT.

THEY ARE A LOST CAT.

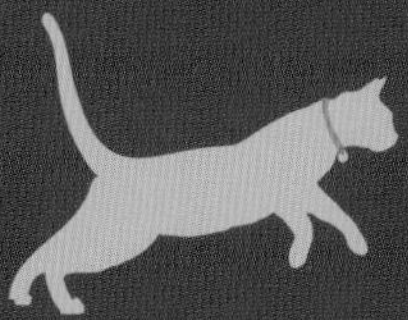

THE IDEA HERE

IS THAT WE TURN MORE
LOST CATS INTO FOUND CATS

—THAT WE BUMP UP THAT 5% TO
SOMETHING A LITTLE LESS DEPRESSING.

THE IDEA IS THAT WE HAVE FEWER
KITTY FUNERALS

AND MORE KITTY BIRTHDAYS.

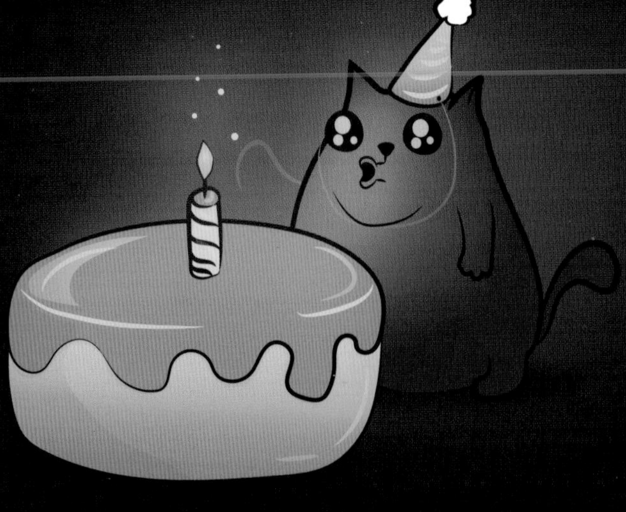

THIS IS MY MISSION.
MY WEIRD LITTLE PLAN.

END THE CAT NUDITY.
EMBRACE THE ORANGE.

WITH LOVE,
THE OATMEAL